THE
ALPHABET ABECEDARIUM

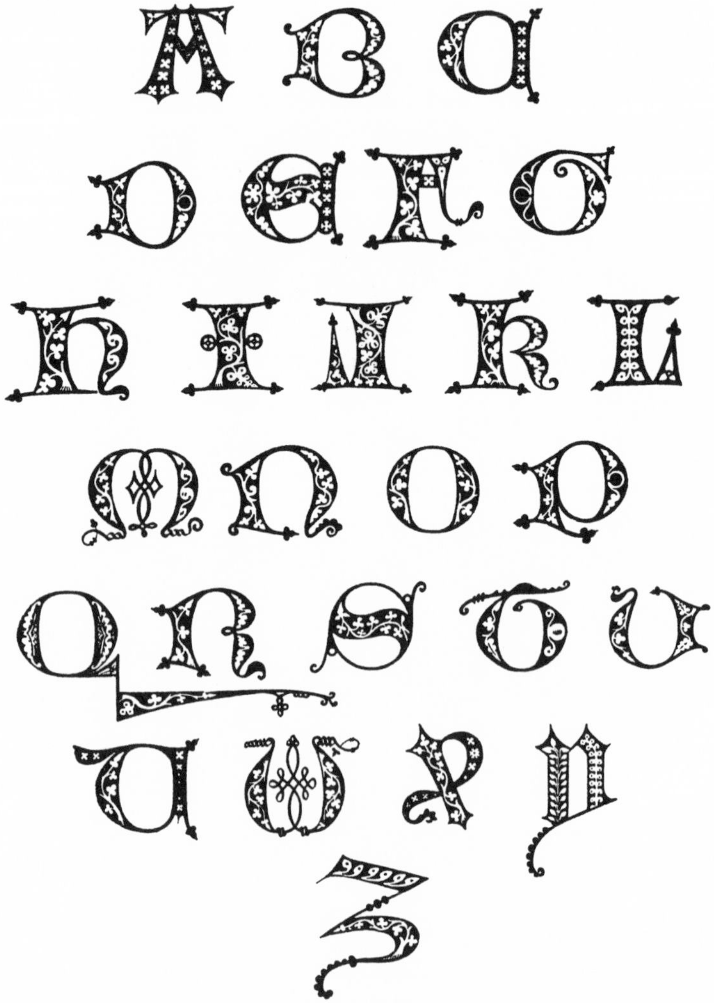

THE ALPHABET ABECEDARIUM

Some Notes on Letters

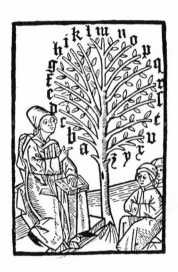

Richard A. Firmage

DAVID R. GODINE, PUBLISHER
BOSTON

for A. and M.

—An allaphbed for the abcedminded—

First published in 1993 by
DAVID R. GODINE, PUBLISHER, INC.
Horticultural Hall, 300 Massachusetts Avenue
Boston, Massachusetts 02115

Library of Congress Cataloging-in-Publication Data
Firmage, Richard A., 1946–
The alphabet abecedarium: some notes on letters / Richard A. Firmage
p. cm.
Includes bibliographical references and index.
1. Alphabet—History. 2. Alphabets. 3. Printing—History. 1. Title
P211.F6 1993   93-26544
411-DC20   CIP

ISBN 0-87923-987-5 (hardcover)   ISBN 0-87923-998-0 (softcover)
First edition a b c d e f g
Printed and bound in the United States of America
Title page illustration: "Teaching the alphabet," woodcut from a book by
Geiler von Keiserberg, printed in 1490.

A Choice of Epigraphs:

"(Stoop) if you are abcedminded ... in this allaphbed!"
—James Joyce

"So, first comes the house of man, and its construction, then the human body, its build and deformities; then justice, music, the church; war, harvest, geometry; the mountain, nomadic life and secluded life, astronomy, toil and rest; the horse and the snake; the hammer and the urn which—turned over and struck—makes a bell; trees, rivers, roads; and finally destiny and God: This is what the alphabet signifies."
—Victor Hugo

"Then he went off sniffing drainpipes and reciting the alphabet."
—Bob Dylan

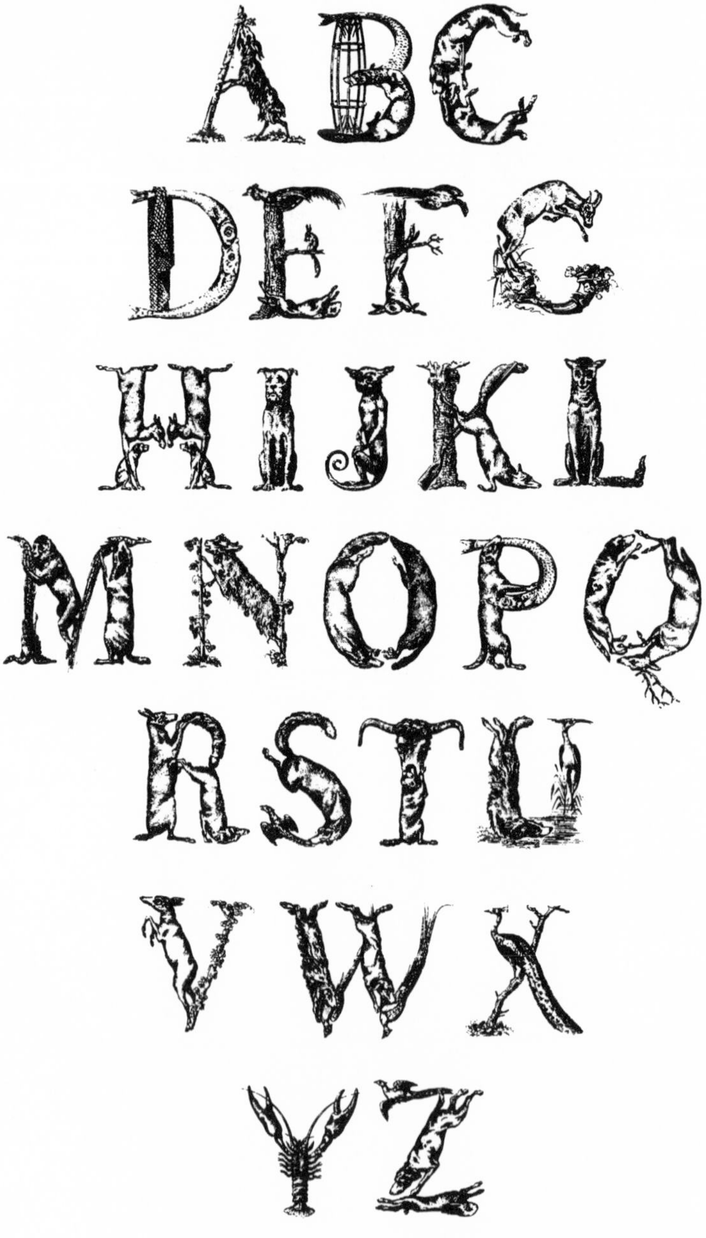
ABC
DEFG
HIJKL
MNOPQ
RSTU
VWX
YZ

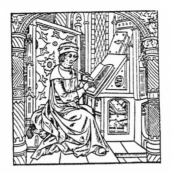

CONTENTS

FOREWORD ix

INTRODUCTION 1

A 47

B 56

C 64

D 72

E 81

F 89

G 98

H 107

I 115

J 124

K 132

L 141

M 150

N 159

O 168

P 177

Q 186

R 196

S 205

T 214

U 223

V 231

W 240

X 249

Y 258

Z 266

A–Z 274

& 284

SELECT BIBLIOGRAPHY 295

INDEX 301

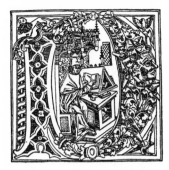

FOREWORD

(A Letter to the Reader)

"'Of course you know your ABC?' said the Red Queen.

'To be sure I do,' said Alice.

'So do I,' the White Queen whispered. 'We'll often say it over together, dear. And I'll tell you a secret—I can read words of one letter! Isn't *that* grand? However, don't be discouraged. You'll come to it in time.'"

The above exchange from Lewis Carroll's *Through the Looking-Glass* happily concerns itself with the subject of this book—the alphabet— and presents both characteristic assumptions and not so usual responses of the sort the reader will find in the pages that follow. I have found that there are common assumptions made upon the mention of an alphabet book. The first, typically, is that the work in question is an abecedary— a child's pictorial instruction book linking the letters with common words which they begin. If the book is not that, then it is most often thought to be an instructional or source manual for calligraphers, or a type specimen book. Told that it fits neither category, one might speculate that the work is a scholarly tome on the origins of writing.

This book cannot fairly claim to be any of the above; however, don't be discouraged, a sympathetic and active imagination may find elements of all in it. It is perhaps best termed a miscellany—an "allaphbed for the abcedminded"—a collection of notes pertaining to our twenty-six letters that have interested this writer. I have called it *The Alphabet Abecedarium*, using the least common form of the word for the child's primer to suggest a more weighty but (hopefully) still delightful instruction book for the more advanced reader such as the White Queen. Interesting lore and information about the Roman alphabet replaces charming illustrations of apples or anteaters. The illustrations included may still delight, but they usually depict the letters in various guises, just as the text concentrates on that subject. A is about A, in other words. A few diversions on the path will be encountered, however. Be prepared for anything … it's quite possible you'll come to it in time. As Victor Hugo wrote: "The alphabet is a source. A is the roof with its rafters and traverse-beam, … or it is like two friends who embrace and shake hands."

This book has held me in its embrace. Conceived originally as a winter's brief exercise, inspired and prompted by my fascination with the graphic forms of the alphabet, the work expanded greatly through years of research, far overstepping its original bounds. The present book is actually a distillation of voluminous notes on the subject, focusing on curious facts and fancies associated with the letters. I have come round to a version of my original concept through the back door, as it were. And, if it remains but a peek at the mansion, the subject still merits the attention. It is not a scholarly dissertation sniffing about for "truth"; yet I think it will reveal much to many who believe they know their ABCs. It cannot pretend to completeness, but within its limits it strives for accuracy—that is, I have faithfully recorded the various statements; whether or not the statements are trustworthy is another matter altogether, and one that concerns this book very little.

In discussing the evolution of the basic letter shapes and the development of the modern capital and lower-case forms, no attempt is made to trace a comprehensive history. Rather, only certain highlights are mentioned. The gradual refinement and alteration of the letters was usually the result of centuries of usage by countless, and frequently anonymous, scribes and type designers. There was great variation even within the major historical styles, and any illustration is only one among innumerable variants. No form of any letter was ever considered definitive—even such often cited examples as the Roman capital letters of the Trajan Column are but very good representative characters and were never considered in Roman times as *the* models against which all other forms were measured. Even within the Column, letters vary.

Instead of an analysis of the various letter changes and forms, the reader will find representative drawings of each of the letters, allowing each letter to be seen at various stages in its history. In the boxes at the bottom of the chapter pages these forms will not be identified, as the intention is to show a part of the vast range of character design and not any particular form. The curious can study type and calligraphy specimen books to identify these and thousands more not shown. However, in the Introduction representative historical styles are illustrated and identified; in each chapter the reader will find many of these letters shown in the first box, which roughly traces the historical letter forms. The subsequent boxes are then filled with random alphabet forms—both upper- and lower-case—grouped into similar classes, such as old style, sans serif, or decorative. Thus, one can see the almost always very interesting metamorphoses the letters have undergone.

A couple of things should be noted here for the concerned reader. It should be understood that in their uses and spellings of words there are many inconsistencies among the writers I have quoted. This understood, I take responsibility for any errors that may be found in the book. There are, however, at least two inconsistent uses that I do not consider errors. The first involves the use of the apostrophe with plural designations of the letters—for clarity I have occasionally inserted the mark (usually with vowels, e.g., O's) although my preference is to be technically correct and omit them. Also, my use of the terms letterform(s) and letter form(s) should be explained. They are intended to mean different things. The first (one word) is synonymous with "letter(s)" and is used for the sake of variety. The second (two words) may often seem to be synonymous (and some uses are ambiguous), but is intended to refer to or stress the form of the letter as a *shape* rather than the letter as an *identity*.

My acknowledgements must include all those who have been concerned with letters—more specifically, those who have written of that interest, endeavoring to share it with others,…like "friends who embrace and shake hands." The Bibliography lists my major indebtedness—a debt that is more truly a treasure—but much cannot be listed, for the world of letters is wide. Friends who have helped make this book possible include Fred Brady, Robert Slimbach, and Mary Cochran at Adobe Systems, and Laura Williams at Aldus Corporation. Direct thanks for many helpful suggestions is cheerfully given to David Godine, to Arthur Nelson, and especially to Anne Shifrer and to Susan Meigs. The book is a better one because of their efforts and concern. Isn't *that* grand?

ABCDEFGH
IJKLMNOPQR
STUVWXYZ
(&.,;:;-"'!?)
abcdeetfghij
klmnopqrstu
vwxyz

An Art Nouveau typographic alphabet named Robur Black Inline

INTRODUCTION

"At the Egyptian city of Naucratis, there was a famous old god, whose name was Theuth; the bird which is called the Ibis is sacred to him, and he was the inventor of many arts, such as arithmetic and calculation and geometry and astronomy and draughts and dice, but his great discovery was the use of letters."

With those words, recorded in Plato's dialogue *Phaedrus*, Socrates begins to relate an ancient legend. The greatest of many great inventions, the use of letters or invention of writing seems to be worthy of a god, being the foundation for the recording and transmitting of all thought and speech.

The legend continues with Theuth (Thoth) showing his inventions to the great king Thamus, "desiring that the other Egyptians might have the benefit of them." Thamus listened, commenting upon the merits of each until they came to the letters. "This, said Theuth, will make the Egyptians wiser and give them better memories." But Thamus disagreed, maintaining that "the parent or inventor of an art is not always the best judge of the utility or inutility of his own inventions to the users of them. And in this instance, you who are the father of letters, from a paternal love of your own children have been led to attribute to them a quality which they cannot have; for this discovery of yours will create forgetfulness in the learners' souls, because they will not use their memories; they will trust to the external written characters and not remember of themselves. The specific which you have discovered is an aid not to memory, but to reminiscence, and you give your disciples not truth, but only the semblance of truth; they will be hearers of many things and will have learned nothing; they will appear to be omniscient

I

and will generally know nothing; they will be tiresome company, having the show of wisdom without the reality."

Here the recitation ends; there is no record of what, if any, reply Theuth made to the opinions of Thamus. Yet perhaps the best reply is right in front of us—the written words without which we would not have even the "show of wisdom" of the attack against writing, let alone the philosophy of Plato. Actually, *Phaedrus* is not an attack on writing; it seeks only to subordinate the written word to philosophical dialogue. But although Socrates stressed verbal discourse, Plato's dialogues were recorded with pen on papyrus. And we are fortunate that they were— the "semblance of truth" is better than nothing at all.

Thamus (or Socrates) was right, however, in maintaining that writing can be misused—it can mislead, deceive and corrupt. It freezes language and does not directly respond to questions as a speaker might. It can be a crib, hindering free thought and personal reflection; yet it can also prompt thought and reflection—something perhaps overlooked by Socrates, doubtless less so by Plato, and appreciated by the students of Platonic thought for the past 2400 years. The "external written characters" are vehicles of human thought and a subject worthy of their own examination.

Reversed writing from the Roman catacombs revealing the illiterate or semi-literate endeavoring to use letters without fully understanding them.

In fact, the development of writing has been called the greatest of all human accomplishments. Although it is true that literacy is not required in order for a person to survive and even prosper in a material sense, it does make possible an enriched intellectual and (perhaps) spiritual life. I must hedge with the spiritual since what glimpses we have of ancient as well as modern preliterate or illiterate societies often reveal rich and vital attitudes and postures in regard to otherworldly concepts as well as one's place in this world—attitudes I often feel to be superior to those of our own supposedly enlightened culture. To me, the oral-based culture of such groups often presents a treasure comparable to the exquisite and marvellous cave paintings created thousands of years before the development of any system of writing.

As Thamus pointed out in our story, humans relied on their memories and other memory-aids (such as notched sticks or knotted strings) before the development of writing systems, and it appears that prodigious feats of memorization were accomplished—major epics and sagas being passed on through generations by bards and storytellers. The Homeric epics in their original form are but one example of marvellous "literary" creation without writing. We will meet later those who extoll the virtues of oral culture; but all will concede that it has limitations most noticeably evident when the sheer mass of accumulated data overwhelms the individual human ability to store and recover it.

Enter for good and/or ill the writing systems. Without them, in the words of Edward Clodd, "all that memory failed to overlap would be an absolute blank; the dateless and otherwise uninscribed monuments which the past had left behind would but deepen the darkness; all knowledge of the strivings and speculations of men of old would have been unattainable; all observation and experience through which science has advanced…irretrievably lost….Save in fragmentary echoes repeated by fugitive bards, the great epics of East and West would have perished, and the immortal literatures of successive ages never have existed. The invention of writing alone made possible the passage from barbarism to civilisation, and secured the continuous progress of the human race." Although I think that a fair mind could question the supposition of continuous progress and the unmitigated merits of "civilisation," it remains true that writing has certainly enriched human society and our intellectual heritage. Though the Word might have been first "in the beginning" and continue to exert remarkable power (as orators have shown throughout recorded time), it is the transcription of the Word, it is writing, that enables it to reverberate and resound through the ages.

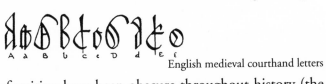

English medieval courthand letters

The origins of writing have been obscure throughout history (the account of Socrates is hardly universally accepted) and are likely to remain so. The present work makes no claim to and little effort at clearing those long-standing mists. Rather, its concern is with the alphabet—specifically, the present English alphabet—and some of the curiosities attendant upon its history and development. At its most basic, the alphabet is a subject that any reader has already committed to memory; once learned, (s)he may be eager to expand that knowledge,… so even a Socrates may give the effort a slight nod of approval.

One of our modern authorities on the subject, David Diringer, has aptly defined writing as "the graphic counterpart of speech, the 'fixing' of spoken language in a permanent or semi-permanent form." He has also written that "with its 22 or 24 or 26 signs, the Alphabet is the most flexible and useful method of writing ever invented." It should be expected that there would be a treasure of lore and commentary concerning something as important to human history and civilization as the alphabet and its component signs, but even this might come as a surprise, accustomed as many of us are to overlooking these basic elements and building blocks of our culture and consciousness. If that does not surprise the reflective reader, perhaps in the pages to follow he or she will find other surprises as we pursue a tour of the alphabet. We can fairly infer that even Socrates would have sanctioned this effort, for he concludes that a man of sense may sow and plant in the garden of letters, "but only for the sake of recreation and amusement…as memorials to be treasured against the forgetfulness of old age, by himself, or by any other old man who is treading the same path."

An invitation is thus here extended to the aging, the lighthearted, the fun-loving, and the freethinking to tread the following path of letters. First, a bit of background information as preparation for the journey.

ABCDEFGHIJKLMNOPQR STUVWXYZ

Most basically, an alphabet is a set of symbols representing sounds. It is composed of letters—each one a visual sign representing a distinctive sound. Alphabets are a late development in history, however. Long before alphabets there existed other systems of writing and, most likely, long before any writing there was language or oral communication between humans. It is commonly agreed that human speech (or language) developed before its graphic representation (or writing, in any of its many forms). There are no people on earth who are without language, but there are languages that have no invented writing.

Writing is a means to communicate of a more than momentary nature, distinguishing it from speaking or gesturing. It is also distinct from objects signifying meaning. Writing is expressed by markings on objects, not by the objects themselves. (The etymology of "to write" in many different languages descends from words for incising, marking, carving and painting.) According to A. Lloyd Jones: "The human brain has done nothing that compares in complexity with this fusion of ideas involved in linking up the two forms of language....Once it is achieved in our early years...we cannot think of sounds without thinking of letters; we believe letters have sounds. We think that the printed page is a picture of what we say." In his *Logic,* Aristotle declared that "spoken words are the symbols of mental experience and written words are the symbols of spoken words." It is important to realize, however, that although writing is connected with speech, it is not an exact equivalent. It was especially distinct in its earliest forms when signs represented objects and ideas rather than sounds.

No document of our parent human language (if there was one) or even the parent Indo-European language of our Western tongues has been or is likely to be found, for that language probably broke up into many others before the invention of writing. The biblical story of the Tower of Babel and the subsequent confusion of tongues is the best-known attempt to account for the multitude of languages historical humans had to deal with in the distant past. This bewildering state of affairs could easily be interpreted as a curse of God; and people longed for the mythical time when all spoke the same language. Hebrew scribes posited such a past before Babel but could say little about the original language. Modern scholars can do no better. Despite this gap in our knowledge, we do know that there existed a great many different forms of writing that developed before the alphabet. They have even been classified into a few broad categories. The development of writing can be basically summarized in the paragraphs that follow.

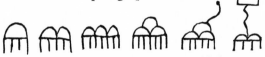

Moki Indian pictographs for rain and lightning

Pictographic, or *Iconographic,* writing was the first actual writing. A simple picture designated an object. These systems developed from isolated markings to a series of connected pictures, or stories, such as those made by nineteenth century American Indians. Generally, the signs were simplified and abstracted; aesthetic quality was subordinated to simplicity.

Ideographic, or *Hieroglyphic*, writing developed from pictographic writing. In this stage, a conventionalized picture also came to represent associated ideas, abstractions, or even metaphors. Thus, a picture of the sun could not only designate that heavenly object but also such ideas as light, brightness, and day. Many modern punctuation marks are actually ideographs—they directly represent ideas. Ideographs were basic to the ancient Egyptian and the Chinese writing systems, many continuing in use throughout the history of each script. In many other scripts their use was only temporary and was gradually superseded by phonetic writing.

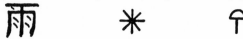

Chinese ideograph for rain, moisture (left), and early pictorial Sumerian ideographs for star, sky, God (center), and eye, to see, face (right)

Phonetic writing is the final major stage in the evolution of writing. It represents the major breakthrough: the realization that written language could correspond to spoken language, that homonyms as well as homophones could be represented by the same sign—for example, the sun sign could now also be used to represent "son." Signs now represented sounds. This has been called the most intellectual achievement ever attained by human beings; and it was a necessary step to halt the otherwise unlimited proliferation of word signs. The next step involved making signs to represent syllables, when it was realized that words could be broken down into abstract sound-component units. (A syllable is a vowel sound or a vowel in combination with one or more consonants.) Each of these stages generally led to a reduction in the number of signs necessary for a language; but even a refined syllabary requires at least three times as many signs as does an alphabet.

Alphabetic writing—the final development—involved a further abstraction: designating signs for individual vowels and consonants, even though the latter cannot technically be sounded by themselves. (Vowels are unstopped voiced sounds—always produced by a vibration of the vocal cords. Consonants are sounds made with a noticeable obstruction of the air stream.) With an alphabet any word can be written, even those—like place or personal names—that could not be suggested by pictures. The alphabetic system was very simple once conceptualized. And, once developed, the idea spread rapidly. A few signs came to represent the comparatively few phonetic sounds in a spoken language, and with them all possible phonetic combinations could be made. The development of writing thus evolved from a picture representing a thing to a symbol representing the name of a thing—the picture of a sound.

An alphabet is not a static or unique system; at the present time there exist dozens, and a study of historical records increases the number. Alphabets not only vary in the signs used to represent sounds, but also in the actual sounds signified—that is, certain alphabets distinguish sounds little used or unsignified in other languages and alphabet systems. An alphabet is also distinct, of course, from the language it is used to represent. The same letterforms can be used for various languages—a prime example being the Roman alphabet used for most modern tongues including our own English language. The written alphabets of languages can be virtually identical, but the sounds represented can differ widely. Consider the spellings "pain" and "dire" in English and French—both constitute words in each language, yet the pronunciation of the same spelling differs greatly.

Although attention is often focused on the alphabet as symbols for language sounds, the present work will also direct attention to the letterforms themselves—the alphabet as writing. The great American type designer Frederic Goudy wrote that the primary function of a letter is to signify what it is itself—its name; only secondary is the part it plays in a word—its sound. "The roman characters we use may be considered not only for their historical development; we may also think of them for themselves alone, quite apart from their function of representing human thought visibly—that is to say, for the unique pleasure that is to be taken in the severe simplicity and beauty of their individual forms."

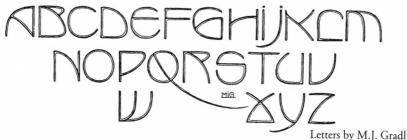

Letters by M.J. Gradl

Alphabets have gradually changed, developed, and been refined through time. Although letters do not alter in "meaning," their forms have undergone great alteration and are still changing (or are capable of it). As William O. Mason wrote in *The History of the Art of Writing*, there is a whole volume of human history behind each one of the letters: "These simple symbols, apparently so arbitrary and meaningless to our latter-day eyes, are replete with the linguistic, even the domestic, history of countless generations of our remote ancestors." The aim of this book is to present to the reader some of that history in one rather slim volume—made possible through the principles of incisive editing and incomprehensive research.

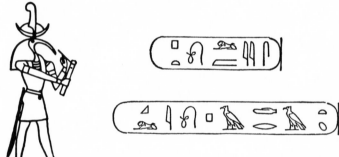

Thoth, the Egyptian god of writing, and hieroglyphic script

That the invention of writing was a momentous achievement seems to have been recognized and appreciated by those who possessed it. Many different ancient societies ascribed the first writing to their gods or to divinely inspired activity. The Babylonians credited the god Nebo with the invention of letters; the Egyptians ascribed it to the god Thoth. A Greek legend credited Hermes (the Greek equivalent of Thoth), who was said to have modeled the letters after the patterns of flights of cranes while he was in exile or traveling in Egypt. In Islamic doctrine, Allah secretly gave the alphabet to Adam, saying that it was not known to the angels. A Dionysian scholastic tradition maintained that the letters fell from heaven; in Irish legend the hero Ogmios is credited with the invention of writing. To the Indians, Brahma was the inventor; to the Scandinavians, Odin.

An ancient Chinese tradition ascribes the invention of writing to Ts'ang Chieh, a dragon-faced, four-eyed sage who lived during the reign of the Emperor Huang Ti (2698–2598 B.C.). He has been called a sage or

柊 熙 誠 焉 閒 方 叛 菴 境

Chinese writing

a demigod, and been given the titles of Prince of Scribes and the God of Writing. He found the models for his characters in the stars, in tortoise-shell markings, and in the footprints of birds in sand. The special style of the 540 most ancient Chinese characters is known as "bird footprints writing." At this invention heaven caused showers of grain to fall from on high, the disembodied spirits wept in the darkness, and the dragons withdrew themselves from sight. Whether the spirits were weeping for joy or in sorrow, most humans considered the event a happy one. As E.T.C. Werner says: "The reverence for the written character was a kind of idolatry. Printed paper was sacred, the sin first mentioned is its misuse, and its preservation the first among meritorious actions. Waste paper was gathered up and burnt in the 'Pity the Written Character' furnace. The ashes were sent to a port and carried out to sea, to be thrown overboard in a storm, so as to cause the waves to be stilled....It was considered an offering to Confucius, and to the God of Literature."

The Judeo-Christian tradition has championed many contenders for the honor of having invented writing. The eighteenth century English writing master Joseph Champion credited the first writing to either God or Adam; but his contemporary William Massey saw "no necessity to suppose that our first parents should be capable of writing as soon as speaking,...for of what use could that have been at the first, when none but Adam and Eve, or a very few others were in the world?" In the early nineteenth century, Gustav Seyffarth claimed that the alphabet was invented the day the Great Flood ended—which he calculated to be September 7, 3446 B.C. In the Talmud, writing is mentioned as one of the ten things created in the twilight of the Sabbath eve. The twenty-two square Hebrew letters, sometimes called the "Writing of Heaven," have been associated with the twenty-two works of creation mentioned in Genesis and also have been believed to contain all knowledge. Although there is no direct mention of writing in the Book of Genesis, there are

ת ש ר ק צ י

Square Hebrew letters by Geofroy Tory

references to language. The story of the writing of the Ten Command-
ments is found in the Book of Exodus, and both Jehovah and Moses can
be read as having written them. The Jewish historian Josepheus said that
the children of Adam invented the letters. Another legend credited
Abraham as the inventor. In a third, Moses is honored for giving letters
to the Israelites, from whom the Phoenicians received them and in turn
passed them on to the Greeks.

Speech is usually taken for granted in ancient myths; it is *writing* that
is considered the important gift of the gods or invention of humans.
Speech does loom more important in the Judeo-Christian tradition,
although, once recorded, the words of the Law or the Prophets were
venerated as though they were the continuously audible word of God:
the world could be destroyed if even one letter was tampered with or
altered. Jewish tradition also forbade the casual destruction of worn and
tattered scriptural writings. It seems evident that as ancient peoples
became literate they were concerned to give writing more than a mundane significance—in part because they recognized the importance of
the accomplishment and perhaps also because they (like us) had no
historical record of a specific inventor to honor. According to archaeological evidence, true writing systems are of relatively recent origin—the
earliest known examples are Sumerian from about 4000 B.C.

Sumerian writing was originally pictographic and the preserve of an
elite priestly class. Literacy was highly honored: writing was called "the
beginning of kingship," and libraries were established. Sumerian writing was impressed on clay, which was not a very suitable medium for
pictorial representation. In time, the pictures became highly stylized and
were made with a wedge-shaped stylus, resulting in what is known as
cuneiform writing. This method continued to be used in successive
scripts of the Fertile Crescent area, including Akkadian, Assyrian,
Babylonian, and Persian—scripts that included phonetic syllabaries but
no true alphabet. Although these scripts lie outside the range of this
work, it should be noted that their users attached great importance to
written records. According to lore, Xisiathros (the Babylonian Noah)
buried all documents before the Deluge in order that they might be
preserved for use after the disaster.

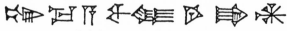

Babylonian cuneiform writing

Egyptian hieroglyphic script is probably the best known of the early writing systems. Many ancient writers ascribed the honor of inventing writing to the Egyptians, although some modern scholars believe that Egyptian writing could have been influenced by Sumerian. The script itself was markedly different. Classic hieroglyphic writing had developed by 3000 B.C. and was pictorial in appearance, most of the signs being derived from heavenly bodies, parts of the human body, natural objects, flora, fauna, furniture, etc. It was pictographic in origin, but also included ideographs and phonetic signs representing words, syllables, and in time even twenty-four consonantal signs developed mainly for the spelling of foreign names. It was not an alphabet, although it might have developed into one; but the Egyptians were conservative about change and they loved their decorative script. Thus, the hundreds of pictographs and ideographs were retained and even used redundantly in conjunction with the alphabetic characters.

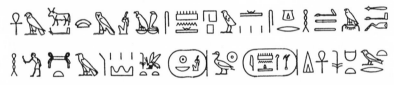

The costliness of papyrus as a writing material led to the practice in ancient Egypt of using both sides of the sheets, and even reusing them by washing off the ink—not only to provide a new writing surface but also, according to James Baikie, because "the ancient Egyptian had a profound belief in the magical virtue of the written word, and one of his favorite ways of possessing himself of knowledge was to wash off in beer the writing of any roll whose contents he wished to make infallibly his own, subsequently drinking the beer. He thus literally absorbed the knowledge which he desired to possess."

An ancient Egyptian papyrus relates the tale of an adventurous son of Ramses II, who resorted to grave robbing in order to possess a magic papyrus belonging to the god Thoth. The scroll was elaborately guarded in a golden box surrounded by seven other boxes of various materials, the whole guarded by serpents and scorpions. What made the effort worthwhile was that the scroll conferred on its possessor the power to understand the birds and animals and to be able to enchant everything that is in heaven or on earth. As usually happens in such tales, our hero was able to gain possession of the papyrus after many trials; however, its possession brought him more troubles than benefits. He was warned by his father, the Pharaoh, to return the papyrus but refused until he found himself naked and destitute, mourning his dead children. Happily, he found that dire scenario to have been only a dream of warning. He hurriedly returned the papyrus and did penance to Thoth, who forgave him. Since that time, it seems that there has been no short road to mastery of the mysteries; but the letters are still available for scholars to use in pursuing knowledge along more traditional paths and for writers to employ to enchant their readers.

Hieroglyphic script—called "writing of divine words"—was originally the possession of the elite, reserved for the highest purposes. One Egyptian official counseled his son to "love letters," for knowing them "you may protect yourself from hard labor of any kind." The illiterate also valued the power of writing. According to the *Book of the Dead*, if certain words were inscribed and buried with a person, (s)he would attain a state of contentment for eternity. In fact, the written words were considered sufficiently powerful to outweigh the sins of the deceased. In time, a cursive variant of the pictorial characters—called hieratic ("priestly") writing—developed. Still later—about 700 B.C.—a further cursive variant developed. It was called demotic ("common") writing and was used for everyday purposes by an increasingly literate populace.

Hieroglyphic, hieratic, and demotic scripts

In most ancient societies literacy generally increased. All writing systems depend upon social conventions, with the letters or signs taught through educational systems and transmitted to successive generations.

Many ancient scripts, including Egyptian, Mycenean, and Semitic, have been championed as the basis for our modern alphabet; but conclusive evidence is lacking. Much less disputed is the historical alphabet lineage from about 1000 B.C. Legend, myth, antique and modern scholarship all agree that the alphabet as we know it came from Phoenicia through Greece to Rome. The Phoenician script was one of a number of early Semitic scripts (ancient Hebrew was another) that, despite minor differences, shared many basic similarities—most were consonantal syllabaries consisting of 20 to 24 signs. Unfortunately, the

$$\text{𐤊 𐤁 𐤂 𐤃 𐤄 𐤅 𐤆 𐤇 𐤈 𐤉 𐤊 𐤋 𐤌 𐤍 𐤎 𐤏 𐤐 𐤑 𐤒 𐤓 𐤔 𐤕}$$

Phoenician letters

origin of these scripts is also shrouded in mystery. One theory is that Semitic mine workers in the Sinai peninsula gained the idea from the consonantal phonetic signs of their Egyptian overlords. Phoenician writing is thought to have developed by 1500 B.C. and perhaps as early as 1850 B.C. From what was most likely a similar source, the Phoenician and the Hebrew scripts began to diverge, becoming quite different in graphic design by 1000 B.C.

In some ways, "Phoenician" is a generic term for northern Semitic scripts of about 1000 B.C. The Phoenicians were the major seafaring and trading people of that age, traveling from Brittany to the Indian Ocean. A simplified writing system would obviously have been of great value to them and to those with whom they traded. One theory holds that they adopted a basic Semitic script that was influenced and altered by other scripts, such as Mycenean, with which they came in contact. In any case, by 1000 B.C. their writing system had become the *lingua franca* of the ancient world. Their basic script consisted of 22 consonantal signs and no vowel signs. The use of consonants only does not mean that vowels were unimportant—they would be sounded in speech—it is just that they were not considered to be necessary in writing, especially in an economizing script. Meanings can often be deduced in sntncs wth th vwls lft t. The direction of Phoenician writing was from right to left. The letters had names and a standard order. Most of the letter names were ordinary Semitic words, and their sound value was that of the first letter of the name—which is called the principle of acrophony, familiar to us through abecedaries ("a is for ape, b is for bird," etc.). Scholars disagree about whether or not the letter names were based on pictographic signs. If not, first a sign would be made, then it would be given a name. If a resemblance to something was noted in the sign's shape, that presumably would prompt the choice of the name—otherwise any word beginning with the required letter would serve the purpose. The reason for the particular order of the letters is not fully clear but is thought to be based on three principles: the similarity of the juxtaposed letters' sounds, the meanings of their names, and the forms of the signs. The letters' order is confirmed by their concurrent use as numbers.

Technically, the Phoenician and Hebrew systems were syllabaries rather than alphabets—a reader would have to supply the necessary vowels according to the context to ascertain the meaning of the words indicated by the letters. Thus *beth*, for example, not only expressed the sound [b], but also [ba], [be], [bi], [bo], [bu]. Yet in its use, simplicity, and regularity it is hardly an exaggeration to call the Phoenician script an alphabet—especially as it is the easily recognized ancestor of all our modern alphabets and expresses the basic alphabetic idea of one sign equaling one basic sound.

In Book Five of his *Histories*, Herodotus wrote that the Phoenicians introduced writing to the Greeks, who at first used the Phoenician characters before gradually altering and modifying them to suit the Greek language. Although he has been called the "Father of Lies" as well as the "Father of History," Herodotus's account is accepted by modern scholars. The oldest forms of the Greek letters are virtually identical with the Phoenician characters. The Ionians, in fact, called the letters "phoenicians." Also, the order of the letters is similar, as are their names, although the Greek letter names were meaningless whereas the Semitic names were actual words. The Greeks thus adopted the acrophonic principle of linking the name of the letter with its sound. The direction of writing was at first from right to left, following the Phoenician. Around the sixth century B.C. Greek writing became *boustrophedon* ("as an ox plows a field"), the direction of the lines alternating from right-to-left to left-to-right. Finally, about 500 B.C., Greek began to be written exclusively from left to right. The date of first Greek borrowing is uncertain—estimates range from 1400 B.C. to about 850 B.C., with the latter date increasing in scholarly favor. Scholars add about two centuries for its adoption and development before the alphabet was extensively used and accepted.

Early Greek
boustrophedon writing

It was the Greeks who created the first true alphabet, improving on the Phoenician original by adding signs for the vowels. (It is interesting to note that the borrower of a writing system often improves upon or simplifies the original, being unencumbered by the forces of tradition.) Besides adding vowels, the Greeks modified letters to signify other sounds that they needed in their language. Some characters thus fell into disuse or dropped out of the alphabet entirely. Always individualistic, the Greek city states developed many local variants of the basic Greek alphabet. As one scholar expressed it: the signs were reversed, elaborated, and stood on end—all treatments likely to befall a meaningless shape with an unintelligible name. Thus, there is no general agreement on the correct shape of the early Greek letters. And, with boustrophedon writing, for almost every letter there existed at least two forms. The early Greek inscriptional forms of the letters were rather stiff and severe geometrical shapes with little variation of line widths and usually little balance in size or positioning along a horizontal reading line.

ΑΒΓΔΕΖΗΘΙΚΛ MNΞΟΠΡΣΤΥΦΧΨΩ

Classic Greek alphabet

Two major variants of the Greek alphabet eventually evolved. One, the eastern or Ionian, was officially adopted by Athens in 403 B.C. and became the basis of the classical Greek, the modern Greek, and the Cyrillic (Slavic) alphabets. The other, the western or Pelasgian (also known as Chalcidian) variant, traveled with Greek colonists to the Italian peninsula where it became the basis for the Etruscan and Roman alphabets. The Greek letters underwent gradual modification through the centuries and developed capital, cursive, minuscule, and uncial forms, much as did the Roman alphabet. However, as the latter belongs to our study while the classical Greek alphabet developed along a different path, we shall turn our attention towards the Roman.

Before we leave mankind's other scripts behind, however, a word or two needs to be said. I would ask the reader to remember that this study is limited to the alphabet used by this writer; but it is not making any claims of superiority. Many people have called Arabic the most beautiful script; others extoll Chinese, Indian or other writing. Cuneiform and other ancient systems still intrigue the mind and delight the eye, while

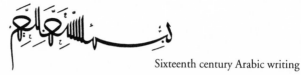

Sixteenth century Arabic writing

New World glyphs of the Aztec and Mayan civilizations open whole new worlds to the imagination. I know from experience that one need not know what is being said by a script to delight in it; yet that delight can be magnified when the script is known.

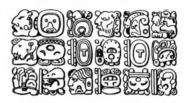

Mayan glyphs

But this is the important part: writing (known or unknown) can also spawn fear. As a weapon, the pen *is* mightier than the sword; writing is a danger as well as a delight, a threat as well as a promise; and whether the script is known or not there will always be some who would try to destroy or hide it from others because of its potential disruptive power. In telling the story of the fanatical Franciscan missionary Diego de Landa, Evan Connell indicts intolerance and misguided zeal for all times and cultures. De Landa almost succeeded in destroying all Mayan writings (and did cause incalculable losses)—all in the name of God and religion. Even at the time, in the sixteenth century, his actions sparked outrage in others and prompted his written defense—a monument to the power of writing. As Connell says, here "we meet the terrible yet familiar justification for book-burning: 'These people use definite signs or letters to record in their books their early history and their lore. By means of those letters, as well as by drawings and figures, they can understand their own story and make others understand and learn from it. We found a great number of books, and since there was nothing in them but superstitions and lies of the devil, we burned them all, to the great woe and lamentation of the people.'"

Ours is "the great woe and lamentation" whenever and wherever such repression is met up with—whether from local school boards banning books to book burnings in cultures near or far. Don't ever think that written signs are trifles—humans kill and die for them daily.

On a happier note, others bless them daily. Another side of missionary zeal is found in the story told by Edward Clodd of how the Cyrillic
alphabet was created when the Greek alphabet came to Russia. "'Formerly,' says John, Exarch of Bulgaria, who wrote in the ninth century,
'the Slavonians had no books, but they read and made divinations by
means of pictures and figures cut on wood, being pagans. After they had
received baptism they were compelled, without any proper rules, to write
their Slavonic tongue by means of Greek and Latin letters. But how
could they write well in Greek letters such words as Bog, Zhivot, Zelo,
or Tserkov, and others like these? And so many years passed by. But then
God, loving the human race, had pity on the Slavonians, and sent them
St. Constantine, the Philosopher, called Cyril, a just and true man, who
made for them an alphabet of thirty-eight letters, of which some were
after the Greek style, and some after the Slavonic language.'"

АБВГДЕЖЗИЙКЛ

Cyrillic alphabet letters

Now, let us proceed with our study of the Roman alphabet.

The Etruscan alphabet provides the link between the Greek and
Roman alphabets. The Etruscans were the dominant culture in Italy
from about 700 B.C. until the rise of Roman power nearly four hundred
years later. In the eighth century B.C., they are thought to have adopted
the western alphabet variant of Greek colonists and then adapted it to fit
the Etruscan language. This language was almost certainly non-Indo-
European and presents scholars today with the curious case that they are
able to "read" it—knowing the sound the letters symbolize—but not
understand it. Originally, the Etruscan alphabet had 26 signs, although
there was great variety in the shapes of the individual signs. It reached its
classic formulation about the year 450 B.C. with 20 letters, including four
vowels. Etruscan writing continued until the first century A.D. but fell
into increasing disuse with the loss of political independence to Rome.

Etruscan alphabet

The Roman alphabet probably originated in the seventh century B.C. and was influenced by early forms of both the Etruscan and western Greek alphabets. The earliest Roman alphabet had 21 letters, including the five basic Greek vowel signs. Like the Etruscans before them, the Romans adapted the various signs to their own language requirements, retaining many of the letters, rejecting some, and restoring and inventing a few others. The earliest known specimen of Roman writing is from about 600 B.C. Early Roman writing was also boustrophedon, the lines alternating direction from left-to-right to right-to-left, and thus in effect almost doubling the number of characters a literate person would have to recognize, since a letter such as B would face either left or right depending on the direction of the line of writing. By 500 B.C., however, Romans began to write exclusively in a left to right direction. The Romans continued to develop their alphabet long after the Greeks and Etruscans considered theirs complete. This we will study later; but it should be noted now that there was much to develop. As Donald Anderson writes: "The early history of Roman letters is scarcely the noble enterprise we might have been led to expect."

Early Roman boustrophedon writing

Ancient Romans commonly carried small wax-covered wooden tablets called pugillares for use in their daily commerce. A sharp metal stylus was used to inscribe letters on the wax. (In emergencies the stylus could be used as a weapon, thus revealing that before the pen became mightier than the sword, the stylus could be the latter's equal!) Pugillares were convenient and reusable; however, the letters inscribed on them were purely functional, with no pretensions of aesthetic excellence. The letters were eventually made beautiful with the more suitable materials of pen and ink on papyrus or parchment, or the careful carving of inscriptional letters on stone monuments.

For some five hundred years Roman writing was irregular and generally unimpressive. Only in the first century B.C. did the script begin to exhibit the mastery with which we are familiar. The outlines and proportions of the letters were gradually improved and refined, resulting in inscriptional capital letters that were individually beautiful as well as rhythmically graceful in combination. To quote the influential printer and scholar Giovanni Mardersteig: "The capital letters used in classic Roman inscription are the most living element in the heritage handed down to us by antiquity. No other civilization has endowed its letters with such an unmistakeable character, familiar to all those who read and write—a form which has lost none of its validity and still constitutes the means of communication in the languages of many peoples." Their letterforms have even been called the Romans' greatest original artistic achievement.

ABCDEF

The Romans created a distinctive alphabet—one that had more variety than its antecedents. Whereas more than two-thirds of the Greek letter signs were rigid and angular, only a little more than half of the Roman capital letters are straight-lined. The Roman alphabet thus has more of a rhythm, with the severity of the straight letters acting as a stabilizing force complementing the grace and variety supplied by the curved forms. Also, the use of the finishing stroke (or serif) on vertical elements gave the lettering a distinctive regularity and formality. It has been said that the Roman alphabet marches along its base line, effectively conveying the idea of power and empire.

TI·CLAVDIVS·DRVSI·F·
TRIBVNICIA·POTES
AQVAS·CLAVDIAM·EX FONT
ITEM·ANIENEM·NOVAM·A

Roman inscription lettering from an aqueduct in Rome

The capital letters were the only forms that existed initially, and the great examples of the Roman capital letters are the monumental inscriptions of the first centuries of the Roman Imperial period, such as the lettering of the Trajan Column. However, even these letters reveal more variety than is generally believed. And common everyday Roman handwriting—like our own—varied greatly in quality and legibility. The history of the alphabet after the beginning of the Christian era involves changes in letters and lettering brought about through writing with pen and ink. In briefly tracing that history it will be useful to realize that some changes in letterforms are considered merely stylistic variants; others are more functional, such as the creation of new letters or the changes that led to the development of the lower-case letter forms—those most commonly used today.

After reaching their elegant formulation in the first century A.D., the classic forms of the capital letters were established, but writing did not long (if ever) remain static. The Roman letter forms began to alter according to the uses to which they were put and the methods used to make them. Although it may be surprising to many who might view the alphabet as essentially stable and unchanging, letter forms are constantly changing—though most often very gradually. Its letter forms often distinguish an era or culture as notably as does its architecture. And, though one could argue that it is only particular representations that change while the ideal (classical Roman) form remains, that is only partly correct, for many people do not acknowledge the classical as the ideal. Also, there is not any particular alphabet inscription that succeeding ages have recognized as the perfect model. The inscriptional capitals were the first flowering of the Roman alphabet, however; and these are the letters that adorned the monuments and were visible to passers-by in the following centuries, as well as the forms that later Renaissance designers used as their models.

The handwritten counterparts of the inscriptional capitals are less known (very few manuscripts featuring them have survived), but they echo them closely in form and feeling although the letters vary in proportion and detail. These letters are known as monumental or square capitals and were considered the highest form of writing during the period of the Empire. This style was known as a formal or "book" hand and its use was reserved only for texts of high distinction—such as the writings of the poet Virgil. Square capitals were very elegant and formal, but the letters were difficult to write rapidly and took up a lot of space on the expensive writing materials of parchment and papyrus. As Nicolete

ABCDEFGHILMNOPQRSTVXY·+
YARIALYENEREARTESLABOR

Roman square capital alphabet (above); used in text of Virgil from the 4th century (below)

Gray points out: "The Roman letter was evolved as an inscriptional letter and its forms come easily to the chisel—but not to the pen.…They are artificial and unnatural to the pen, beautiful, but very difficult to write."

The desire for a more economical script coupled with the scribe's natural tendency to write faster and easier letterforms led to the development of the Rustic capitals. These letters retained most of the basic capital shapes but were very different in appearance en masse. Better adapted to the use of pen and ink, the Rustic script was easier to write rapidly. It exhibited a more cursive style and used ligatures (joined letters) in the interest of speed. Rustic was also a book hand, chosen for important manuscripts. (Its name was a creation of eighteenth century scholar⸍ who considered it somewhat primitive, something its Roman originators did not.)

ABCDEFGHILMNOPQRSTVXY
NYMPHASQVESORORESILIVMNONPOPVLI

Roman Rustic alphabet and example

It should not be forgotten that throughout Roman history there also existed common writing used for everyday purposes. This writing was much more cursive than the book scripts and showed the irregularity that any personal handwriting reveals in contrast to the regularity of our formal typographic or calligraphic forms. Throughout the history of the alphabet, cursive writing has tended to modify the more formal styles by substituting simpler and more rapidly executed forms.

Roman imperial cursive script (left), and graffiti from Pompeii

By the fourth century, letter changes had become so dramatic as to constitute the beginning of a new style—the uncial. The established capital letters were not wholly abandoned—they were occasionally used for texts—but they soon came to be used with uncial letters only as initial letters at the beginnings of sections, for the first letters of names, or wherever emphasis was required. This set a precedent for the later use of capitals (or majuscules) and minuscules in combination. The uncial was commonly a large letter—the name implies one inch, although no examples that large are known to exist. This style was also named in the eighteenth century; the name was taken from a term used by St. Jerome some fourteen hundred years earlier. The saint was unhappy with the elaborate Bibles of his day, feeling that they were outside the spirit of the simple gospel message. He inveighed against the costly materials and large elaborate lettering, which he called uncial letters—though it is possible he was not referring to the style of lettering that now bears the name. Uncials resembled classic capitals, but with a strong tendency to rounded forms—especially A, D, E, H, M, and U.

ABCDEFGHILMNOPQRSTUXYZ
PRIMUMSPECTANTIBUSUFFERT

Roman uncial alphabet and sample text

The uncial script, revealing the influence of the square-nibbed pen and its movements, was the first to use ascenders and descenders for certain letters, leading eventually to lower-case letterforms. It was used in literary and official writing until the eighth or ninth centuries and was especially common in the growing body of Christian writing. According to B. L. Ullman, "the uncial script was in a peculiar sense a Christian development. The hand was formalized by the early copyists of the Bible." It should be mentioned that some scholars believe that this style was expressly formulated by early Christian writers who wanted their manuscripts to look different from the pagan works written in Roman square capital and Rustic styles. Later, with the official establishment of Christianity as the state religion, the style gained greater secular promi-nence as well. In any case, it is recognized by scholars as being closely linked with the Christian religion.

In early manuscripts (as well as in much previous Greek and Roman writing) the text was often written continuously—apparently because of a feeling that spaces at uneven intervals marred the beauty of a line. Separation of words began to be popular about A.D. 600 and, needless to say, helped increase writing legibility.

Scribes continued to modify the letter forms, so that by the seventh century there developed what scholars have distinguished as the half-

abcdepȝhilmnopqrſꞇux

Roman semi-uncial alphabet

uncial or semi-uncial style. The letters most affected were A, B, D, E, G, L, M, N, Q, R, and S—letters that were rapidly assuming a modern minuscule or lower-case form. The development of minuscules was influenced by the need for legibility as writing became more rapidly executed. To increase legibility, certain letters were carried either above or below the text line to make them more immediately recognizable. But the great variety of early writing styles makes it impossible to consider any one example a model.

No writing survives from England during the period of Roman domination. The Roman alphabet was reintroduced to the British Isles by Christian missionaries (including St. Patrick) in the fourth and fifth centuries. These monks and scribes developed their religion and writing in relative isolation and employed both to help rekindle Europe's dim lamp of culture a few centuries later. A high point of scribal art was the uncial and semi-uncial forms written by Irish monks and, later, Anglo-Saxon scribes of the seventh and eighth centuries. Not only was their scribal work exquisite for such troubled and somewhat degenerate times—their isolated monasteries were truly outposts of learning and Christianity—but many people consider their most famous work, *The Book of Kells*, to be the most beautiful manuscript ever written. The modern authority Nicolete Gray calls their school of letter design the "most inventive" in the history of Western lettering: "A background of

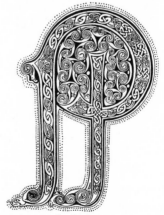

Insular semi-uncial alphabet and decorated initial

abstract art has inspired an approach to lettering which is completely different from that of the classical tradition."

Writing on the Continent at the time was not nearly as aesthetically accomplished as Insular (Irish and Anglo-Saxon) writing. There was no widely diffused style and few centers of scribal learning or practice. A hodge-podge of personal and regional variants of the Roman alphabet developed, some similar enough to be known as styles—such as the Visigothic script of Spain and the Merovingian script of France. All were highly stylized and often very complicated, employing a wide range of ligatures, special signs, and abbreviations, which make them virtually illegible to modern eyes. Many of these ligatures and abbreviations were the result of the scribes' laziness—using them made it unnecessary to raise the hand from the page as often in writing. To call the scribes weary rather than lazy would probably be more fair, for theirs was a hard task. As one wrote: "The man who cannot write, thinks little of the writer's toil, but those who have tried it know what hard work it is."

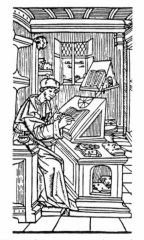 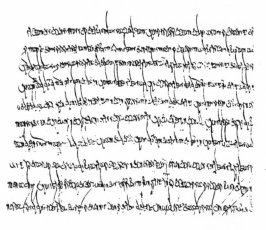

Sixteenth century woodcut of a scribe, and Merovingian writing from the seventh century

The drawing of ornate or decorative letters became well-established during this period. Eastern peoples (especially the Chinese) look upon writing as drawing—as moving and expressive line. According to Gray, Western lettering generally lacks this tradition but most closely approached it during the Middle Ages—one of the few times that calligraphic expression took precedence over legibility. As she writes: there are few if any decorations in surviving classical manuscripts; but "by the

eighth century lettering is the primary embellishment of books....The
idea of a letter has become something very different from the straightforward pen-written rustic, or the linear structure of monumental lettering.
It is now a starting point out of which the artist can begin to make all
sorts of formal and imaginative creations." In both Insular and Conti-
nental writing, letters began to be turned into representational drawings
or frames for illustrations, with more emphasis given to the representation than to the letter as a legible sign. This was the first (and greatest)
period of the metamorphosis of letter forms. Letters became intricate
geometrical patterns, human heads, animals, plants, and more. They no
longer had a strict separate identity nor were they locked into a particular
spatial construct; they had become two-dimensional forms on a page.

Insular decorative letters from the early medieval period (redrawn by George Bain)

This development helps to demonstrate that throughout history
there has been great diversity in letter forms. During some periods,
invention and personal expression in manipulating the forms of the
letters are valued. Ancient and medieval writings reveal such a diversity
of forms that some are barely (if at all) recognizable. At other times,
order and uniformity are honored. The emphasis on independent,
structured signs is generally a feature of classicizing periods such as
Imperial Rome, the Carolingian era, or the Italian Renaissance. It is
these periods, however, that have most greatly influenced the history of
the alphabet; and it is to the second of these that we turn next.

With the reign of Charlemagne (768–814), a measure of stability and
order was brought back to the political realm as well as to the world of
letters. Neither task was easy. In his biography of Charlemagne, Einhard
relates that despite his efforts to learn to write by placing "tablets and
sheets of parchment beneath the pillows of his bed in order to profit
from his moments of leisure to practise tracing the letters," Charlemagne

took up the study too late in life and "the results were not a success." Perhaps that only made the emperor more determined to make the letters easier to trace. Imperial decree ordered an improvement of writing based on a model developed by the emperor's councilor, an Englishman, Alcuin of York. This model alphabet was actually an amalgam of the Insular semi-uncial and various elements of other book scripts. It is called the Carolingian minuscule and was one of the most influential developments in the history of the alphabet, as well as being a unifying force in Charlemagne's Holy Roman Empire. The Carolingian could be called the first popular minuscule alphabet—that is, it was constructed as though between four imaginary lines (with true ascenders and descenders) rather than the two imaginary lines of majuscule (capital letter) scripts. Some scholars maintain, however, that technically it was not a true minuscule since it was not used consistently in combination with capitals. In any case, it came to have a great influence on our modern lower-case letter forms. The Carolingian featured small, somewhat rounded letters, very legible and rapidly executed—which made it an excellent book hand.

abcdefghilmnopqrfʃtuxz
aliquif ex eif extollitur pro ʃcientia
artif ʃuae hic alif erigatur ab ipʃa

Carolingian minuscule alphabet and text example

The Carolingian flourished until about the twelfth century when, despite its excellence, it was effectively displaced by the gothic or black letter styles. ("Gothic" was originally a Renaissance term of some scorn, associating the medieval style that was thought somewhat rude and barbaric with the earlier barbarian Goths who helped destroy the Roman Empire. "Black letter" referred simply to the density of the letter forms which en masse made a page of writing very dark.) This displacement illustrates a repeated development in the history of letters: no matter how effective a script is, the demand for novelty or for a writing style that reflects the "spirit" of a period or a place often leads to the creation of new forms. And, whatever else can be said about the black letter styles, they did reflect the architecture and spirit of the late medieval period.

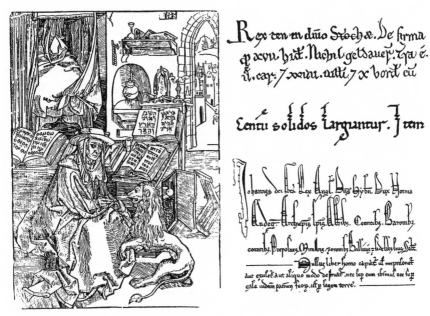

Dürer woodcut of St. Jerome (note the various scripts); right: writing from the Domesday Book (1087), a 12th century Italian charter, and the Magna Charta of 1215 (bottom)

Although the gothic style appears to be a radical break from the Carolingian, its full blossoming was accomplished gradually. Romanesque artists especially experimented with the forms of the letters, creating unique combinations and intricately interwoven patterns. Through the centuries, the rounded Anglo-Saxon minuscule had gradually become more angular and vertical. By the thirteenth century it had developed into the full black letter or Old English letter. Many different varieties developed: Textur, Fraktur, and Schwabacher, among others. Textur was named for its appearance en masse—similar to a woven fabric. Fraktur, with its sharp angles and thin hairlines, appeared almost as broken letters. Schwabacher was a generic name for a more rounded informal gothic. The various black letter forms, being quite condensed, were all economical; but this also made them rather illegible due to the

gaudium manet. Memento illius frequenter

zů einem ſiechen / ſo erkennt menſch ſterbē ſoll oder gene

qui defendat me hodie:et pte= gat ab oīibus inimicis meis

Black letter scripts: Textur (top), Schwabacher (bottom left), and Fraktur (bottom right)

similarity of the individual letters. B.L. Ullman writes that: "At its best Gothic is beautiful but hard to read, at its worst it is extremely ugly and illegible." Confusion of letters—especially i, u, m, n—occurred as they were juxtaposed together. These were the first true dual-alphabet scripts, with majuscules and minuscules used consistently together. Gothic capitals were often large and elaborate.

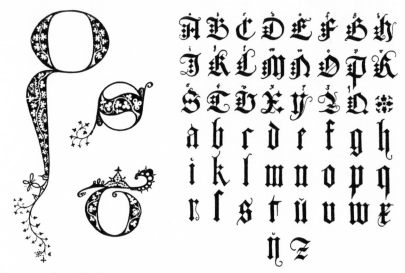

Ornate medieval display capitals (left), and Textur alphabet designed by Albrecht Dürer

A great many contractions, abbreviations and ligatures are found in the black letter scripts, which reflected increasing literacy as well as the rise of the universities. Scribes were no longer only transcribing the word of God for a few fellows; they were now churning out books as rapidly as possible for a growing secular and scholarly audience, and all these measures saved time and materials.

Black letter was the dominant writing style in the mid-fifteenth century when printing with moveable metal type was invented, and it was used in the earliest printed books—including the Gutenberg Bible—which were modeled after the manuscript books of the period. Many of that era's book lovers frowned on the very idea of printed books, one maintaining that he would never allow a printed book in his library. In his book *In Praise of Scribes,* the abbot Johannes Trithemius extolled writing over printing because he felt that it kept the monastic scribes busy, encouraged diligence, and fostered knowledge of the scriptures.

However, he had his book printed (let us charitably presume simply because he wished it to reach more readers).

In the course of the fifteenth and sixteenth centuries, printers and type designers began to stress the independent merits of their work and no longer tried to imitate the look of manuscripts. The unwieldy black letter types began to be supplanted by more rounded forms. This did not happen overnight, however, nor without some resistance. As Nicolete Gray writes: "It is difficult for us to imagine what it must have been like to find Gothic writing familiar and easy to read, and romans foreign, yet the roman letter had been obsolete for two centuries and there is evidence that people found them difficult to read." In most parts of Europe black letter fell into disuse as a text type except in some legal and religious texts, although in Germany it continued in common use into the twentieth century. In John Lewis's opinion, "the gothic letter was fit only for the writings of the Church. The strongly humanistic Renaissance needed the open round letters to express the Florentines' new open-ended thoughts…the archaic phraseology of the law needed the archaic gothic typeface."

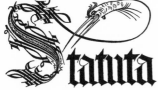

werbé/ als Hertzog Eberhard/ Keyser Conrads/Hertzogen
zu Francken/ vnd Heinrici vorfahr/ Bruder/ vnd vnder
andern Hertzog Arnold auß Bayern/ die jhm zuvor nach
Leib vnd Leben stunden/ hernach seine beste vertrauwete
Freunde worden/ vnd jn für jren Herrn vnd Röm. Keyser
erkannt vnd gehalten. Als nun dieser Heinricus in ver-
waltung seines Reichs gemeynem Teutsch vnd Vatter-
land vorzusehen allen fleyß fürwandte/ alle abtrünnige
vnd widerspenstigen straffte/ die auffrühren vil embörun-
gen/ so sich hin vnd wider erhuben/ stillete/ die vngläubigen
zum gehorsam vñ Christlichen Glauben verursachete/ vnd
darzu alle best Reichs Fürste jm hierinn behülfflich zu seyn

Display letter with Textur type printed in London by Richard Pynson in 1515 (left);
German Fraktur type of mid-16th century (right)

Although printing originated in Germany, Italy soon became its main center of influence. Italian scribes had never fully accepted the black letter styles, and they soon developed other typefaces based on the Chancery or Humanistic handwriting of early Renaissance humanists. Many of those scribes had a special interest in classical Latin literature. They were critical of gothic scripts and reformed their handwriting— that of Petrarch and Salutari has been called *fere humanistica* (almost humanistic). Poggio Bracciolini is credited with the later invention, in 1402, of roman lower-case forms that were in proper relation to the capitals. His Humanistic script was based on the Carolingian minuscule, which Renaissance scholars called *lettera antiqua*, mistakenly thinking that it had existed in antiquity because of their acquaintance with it in

cruce·Tamquam nouellus uitulus ·p.
peccatis ppti uoluntatie mactatus in

Humanistic writing

ninth century copies of classical writings. (It has been said that the history of lettering can be seen as the repeated revival or rediscovery of the Roman letters.) Niccoli of Florence further refined the script, preparing the way for the triumph of roman over gothic letters.

According to Alexander Nesbitt, the union of Roman capitals (incised letters) with Carolingian minuscules (pen and ink forms) was one of the illogical passages of alphabet history. Scribes noticed that the two did not fit together perfectly and so they modified the minuscules by adding serifs and by lengthening ascenders and descenders to make them more compatible. Humanistic manuscripts of the fifteenth century are among the finest ever produced. Ornaments and ligatures were used sparingly, and the manuscripts had a clarity, cleanness and precision distinguishing them from medieval writing. By the time printing reached Italy, the Humanistic script was fully developed into a type style soon known throughout the world as "roman." It was masterfully translated into type by Nicolas Jensen in 1471 and soon thereafter by others—designers of excellent forms that, according to one scholar, "gave the gothic character its deathblow." Thus, by a rather circuitous route, the letters we now take for granted returned to their original capital forms accompanied by harmonious lower-case letters. And these designs have served as typographic models for more than five hundred years. At the other end of the writing spectrum, the related Chancery cursive script of that period also led directly (though not as successfully) to our modern popular cursive handwriting styles in which all the letters of a word are joined to facilitate rapid writing.

qui de lydis fcripfit: Xanthûq; breuiauit. Secûdus hic ipfe.
Tertius ftratonicus fophifta. Quartus fculptor. Quintus
& fextus pictores: utrofq; memorat apollodorus. Cynici au
tem uolumina tredeci funt. Neniæ: teftamenta: epiftolæ cô
pofitæ ex deorum pfona ad phyficos & mathematicos grá-

ad rectam uitam
totius generis ori

Roman type of Nicolas Jensen

With the development of printing, the shapes of the letters were no longer dictated by the pen; they would henceforth be determined by punch-cutting and its more rigid and less variable cast metal forms.

Uniformity would now be the rule. Printing helped freeze the development of letter forms, and Humanistic writing was thus well-timed for its ascendance to prominence—otherwise, alphabet forms may have developed more radically. But it should be noted that printers tried many other type styles and rejected them. According to one authority, even in type there existed a process of natural selection or "survival of the fittest." D. B. Updike felt that early printers, in trying to copy the look of manuscripts in their first productions, made some unfortunate errors in type design that would have been eliminated if they had realized that "they could never successfully reproduce in metal all the forms derived from the pen."

Textur type from the 42-line Gutenberg Bible (left), and some of the alternate letters and ligatures cut by Gutenberg to imitate the look of handwritten manuscripts

Printers and type designers soon learned from their mistakes, and awkward forms were in great measure eliminated. The basic designs differed only in minor points, the average reader unable to discern them except as a slightly different look or "feel" of a printed page. But it is these subtle differences that have occupied printers, type designers and scholars ever since. However, in many ways, the type designs of the first fifty years of printing have seldom if ever been equaled or surpassed for their beauty and general look or "presence" on the page.

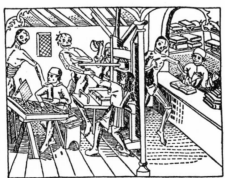

An early woodcut of printers, type compositor and bookseller from the
Dance of Death printed in Lyon by Matthias Huss in 1499

At about the time of the invention of printing, there was a corresponding interest in the ancient Roman letter forms that accompanied the Renaissance revival of classical learning. Felice Feliciano was probably the first to make a thorough study of Roman letters, and in about 1463 he designed an alphabet based on classical models. He felt that the writing of the Augustan period was based on exact geometrical proportion and that the subsequent decline of the Roman Empire was reflected in its letters: "The geometrical foundation and the serifs disappeared, the aesthetic canon was forgotten, and block-letters became, apart from a few exceptions, the expression of an age deprived of spiritual and civic leadership." Others soon began creating their own model alphabets—usually by compass and ruler on a grid framework. Luca Pacioli, Albrecht Dürer, and Geofroy Tory all designed such alphabets; and with the third especially we shall become better acquainted. It is instructive to note, however, that Dürer, the most accomplished artist of the group, said that it is impossible to reduce all letters to simple geometric formulae. The letter shapes are more subtle. Some lines have to be shaped "to a juster proportion." In the years that followed, others periodically arose to remind the strict theoreticians of this.

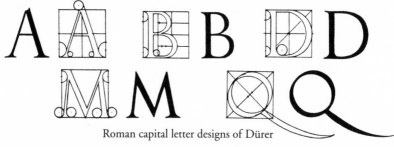

Roman capital letter designs of Dürer

Although they may have erred in seeking total geometrical exactitude, the Renaissance letter designers did foster interest in the forms of the letters. Soon after Jensen introduced his masterful roman type design, Aldus Manutius created the italic type—a more slanted cursive set of forms. After a brief period as a book type, it became generally relegated to auxiliary text uses—a practice which has continued up to this day. The generic names of the two basic type forms—roman and italic—were early employed by printers throughout Europe to characterize their Italian origin and have remained as a tribute to the excellent creations of the early type designers. S. H. Steinberg claims that these

F ertur equis, rapidoq; uolans obit omnia curru.
I amq; hic germanum, iamq; hic oftendit ouantem
N ec conferre manum patitur, uolat auia longe.

First italic type cut by Francesco Griffo for Aldus Manutius (from text printed in 1501)

type designs were linked to the spirit of humanism penetrating western Europe, and resistance to that spirit caused other groups to cling to the isolationism of their alphabet forms.

Broadly speaking, the Old Style roman typefaces (as these first designs have come to be called) have a less mechanical feel than later type designs. There is more "drawing" in them. They echoed their handwritten models to a great extent, yet at the same time the letter shapes were gradually refined to more standardized and independent forms. Their basic characteristics include a basic axial bias to the rounded letters; very little contrast between thick and thin strokes; heavy, bracketed serifs; and a general heaviness in appearance. With italics, major changes involved round letters becoming compressed and elliptical; letters slanting to the right; and letters being very closely spaced or joined together as ligatures. Other typecutters refined and designed other early roman and italic forms: Claude Garamond, Robert Granjon, Christophe Plantin, Francesco Griffo, and William Caslon were important designers during the 250-year period when Old Style typefaces reigned supreme. Unfortunately, after the sixteenth century, the general quality of printing and care in type punch-cutting were much inferior to that in the century that followed the first flowering, even though punch-cutting especially was a trade jealously guarded by its practitioners. Writing in 1683, the knowledgeable Joseph Moxon called it a mystery, while a punch-cutter of the period said that he would not divulge the art for 100,000 florins.

Governments also found it useful to control the typefounding and printing industries to help control the dissemination of information, especially in England, where in the sixteenth and again in the seventeenth century the number of typefounders and printers licensed to practice their trades was severely limited. This prompted John Milton to protest with his justly famous treatise on freedom of the press, the *Areopagitica*, which eventually helped lead to an easing of the restrictions. The increased possibilities of competition also again gave printers and typefounders reason to care about the quality of their work.

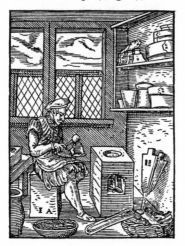

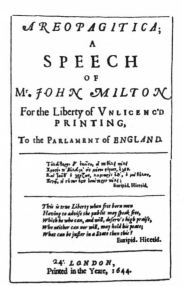

Woodcut of a typefounder from Jost Amman's *Book of Trades*, printed in Germany in 1568 (left); and title page of *Areopagitica* (showing inferior quality of printing and typefounding)

Towards the end of the eighteenth century there was a development in type design that scholars consider sufficiently distinctive to constitute a new style. This style is now called Transitional, and its major practitioner was the English printer John Baskerville. Although he was a successful manufacturer, Baskerville found himself with a curious passion, one shared by this writer and many others—perhaps including you, gentle reader. As Baskerville expressed it: "Having been an early admirer of the beauty of Letters, I became insensibly desirous of contributing to the perfection of them." More fortunately, he was able to implement his ideas. His design featured greater contrast of line widths, thinner serifs, and a lighter feel or "color." It met with early criticism; many claimed that it was difficult to read, even causing blindness! But, in a letter to Baskerville, Benjamin Franklin reported that he tested one critic by calling a Caslon Old Style type a Baskerville sample, at which the

Double Pica Roman.

TANDEMaliquando, Quirites! L. Catilinam furentem audacia, fcelus anhelantem, pe-
ABCDEFGHIJKLMN.

Double Pica Italic.

TANDEM aliquando, Quirites! L. Catilinam furentem audacia, fcelus anhelantem, peftem patriæ nefarie moli-
ABCDEFGHIJKLMN.

Baskerville type from Specimen of 1762

"connoisseur" damned it as much inferior, though it was the same type he had praised when it was correctly labeled. What's in a name?

Within a few years another type style developed to which the Transitional was transitional. It was called Modern, and it has been called a "complete expression of the Age of Reason" because it took advantage of technology and freed type design from characteristics that were irrelevant or unnecessary in its manufacture—no longer did type seek to imitate the pen and ink drawn letter. Two of its representative typefaces are Didot and Bodoni—named after their respective designers. In many ways, modern type was the result of technological improvements in engraving, printing techniques, and paper finishes, which allowed design characteristics theretofore impossible. Modern type is distinguished by great contrast between thick and thin strokes; straight, hairline serifs; and narrower letters having a vertical emphasis.

HoMe HoMe HoMe
Old Style (left), Transitional (center), and Modern type

Modern types, although dominant throughout the nineteenth century, have generally not been looked upon with great favor by subsequent type designers because their extreme contrast of line widths makes them difficult to read. William Morris, for example, thought the Bodoni type the most illegible ever cut with its "preposterous" thicks and thins. "The sweltering hideousness of the Bodoni letter" was one of his more memorable descriptions of it. When printed with extreme care in large sizes, some modern typefaces could be very elegant, and certain books featuring them are considered triumphs of the printer's craft. Generally, however, the type sizes used were rather small and the printing was not of the highest quality—a combination always guaranteed to produce a book difficult to read.

The Industrial Revolution greatly affected the printing and type-founding industries, leading, as Alexander Lawson claims, to a degradation of the basic letterforms. The goals of increasing speed and output led to a general decline in quality, and less attention was given to detail in text and newspaper typefaces; but, conversely, advertisers and designers began to see type as a means to gain readers' attention. As Lawson says: "Visual relief depended on the development at this time of the myriad display types of kaleidoscopic variety that characterize for us nineteenth century typography."

The nineteenth century was typographically wild. Advertising and other ephemera replaced books as the printers' major product, and designers' attention turned to display typefaces. As society became more consumer-oriented, advertisers saw in type new opportunities. A whole class of type designs developed along unconventional lines. The ability of a typeface to claim attention was more important than its legibility or sedate beauty. And typefaces began to howl for attention. As political caricature exaggerated features to create an impact, type designers similarly exaggerated type features. Modern type was already distinguished by its great contrast between thick and thin lines; designers of display type made the contrast even greater, creating what are now known as Egyptian or Fat-face types. Other major type innovations of the century were square serif and sans serif type designs (although the latter did not achieve prominence until well into the twentieth century).

This was the great era of decorative and advertising type. Very large letter designs were cut in wood and used to print posters and placards. The designs were often as crude and vulgar as their employment, with

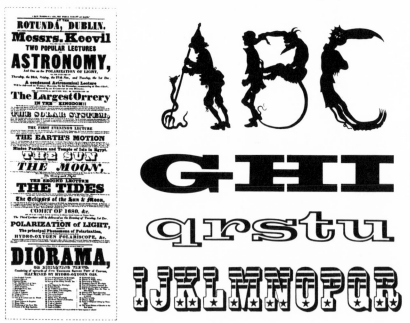

Advertisement and various nineteenth century typefaces

very little sensitivity and considerable decoration displayed. Especially in the United States, a great many typefaces were often mixed in the same advertisement—which sometimes (surprisingly) had a charm of its own. As Donald Anderson has said, often "the piece communicates a dazzling vulgarity quite in keeping with the entertainments announced, and in this sense nineteenth century typography reflected life on the frontier—brashly improvised." In other words, poor type poorly used (in a more pure sense) could be very effective in communicating a message or idea. But, as Frank Denman says of Victorian typography, it could also be hideously vulgar: "Type was tortured into wretched shapes and covered with gingerbread. It was set in twisted lines surrounded by curiously bent rules. Typography had long since ceased to be an art and had become an exercise in ingenuity." Nicolete Gray more kindly calls it a "folk art" of early industrial society. Another commentator, Seán Jennett, adds: "Nothing was too strange or too far-fetched to be made into the letters of the alphabet....Most of these queer types were mania types; they were produced to satisfy a demand for novelty, and when the taste cloyed they wore away in disgrace and a later novelty took their place." And D.B. Updike labeled almost all decorative faces under the heading "types we ought not to want."

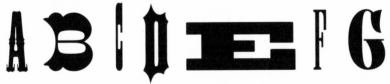

Modern versions of nineteenth century wood display typefaces

The late nineteenth century also saw important developments in typecasting which revolutionized the industry. With the creation of keyboard hot-metal systems such as Monotype and Linotype, a keyboard operator could create type on demand, independent of the old cases of foundry type which had heretofore characterized the industry. The machines held matrices into which hot metal was poured, forming letters which could be remelted at the conclusion of the project. The different machines' suppliers developed hundreds of typefaces, making an immense variety of letterforms more easily available to printers.

Another important development of the late nineteenth century was the revival of Old Style printing typefaces. With the Arts and Crafts

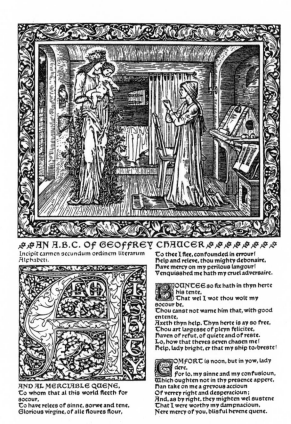

Portion of page of *Kelmscott Chaucer* (1896) with type designs by William Morris and illustration by Sir Edward Burne-Jones

movement there was a renewed interest in quality printing and type forms—both from the past as well as new designs based on traditional forms. William Morris and his Kelmscott Press were major forces of reform towards the end of the century, and their influence has extended to the present. Other quality small private presses soon were founded, sparking a new interest in typography which even carried over to larger commercial publishing houses. In the words of one of our foremost contemporary designers, Warren Chappell: "Within a decade after the founding of the Kelmscott Press, the alphabet was being reexamined as it had not been for decades, even centuries."

The twentieth century has witnessed both the revival of type from all periods and the development of new designs. Many variants of classic types exist, with different typographic companies offering their particu-

lar version. Some are so close to each other as to be almost indistinguishable; others carrying the same name—Garamond, for example—appear
very different when set in full pages of text. Unfortunately, many
variants of these typefaces have simply been stolen, slightly altered, and
renamed—a problem which has plagued designers since the fifteenth
century, but which certainly worsened in the nineteenth century when
punch-cutters were no longer needed for the creation of type. Succeeding technologies have made potential theft even easier, although the
design of typefaces remains as challenging as ever—a fact which should
help make the proprietary nature of type manufacturers (in whatever
medium they develop their products) understandable.

One of the major developments of the first half of the twentieth
century was the use and design of sans serif types. Certain designers—
such as those of the Bauhaus school—saw sans serif type as clean and
functional, typifying the "modern" spirit of the era. Many different sans
serif designs were developed for both text and advertising uses, and in
certain quarters the style was misnamed "gothic," although there is no
connection between it and the black letter types of the medieval period.
As stated by Walter Gropius, the Bauhaus type ideal was "a restriction to
typical basic form and color, intelligible to all." Hence, what were
considered extraneous features (serifs, for example) were dropped from
the letters, reducing them to stark, rationally constructed skeletal forms.
They were seen as eminently functional and unencumbered by historic
baggage—that is, they echoed no tradition, proclaiming instead the
impersonal machine age community of mankind and not a particular
individual or period. In practice, however, though sans serif types have
achieved a great measure of popularity, they have not supplanted the
older romans in general use, beauty, or legibility. And they have also
elicited some scorn. The important American graphic designer (and
curmudgeon) T. M. Cleland said this about sans serif type: "Cutting the
serifs off roman letters in the name of 'simplicity' may well be compared
to simplifying a man by cutting off his hands and feet!"

Another major development of twentieth century typography was the
introduction of type "families," the variations on a basic design accomplished by thickening, thinning, elongating or compressing the letter
forms: "the distortions of weight and width manipulations," as Alexander Lawson puts it. With some types many variants have developed—

ABCDEFGHIJ opqrstuvwxyz

DEFGHIJKLMNO QRSTUVWXYZ&a
DEFGHIJKLMNOP QRSTUVWXYZ&a
DEFGHIJKLMNO QRSTUVWXYZ&a
DEFGHIJKLMNO QRSTUVWXYZ&
DEFGHIJKLMN QRSTUVWXYZ
ABCDEFGHIJKLMNOPQRSTUVWXYZ&abcdef
ABCDEFGHIJKLMNOPQRSTUVWXYZ &
ABCDEFGHIJKLMNOPQRSTUVWX
ABCDEFGHIJKLMNOPQRS
ABCDEFGHIJKLMNOPQ

A portion of the Futura typeface family

from Light to Regular to Semi-Bold to Bold to Extra Bold to Extended
and Condensed versions in their own various weights, etc., etc. To compli-
cate things further, there is no uniform standard terminology—one
face's bold can be lighter than another's medium, for example. The great
designer Eric Gill once commented wryly that "there are now about as
many different varieties of letters as there are fools," and he went on to
say that "the only way to reform modern lettering is to abolish it."

Sans serif types are more adaptable to familial treatment than are
regular romans; but almost all text types have families of some size, if
only a bold form, an italic, and a bold italic. Akin to the Malthusian who
fears overpopulation, some feel that keeping families of type small may
be the only responsible way to act in this day and age. Though one might
concede that the designer had fun creating twenty different variants of
his or her basic idea, it is difficult to imagine knowing what to do with
them all, and it is even frightening to imagine everyone else spawning
their own in a like manner.

Technologically, the development of photomechanical type facilitated the typographic expansion of this century. Instead of having to be cast in metal in all necessary sizes, the phototype letter could be drawn, photographed, and then enlarged or reduced optically on photographic paper. At least theoretically. In practice, other design considerations sometimes obtrude; but the process is still immensely more simple, economical and rapid than using either foundry type or hot-metal composition systems. This was a tremendous development, revolutionizing typography and freeing letter design almost completely from its mechanical roots and constraints.

Tremendous as this development was, within just a few years it was challenged and is now being displaced. Most recently, type designs made through computers on a cathode-ray display screen grid system hearken back to Renaissance letter design systems but promise tremendous speed and an almost infinite variety and malleability of letter forms, forms now adapted to new materials and often not even thought of as drawn, carved or printed—"a very important innovation in the history of lettering," in the words of Nicolete Gray. Technologies are being created or improved upon constantly, and new computer display and printing systems are providing very high quality typography while attracting extremely talented designers to create and interpret type designs.

With the development of personal computers and the accompanying revolution in typography that allows letters to be twisted, turned, sized, shrunk, and stretched in ways impossible and even undreamed of only a decade ago, virtually anyone with a computer can manipulate typographic forms with few restraints and can even create his or her own letter forms with regular precision (or lack thereof). The possibilities are staggering, and although the new computer information revolution

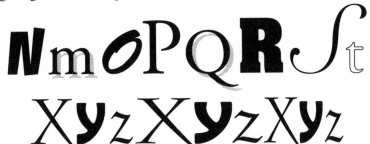

Computer generated and (very simple) manipulated type—tremendous (virtually infinite) variation is possible in shape, shade, pattern, and distortion, just for starters.

should enhance and facilitate some important creative projects (such as, ahem, this present effort, composed on computer and laid out in great part with the aid of the new technology), it is also very easy to imagine the great potential for mischief in the misuse of these new tools. If Eric Gill were alive today, I would be willing to wager that he would find *more* letter varieties than there are fools,…although fools still seem to be increasing in number.

From our perspective in the late twentieth century, we are able to view the history of the alphabet through millenia, and we can make use of much of it. There are currently thousands of variant letter forms (not counting handwriting) in use in the English speaking world, all based on the Roman alphabet. Although any form of classification is somewhat arbitrary, the Printing Industries of America has established eight general groups of typefaces, roughly classified according to difference in stroke (thick and thin relation and balance), formation of serifs, and curve stress or axis of the type design. The eight are: 1) Old Style; 2) Transitional; 3) Modern; 4) Square serif; 5) Sans serif; 6) Black letter; 7) Cursive and Script; and 8) Decorative typefaces. All have numerous variants, but the last two especially are "catch-all" categories based on no fixed design elements and containing all sorts of otherwise unrelated

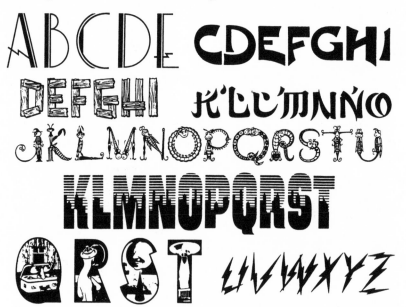

Decorative and display type

forms. Some type designs are *tours de force* only; others are meant to be silly and to entertain or amuse. Our decorative types, for example, have taken flights of fancy beyond nineteenth century horizons, and further explorations are probable, especially with the incredible power of computer-aided design becoming ever more widely accessible.

For more than two thousand years there has been a gradual development of the forms of the letters from the Roman capitals—sometimes as conscious design, but often as a gradual outgrowth of function influenced by the materials used to make the letters, their prospective use, and the desire for speed in writing them, among other things. It goes without saying that not all forms were equally attractive or useful. Although the basic forms of the letters are not "fixed," nonetheless they cannot be altered with impunity outside of a general range that cannot be defined yet exists as a convention among literate people.

This question, "When does a letter cease to be itself?" has been asked by many people and studied by many experts, including Eric Gill in *An Essay on Typography*. Although no definitive answers have been established, the "essential character" (or basic skeleton) of a letter is the focus of the study. Sometimes great elaborations or distortions do not affect a letter's recognizability, while a tiny change of stroke or elimination of a letter part may make it unrecognizable. It is instructive to view some of the ingenious monograms and ciphers artists and designers have created since ancient times, as well as the more recent work of Scott Kim, John Langdon, and others who attempt to construct designs of words ("ambigrams," as Langdon calls them) that will read the same when reversed, turned or otherwise inverted. In this work we often find the

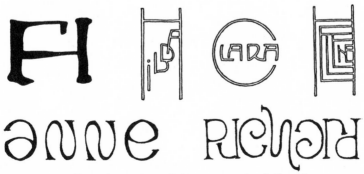

The malleability of letter shapes: Franz Hals monogram (top left), and name monogram constructions by H. Nowack (top right); two basic "ambigrams" by the author (below).

letter forms distorted beyond all normal parameters, yet the eye endeavors (generally successfully) to see as a letter a form that would never be considered such if it were isolated or out of a context. If nothing else (besides admiration for the designers' ingenuity), we see here that a letter form in isolation is much more limited than one in the context of a word where it can be influenced, molded, and even recognized by its relation to the other letters.

As basic shapes, letter forms have been used as decorative elements for centuries; but such is the power of the forms that Adrian Frutiger states: "When a sign image resembles a letter of the alphabet it is difficult to see it as anything else." This can certainly be disruptive if the designer had no such intent, but often it is intentional and adds to the meaning or distinctiveness of the piece—particularly in monograms or logos which play off of distinctive letter forms as both picture and symbol. Frutiger points out the resonance gained from the double meaning, and in some ways it can almost be seen as coming full-circle back to the pictograph as the origin of writing.

The basic skeleton of the letters did not alter much with the advent of printing; but the development of the roman typeface follows the tendency to refine the letters away from handwritten models to independent forms. Many design elements affect the basic "look" of a typeface; but certain general features are considered essential. As Warren Chappell explains: "It has been noted that despite numerous digressions from the basically geometric, the alphabet has managed to remain essentially Roman because of repeated efforts to reestablish the classic concept."

ABCDEFGHIJKLM NOPQRSTUVWXYZ

Classic Roman alphabet drawn by Edward Johnston

In the pages to follow, both the "classic concept" and "numerous digressions" will be examined. There are hundreds of languages in the world today, many dependent upon the Roman alphabet. Eugen Nerdinger claims that today "the world becomes strange or foreign

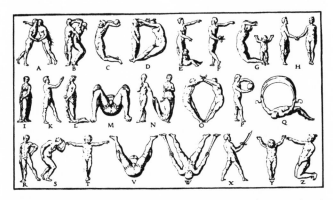

Alphabet of human figures by J. Theodor and J. Israel De Bry (1596)

where there is no roman alphabet." We shall soon see how "strange or foreign" itself is the history of the letters of the Roman alphabet.

Letters were originally regarded as sacred signs. Karl Gerstner maintains that "our signs have lost their magic and therefore their power....As literates we are initiates but not the elect." John Barth, however, reminds us that letters still have immense power—enabling us, among other things, to say the unseeable, such as "that green house is brown." "Mere nonsense," scoffers might exclaim. Perhaps;...but then again, perhaps not always. And, among other things, letters regularly still enable the magic of literary creation.

"Human society, the world, man in his entirety is in the alphabet. Masonry, astronomy, philosophy, all the sciences start here, imperceptible but real, and it must be so," wrote Victor Hugo. The reader is invited to cross the threshold into the magical, powerful world of the alphabet. In times past anyone reading abecedaries was considered ignorant; it was no compliment to call a person an abecedarian. But abecedaries have always been a path for beginners, and this one is for initiates seeking literally to become more literate (perhaps even elect). So read it openly. Enjoy it. Although the course may get complicated at times, the view is wonderful and you can travel at your own pace. Feel free to pause amidst the flowers.

We begin with an old riddle: "There are twenty-six regents upon the earth; through them must the whole world be ordered. They eat no bread; they drink no wine. Tell, what kind of rulers are they?"

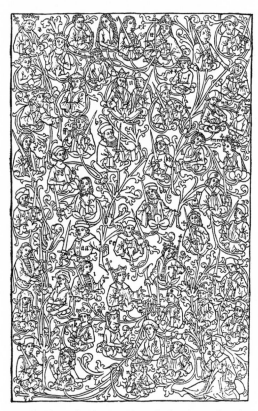

A Hapsburg family tree using the letters to identify
the ruling family; printed in Augsburg in 1475–78
from *Spiegel des menschlichen Lebens* (*Mirror of
Human Life*)

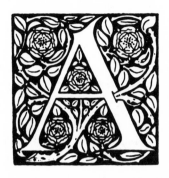

A IS THE FIRST LETTER of the English alphabet, the first letter of the Roman alphabet, and corresponds to the first letter of the Phoenician where it represented a breathing sound that was neither a vowel nor a consonant. Its name in the Phoenician was *aleph*, which meant "ox," and paleographers have made efforts to relate the sign to a stylized pictograph of that animal's head. Otto Ege speculated that this sign was placed first in order to honor the great domesticated animal—valued for both the work and the food it provided humankind—as food is the most important of human needs. The pictorial sign was thus more important than any associated sound.

Another scholar, Hugh Moran, relates the ox sign *aleph* to the Taurian Age—that period (c. 4000–2000 B.C.) when the sun at the vernal equinox appeared in the constellation of Taurus and during which the proto-alphabets of many cultures were formulated (or, as he believes, the universal proto-alphabet was devised). He theorizes that the letters of this ancient phonetic alphabet were derived from the form or astrological meaning of heavenly constellations. According to his research, Egypt, Sumer, and China shared ancient cosmological concepts, and all considered the bull to be a sacred animal; he also believes that religion is the only possible widespread organizing principle that could have united early people before they diverged into separate areas and civilizations. Basic symbols associated with the seasons and the movement of the heavenly bodies related the gods to the affairs of humans,

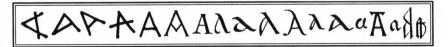

47

and the letters were among the most important of these symbols. Moran relates *aleph* etymologically to the names of the ox or bull in Assyrian (*alpu*) and Sumerian (*alam*), which gives the root *al* or *el* found in ancient names of the deity—for example, *Alam* of the Sumerians and *Elohim* of the Hebrews.

Modern astrologers and mystics have also sought the ancient mystical significance of early Semitic letters. According to Zolar, the Hebrew *aleph* stands for man as a collective unity, as lord and master of the earth. Its numerical value is one. *Aleph* was one of the three Hebrew "mother" letters, and it corresponded to the element air (because it made a slight hissing sound when pronounced) and to the seasons of spring and autumn. Hebrew is rather unusual among ancient cultures in having only three basic elements instead of the usual four, thus one letter corresponding to an element had to do double duty and serve to represent two seasons. This honor was accorded *aleph*.

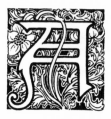 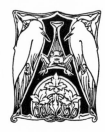 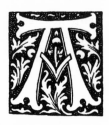

In borrowing the basic form and idea of the alphabet from the Phoenicians, the Greeks slightly altered the first letter, assigned to it a true vowel sound (thus creating the first true phonetic alphabet), and gave it the name *alpha*. According to most scholars, this was a meaningless name referring to no actual object (unlike the Phoenician) but instead meant only as an approximation of or reference to the Phoenician name. Speaking of the Greek alphabet, Robert Graves maintains that "*Alpha* was the first of the eighteen letters because *alpha* means honour, and *alphainein* is to invent." As is common, there is some disagreement over facts and interpretations here; but the position and tradition of honor accorded the first letter is reinforced.

The Romans began the practice of having no name for the letters except their basic sound. Almost all alphabet descendants from the Roman—including English—have followed the practice, although the actual names accorded the letters vary with the languages and with which of the letters' sounds are used. According to the *Oxford English Dictionary* there are at least thirteen separate sounds represented by the letter A. Technically, it is termed the "low-back-wide" vowel, formed with the widest opening of jaws, pharnyx, and lips.

The Renaissance designer Geofroy Tory believed that the first letter was especially meaningful for the ancient Romans, who created its classic (and still current) capital form. In tracing the construction of the letters he inferred a number of spiritual and allegorical meanings. The A was created in the form of a triangle, which led to Tory's observation that the "ancients, wishing to demonstrate the extraordinary perfectness of their letters, formed and fashioned them according to the proper proportions of the three most perfect figures of geometry—the circle, the square, and the triangle. And because an odd number was always considered among the ancients as a lucky number... they made their first letter in the image of an odd number placed upon the square, which is an even number, to give a good opening and fortunate approach to those who may love and wish to study well-made letters."

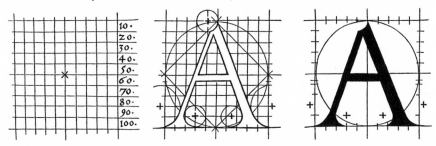

Design grid and letter A of Geofroy Tory

Tory's *Champ Fleury* (written in 1529) is filled with this sort of curious, highly imaginative, allegorical and entertaining information. He constructed his letter designs on a square grid which occasionally contained a drawing of a naked human figure. With the A, the transverse

AaAAaAaAaAaAaAaAaAa

stroke of the capital letter serves modesty while also helping to establish an attractive letterform. "Thus this cross-stroke covers the man's organ of generation, to signify that Modesty and Chastity are required, before all else, in those who seek acquaintance with well-shaped letters, of which A is the gateway and the first of all in alphabetical order." Contemporary authorities use different images but agree on the importance of the placement of the letter parts. Walter Tracy maintains that if the legs of A sprawl the letter will look vulgar, while if the bar is too low it will look dull; too high and it may print poorly. He continues: "So there is a desirable, even obligatory, arrangement of the three strokes if the letter is to be acceptable. Most of the other capitals have structural rules that are just as fundamental to their aesthetic effect."

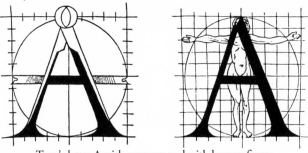

Tory's letter A with compass and with human figure

Tory also relates the alphabet to the human body and finds a correspondence with the nine classical Muses, the seven Liberal Arts, the four Cardinal Virtues, and the three Graces. He claims that the twenty-three letters of the Roman alphabet were "secretly constituted and made to agree with the number of vital channels and the noblest organs of the human body.... Thus we shall find the human body and perfectly formed man to be the model for the disposition of the number of our letters,... for our worthy Ancient Fathers were so virtuous in their speculations that they determined secretly to make clear that the perfect man is he in who fine letters and goodly learning are so closely and intimately instilled that all parts and motions of his body are attended by the noble quality... *decorum*." In his scheme of relations, Tory drew the figure of a man with his body parts related to the various letters. In this "man of letters" A

AaAaAaAA*Aa*AaAAaAa

LHOMME LETRE   LHOMME SCIENTIFIQUE

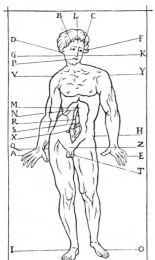
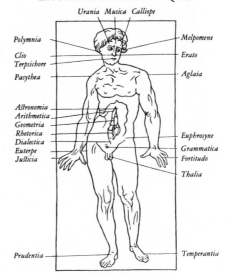

Tory's man of letters and man of science

related to the right hand, and it also corresponded to the cardinal virtue Justicia—justice or justness.

Centuries before Tory, Plato discussed the letter *alpha* in his dialogue *Cratylus,* where the idea was suggested that the first letter was "assigned to the expression of size" by the original "imposer of names" because it is a "great" letter. Exactly what was meant by this I find hard to comprehend; but I believe that the "spirit" of the idea was to establish a position of honor for this gateway sign to one of mankind's greatest inventions. Thus, also, the seventeenth century French Franciscan and mystic John Chrysostom claimed that *alpha* holds the whole alphabet together and is the foundation stone of the entire structure, even as belief is to human life. In a somewhat related, more modern application George Steiner claims that the fiction of Jorge Luis Borges contains "every motif present in the language mystique of kabbalists and gnostics: the image of the world as a concatenation of secret syllables, the notion of an abstract idiom or cosmic letter—alpha and aleph—which underlies the rent fabric of human tongues, the supposition that the entirety of

AaAaAAaAaAaAAaAaA

 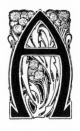 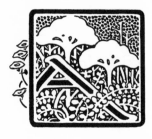

knowledge and experience is prefigured in a final tome containing all conceivable permutations of the alphabet."

A, *alpha*, *aleph*: the first letter has occasionally been used by itself to represent or signify the essence of the whole alphabet—an idea somewhat similar to the Islamic conception that God's essence resides in the Koran; the essence of the Koran can be found in the first chapter; that essence can be distilled in the first verse, and the essence of the first verse can be found in the first letter. The magic formula "Abracadabra" appears similar in some respects. Of disputed but ancient origin, it was originally intended to cure a person of fever and was used both in written and oral forms. When written, it was worn as a protective amulet. Its form was triangular: the complete word being written on the top line, the last letter dropped on the next line and, in turn, on subsequent lines until all that remained at the point was the initial A. When recited, the entire word was first pronounced, and then the ever-decreasing fragments, until only the vowel remained. In either case, the patient's fever was

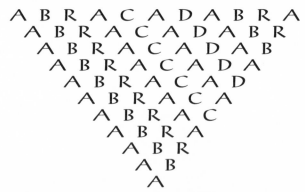

supposed to diminish progressively until the first letter—the letter of good health—remained. As it has come down through the centuries, the charm has supposedly been effective for much else besides fevers.

In the theological realm, A often has been important. Among the ancient Romans some claimed that it was invented by the archaic goddess Carmenta, mother of "charms." In manuscripts of the Middle Ages, A was sometimes used to represent the name of Christ (probably following from the biblical phrase, "I am Alpha …"). A.a.A. was also used to represent God. This came about as an abbreviation of "*AHYH ashr AHYH*" ("I AM that I AM," God's designation of Himself in the King James translation of Exodus 3:14). In his *Romance of Rosenkranz,* Clemens Brentano maintained that the triangular form of A symbolized the tripartite unity of God. Geofroy Tory could certainly understand how. Hegel, however, in his *Encyclopaedia,* compared A to the pyramids, which shape it echoes.

The French poet Arthur Rimbaud wrote that "the weak-minded, applying themselves to *thinking* about the first letter of the alphabet can be quickly hurled into madness." The reader at this point may feel (think?) that there has been much questionable thought devoted to this letter. Rimbaud himself may have thought too much about it. In "A Season in Hell" he claimed to have found correspondences between the vowels—especially their sounds—and colors; although more modestly he prefaced his "invention" as "the story of one of my follies." "I invented the color of the vowels!—*A* black, *E* white, *I* red, *O* blue, *U* green.—I regulated the form and movement of each consonant, and, with instinctive rhythms, I prided myself on inventing a poetic language accessible some day to all the senses. I reserved translation rights." Taking up the baton, I have imagined copyrighting the alphabet.

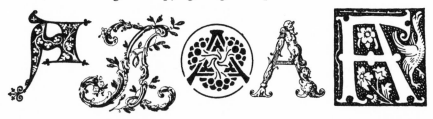

Our first letter does not have a history and connotations of unrelieved brilliance. In his poem "Vowels," Rimbaud again assigned the color black to A and associated it with "gulfs of darkness." For the Greeks, *alpha* was a symbol of a bad augury in the divinatory sacrifices. Most of us are also aware, thanks to Nathaniel Hawthorne's *The Scarlet Letter*, that A was used to distinguish the adulterous. But things could have been worse for Hester Prynne: in the medieval period A was sometimes branded on those caught breaking the Seventh Commandment.

Yet, on the whole, our first letter has happy or prestigious associations. In Logic, A denotes a universal affirmative. It is commonly used in many fields as the first of any series, such as book signatures or quires, geometrical lines, etc. In algebra it is used to represent a known quantity, while in music it is the name of the sixth note of the diatonic scale of C major. The letter commonly stands for excellence and is the highest mark given on report cards, examinations, and pork chops.

A was one of the letters that with the development of the uncial script began to be rounded, a tendency that became more pronounced with the semi-uncial form, which closely approximated and eventually influenced our modern lower-case form of the letter. *One* of our modern lower-case forms, that is; a has two—one a closed bowl with an open loop above, the other a single closed bowl joined to the stem. Both have existed since medieval black letter scripts, although today the former is almost always found in serif typefaces and the latter in sans serif and italic fonts.

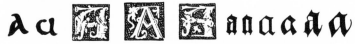

Uncial, semi-uncial, medieval ornamental, and various black letter forms of A

Robert Graves reports that in an ancient Irish calendrical tree alphabet, A (*ailm*) related to the silver fir—or birth tree—and shared the winter solstice with its fellow vowel I. The Old English runic sign for A was named *ac*, meaning oak. In 1340, the English writer Richard Rolle of Hampole maintained that people could know the sex of a newborn infant from its first cry: if a boy, the cry was *a! a!*—which is the first letter of the name of Adam. If a girl ... well, everything in its order.

AaAaA Aa AAa Aa Aa AaA

Jacob Grimm called A the first sound, the king of vowels, associated with the color purple and representative of that which is first and highest. More recently, another writer with an eye and ear for such things, Ernst Jünger, came to similar conclusions. He claimed that A is the true "fatherly" sound—the king. It comprises the highest and broadest of life; its sound or harmony is a type of high, jovial, bright laughter. It is the "eagle" of the world of sound.

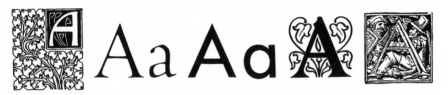

Our first letter has indeed inspired high flights of fancy; but let us return to earth. In his poem "An Ordinary Evening in New Haven," Wallace Stevens wrote of "the infant A standing on infant legs." Geofroy Tory considered his classic Roman capital form of the A to be more mature: "A has its legs thickened and furnished with feet,—just as a man has his legs and feet for walking and passing on,—to tell us covertly that from it, the first letter in alphabetical order, we must pass on to B, and C, and all the other letters."

Accepting that, we shall.

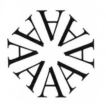

AAaAAAaAAAAaAaAAa

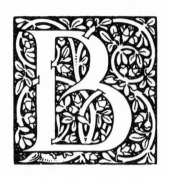

THE LETTER B IS THE SECOND of both the English and Roman alphabets. It corresponds to the Phoenician *beth* and the Greek letter *beta*, both of which were also second in the order of their respective alphabets. It is the first consonant in the alphabet—a consonant representing a sound that cannot be pronounced by itself, needing to be combined with a vowel in order to be clearly articulated. (Vowels represent sounds that can be independently articulated.) As they did with most of their letters, the Romans signified B using its basic sound in combination with a vowel and assigned no other name to it. In English letter names, a long [e] sound is usually used when it follows the consonant (as in B), and a short [e] sound is used when it precedes the consonant (such as F). The technical term for the sound B represents is the "sonant labial mute, or lip-voice stop consonant." Sort of makes you appreciate the Roman name more, doesn't it?

The Phoenician word *beth* is commonly taken to mean a house or dwelling. Some commentators point out that this may more properly and easily be seen as a tent. Otto Ege claimed that *beth* was given second place in the alphabet to honor the second most important of human needs—shelter. In speaking of the ancient Semitic *beth*, Dr. Moran gives the word multiple meanings: "house, temple, daughter, woman, place." He then theorizes that it was the female counterpart of *al* in a dualistic concept of creation—a notion that is widespread in many different ancient cultures. Perhaps most famous and well-known in the Chinese yin-yang principles, it is here given prominence in the ancient conception of the alphabet. B thus symbolizes the idea of expanding creation, the division of one into two—the beginnings of dualism—a notion which the Greek and Roman forms of the letter coincidentally, but happily, illustrate.

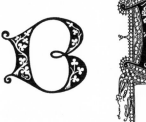 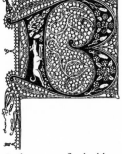 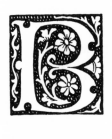

Middle letter from Mainz Psalter, 1457, flanked by 15th and 16th century letters

According to a Hebrew legend from the *Sefer Ha-Zohar* (*The Book of Splendor*), written by the thirteenth century Spanish scholar Moses de Leon and retold by Ben Shahn in *The Alphabet of Creation,* before this world existed the various letters applied to God to assist in the work of creation. "The twenty-two letters of the alphabet descended from the crown of God whereon they were engraved with a pen of flaming fire. They gathered around about God and one after another spoke and entreated, each one, that the world be created through him." As God considered their various petitions, their merits and faults were linked with the meaning of words they begin. For example, "Heth, although it is the first letter of Hanun, the Gracious One, is also first in the word for sin—Hattat. So the letter Heth was rejected....And Gimel, although it reminds one of Gadol, great, would not do, because it also stands at the head of Gemul—retribution." Finally, the letter B (*beth*) applied for the honor. "Beth stepped before the Holy One, blessed be He, and pleaded, 'O Lord of the World! May it be Thy will to create the world through

חדגבא

Hebrew letters by Geofroy Tory

𝕭𝖇𝕭𝖇𝕭𝖇𝖇𝕭𝖇𝕭𝖇𝕭𝖇𝕭𝖇𝕭𝖇𝕭

me, seeing that all the dwellers in the world daily give praise unto Thee through me. For it is said, "Baruch—blessed—be the Lord forever: Amen and Amen!"' The Holy One, blessed be He, immediately granted the petition of Beth, saying, 'Blessed be he that cometh in the name of the Lord!' And He created the world through Beth; as it is said, 'Bereshith—in the beginning—God created the Heaven and the Earth.'" A modern writer, A. B. Kuhn, Ph.D., echoes the idea: "Yes, creation begins with B, not a-gins with A."

The modern popularizer of mystical lore, Zolar, links the letter *beth* with man's mouth, his interior, and his habitation. "It denotes virility, paternal protection, and interior action and movement....This letter in conjunction with ... *Aleph* forms all ideas of progress, of graduated advance, the passage from one state to another: locomotion." Its numerical value is two.

It is perhaps appropriate to remark here that our word for the whole series of letters—"alphabet"—comes from a combination of the Greek names of the first two letters. And, although this can be considered (and originated as) only a shorthand name for the whole, if we reflect on the ideas of Moran and Zolar of a dynamic, expanding creation, our first two letters in combination can be thought of as happily and rightly representing the whole series.

Curiously, though now it seems such a natural designation, the word "alphabet" for the set of letters did not come into use until the third century of the Christian era. According to David Diringer, prior to this time the Romans seemed to call the letters *literae* or *elementa*, which were translations of corresponding Greek designations. A third century Latin work at one time attributed to Tertullian mentions the word, and it seems to have been familiar to St. Jerome writing a few decades later— *alphabeta* and *alphabetum* being found in his works. It was soon commonly used in both Latin and Greek writings.

The word "alphabet" appears to have been introduced into English from the French. It was becoming commonly used by the sixteenth century, but not without a struggle. The Old English term was "abecede," which by the mid-fourteenth century had been shortened in Middle

BbBbBb*b*BbBBbBBBb*Bb*BbB

English to "abece," "abse," or "ABC." "Alphabete" was used in 1425 but
to mean lore and learning acquired through reading, *not* the set of
letters. Within a few years it was used with the latter meaning, and in 1513
it appeared in the title of one of the books printed by Wynkyn de Worde.
Yet, in 1611, in his *Dictionarie* of French and English, Randle Cotgrave
wrote: "Touching the French *abece*, for alphabet I will not call it,
according to the vulgar error, that word being peculiar only to the Greek
tongue." The "vulgar error" continued to gain currency, however, and
in the 1632 edition of Cotgrave's work the above passage was omitted—
"alphabet" had essentially won out out over its synonyms "abece" and
"crossrow" (also crosserow or Christ's cross row). This latter word had
been commonly given to the alphabet because in the early hornbooks
(or letter primers) A was preceded by a cross, and it is found in the
writings of Skelton, Tyndale, and Shakespeare (*Richard III*); but the
Bard also used "alphabet" in *Titus Andronicus*. Milton, Pepys, and Pope
helped insure the victory of the word, employing it in their writings; and
by the time of Dr. Johnson's *Dictionary* of the mid-eighteenth century
its usage was secure.

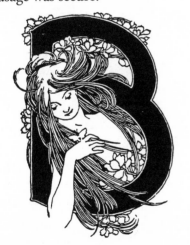

Art Nouveau B (left), and hornbook text showing alphabet preceded by a cross (right)

Although the ancient Egyptians never used a true phonetic alphabet,
they did develop twenty-four hieroglyphs representing consonantal

BbBbBBBbBbBBBbBBbBb

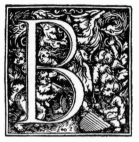

sounds. According to one authority, the pictorial hieroglyph for the [b] sound was a crane or ibis, the bird whose formations in flight (as Greek legend tells it) inspired Hermes to invent the letters; while the Egyptian inventor of writing—the god Thoth—was ibis-headed. Another writer, however, claims that the Egyptian hieroglyph for the [b] sound was a human leg. Perhaps our "authorities" read different manuscripts. I don't claim scholarly authority in this matter, so I will report both opinions; but I know which one I prefer, and I trust that the reader does too. Fortunately, it is not our task to determine "truth," but just to reflect upon the vast literature of letters.

Robert Graves claimed that B was one of the thirteen letters related to the precious stones set in the breastplate of the ancient Israelites mentioned in the Book of Exodus. Its corresponding gem was a red sard. In his fascinating book *The White Goddess*, Graves also wrote at length about an ancient Irish Ogham alphabet called the *Beth-luis-nion* after its first three letters. B (or *beth*) was the first letter of this alphabet and related to the idea of inception. The *Beth-luis-nion* was a calendrical "tree" alphabet, with each letter corresponding to a tree and having many mystic and poetic associations. The story is complicated; but very roughly, about 400 B.C. the *Beth-luis-nion* replaced an earlier order of the letters, the new order symbolizing a major religious change. Graves believes that the letters possibly originally descended from a Mycenean script antedating the familiar ancient Greek alphabet. This tree alphabet was composed of thirteen consonants and five vowels—each consonant

Inscription form of a 20-character Ogham script similar to the earlier *Beth-luis-nion* alphabet

BbBb**B***B*bbBbbBb**Bb***Bb*B

represented a 28-day lunar month and the vowels represented the quarters or seasons of the year (as we have seen with A). B was linked with the birch, which is self-propagating and the earliest foliating forest tree. Its month began on December 24—the beginning of the new year. It was considered one of the seven most important letters of this alphabet. The seven sacred trees of the *Beth-luis-nion* were also linked with the seven pillars of wisdom, the planets, the days of the week, and the days of Creation. B was linked with the sun and Sunday.

It was a script of great symbolic religious importance. According to Graves: "The names of the letters preserved in the Irish ¡*Beth-luis-nion*, which are traditionally reported to have come from Greece and reached Ireland by way of Spain, formed an archaic Greek charm in honor of the Arcadian White Goddess Alphito who, by Classical times, had degenerated into a mere nursery bogey. The Cadmean order of letters, perpetuated in the familiar ABC, seems to be a deliberate mis-arrangement by Phoenician merchants; they used the secret alphabet for trade purposes but feared to offend the goddess by revealing its true order."

Having no desire to offend any goddess myself, I am content to pursue this study along the standard alphabet order. Readers who wish to practice other arrangements can consider themselves warned. In seriousness, whether this particular thesis holds or not, it is a good example of the awe with which most ancient peoples approached the power of the alphabet. It was a tool of divine magnitude—akin to Promethean fire. In those times an abecedarium was no child's amusement—the meanings and relations of the letters could have universal religious importance.

According to an ancient Greco-Roman tradition, B was invented by the goddess Carmenta and introduced half of her year. She was said to

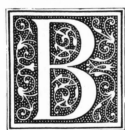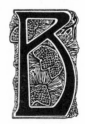

have formed the first fifteen Roman letters in Italy, adapting them from the Pelasgian or western Greek alphabet. The Etruscans had no use for B in their language, and perhaps this myth relates to the difference between Roman and Etruscan alphabet usage. The Etruscans kept the letter, however, and it became part of the runic script of northern Europe thought by many scholars to have descended from the Etruscan alphabet. In runic writing B (*beorc*) also related to the birch tree, an important fertility symbol.

Geofroy Tory devoted most of his discussion of B to describing how it should be made with compass and rule, this letter being one of the most complex and difficult to construct. Ever the French pedagogue, Tory also criticized the pronunciation of the letter by other people. In his "man of letters," B corresponds to the right eye; the letter is also linked to the Muse Urania—in classical times the Muse of astronomy, although considered the Muse of poetry by Milton and other Renaissance and Elizabethan poets.

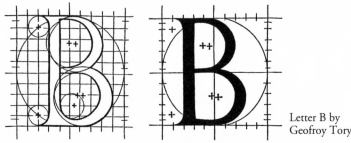

Letter B by
Geofroy Tory

Our basic form of the capital letter was developed by the Romans, who rounded the angular letterform of the Greeks. Tory remarks that it is formed by the pure geometric figures of the straight line and the circle. It is not a perfectly symmetrical letter, however; virtually all of our classic letterforms have slight mathematical irregularities which contribute to a more aesthetically pleasing whole. Donald Jackson has commented that "The top half of the well-fed and well-bred letter B invariably follows slightly behind its rotund 'belly.'"

With the development of the Rustic script, B was often written slightly above the level of most of the other letters. This custom of

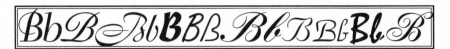

elongating certain letters (F and L were similarly treated) was continued in later scripts and eventually influenced the development of the minuscule form. With the semi-uncial script, the upper bowl of B had merged with the stem, leaving a form close to that of our modern lower-case b.

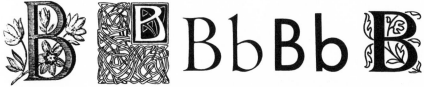

Rustic script (left), and uncial, semi-uncial and black letter variants of B

In our common usage and tradition B has generally followed A—becoming slightly less honored in the process. Grade B is inferior to grade A in virtually all cases, although it is still generally considered above average. B commonly represents the second element in a lettered series and, like A, also represents a known quantity in algebra. In music it stands for the seventh note of the scale of C major. It was somewhat distressingly employed in the Middle Ages, being branded on the foreheads of the blasphemous. (It would seem a true challenge for them not to swear because of their pain from the hot iron!) B does have one usage that A does not: it is the symbol of a chemical element—Boron.

Trusting that we are now somewhat better informed about this letter, we shall move on to the next, pleasantly recalling the old phrase applied to the ignorant and illiterate who "do not know B from a battledore." We, happily, do know something about B. Battledores? …Well, literacy (the mastery of *letters*) is not attained without following the entire path. Let us battle on, striving not to be deflected this way and that from our goal.

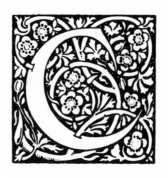

WITH THE LETTER C our survey begins to get a bit more complicated. Although C is the third letter of both the English and Roman alphabets, it was not always so—or perhaps we could better say that it was not always (or only) C.

The Roman letter is descended from and corresponds in alphabet position to the ancient Phoenician letter *gimel* and the Greek letter *gamma*. The Phoenician word for their letter is thought by many scholars to mean a camel; and the *gimel* sign in its original position—tilted 90° clockwise of our modern form—can be thought of as depicting a camel's hump. It would have been a very difficult camel to ride, however, as most forms of the ancient letter depict two lines set at about a 45° angle—resembling an upside down V positioned slightly awry on the page. One authority, however, believes that the sign originally designated a throwing stick somewhat like a boomerang. Zolar says that in the mystic tradition the Hebrew *gimel* represents "the throat and everything that is hollow ... and profound." Its number is three. The classical Greek shape of *gamma* widened the angle of the Phoenician and early Greek forms of the letter, setting the two lines at the perpendicular angle of 90° and positioning them so that they resemble an upside down L (Γ). According to Sir Wallis Budge: "Some of the early Christian mystics saw in the two lines at right angles a symbol of Christ as the corner-stone, and the architects and designers of the Middle Ages used the Gamma freely in their reliefs and patterns."

11)⟨⟨ΓΓCC CccⲤ CꞀ ⳁꝺ Ccꞓ

The reader has probably noticed that both the Phoenician and Greek names for the letter begin with a G—not a C—and this suggests part of the unusual history of our third letter. The Roman C, like the Greek *gamma*, originally had the phonetic value of a hard [g]. In the course of time it also came to take the sound of K—a letter that became virtually obsolete in Roman writing (but more on this topic later). C kept both of these sounds until approximately 300–250 B.C., when the letter G was introduced into the alphabet to represent the [g] sound. (Again, the reader who perseveres will find further enlightenment. Perhaps the phrase "as easy as ABC" is somewhat misleading!) The letter C continued to occupy the place of *gamma* in the alphabet, even though (at least for the Romans) it did not properly belong there. During the period of classical Latin (c. 200 B.C.–A.D. 300) it was pronounced [k]. When the Roman alphabet was reintroduced in the British Isles in the fourth century, C generally had a [k] sound; but through the centuries it underwent a rather complicated metamorphosis—partly due to the Norman French influence after the eleventh century. It gradually gained a more familiar [c] (softer [k]) sound while also retaining the [k] and even adding an [s] sound before certain vowels (E, I, Y)—for example, in the word "cent."

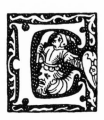 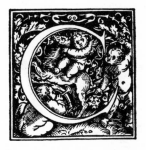 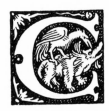

If the reader is somewhat disgruntled over this history that has left us with a letter that does not really seem to be necessary—its basic sounds well-covered by other letters—he or she is not alone. In 1662, James Howell wrote in his *New Grammar* that there were "some critical authors who bear no good will to C, calling it the mongrel androgynous letter, nor male nor female but rather a spirit or monster" because "by her impostures she trencheth upon the rights of s, k, q, assuming their sounds." And, more recently, Hans Jensen reports that C "is a letter, which our Fore-fathers might very well have spared in our tongue."

However, if C may well be considered unnecessary in our alphabet, the *Oxford English Dictionary* maintains that one of its consonantal combinations, the digraph CH, "virtually constitutes a distinct letter, having a history and sound of its own, and as such it receives a separate place in the alphabet of some languages, e.g. Spanish, Welsh....C is virtually two letters in one." The [ch] sound was foreign to native Latin and was introduced to represent the Greek letter X (*chi*). It was brought into English through the Norman Conquest and was fostered by the spread and triumph of Christianity (which name it begins) in England and throughout Europe. Like C, the CH digraph has many pronunciation variants.

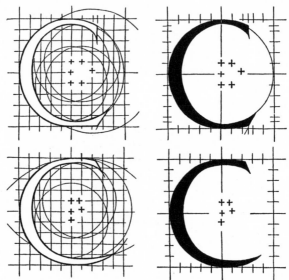

Two versions of the letter C designed by Geofroy Tory

The Roman form of the letter C diverged widely from the classical Greek form of *gamma*; but this form was used in the western Greek alphabet variants from whence it was adopted by the Etruscans and then the Romans. The classic Roman form of the letter is basically a large

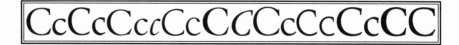

circular arc, but with some divergence from a perfect circle. Tory comments that the tail of C is not just a circle cut on the right but should be opened out, "giving it a graceful tail which imparts charm and spirit." Donald Jackson also remarks that "the top of the rounded C and G would appear to wilt if they did not refuse to bow their heads beneath the invisible roof delineated by the unfeeling compasses."

The basic Roman form of the capital letter C is simple and pleasing and has remained generally unchanged through time. A smaller version of the capital was employed when the minuscule letterforms came into being, and only in black letter scripts did the familiar form become more squared and unusual. Discussing the letter gives us a natural opportunity to comment more extensively on Capitals, however. Our written alphabet combines movement and stability. It expresses a rhythm—curves contrasting with verticals and angles within a horizontal track. Good typefaces establish a "flow" or "current." Capitals seem to set the basic form and measure while lower-case letters create the rhythm. Capitalized nouns have been called "islands in the water of words." Larger, capital-like letters were used at the beginning of lines of poetry in the eighth century. By the eleventh century, with dual alphabets, true capitals were used to distinguish important words, a custom that was common by the thirteenth century and carried to excess in English by the nineteenth. The capitalization of proper names was fixed by the sixteenth century.

In classic capitals, the medial line should be just a little above the mathematical halfway point. This is because we habitually read letters from the top down, and also because this gives the bottom half of the letters more size and greater stability. Donald Anderson observes that the lower-case letters tend to fall into horizontal patterns. "The capitals, clearly more architectural in feeling, complement the small letters. Modern typographers like to play visual games with letters, but the Old Style Roman capitals present a wall of dignity that is difficult to assault. These ancient letters say *ain't* with obvious reluctance."

A relatively recent typographic creation—the small capital letter—has been used for emphasis and variety in texts and headings (such as the running heads of this book), and combines some of the feel of lower-case

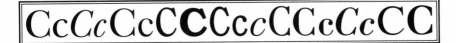

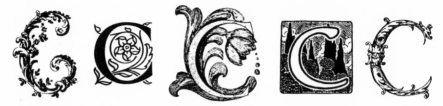

letters with the dignity of the capital forms. In good typography, small caps are not just smaller sizes of the regular caps, but instead are redesigned and proportioned for better readability.

Thousands of times daily we can notice that each of our letters has been made in hundreds of variant forms, often assuming shapes that have only the barest structural resemblance to their classical models. In view of this, is it overly fanciful to liken C to the crescent moon—waxing and waning according to its various scripts? Unfortunately for my poetic speculations, Robert Graves informs us that in the Irish tree-alphabet C was related to the planet Mercury. Its corresponding day was Wednesday. Its tree was the nut—but before applauding that correspondence with my fancies, it was specifically the hazel, considered the Tree of Wisdom. C (named *coll*) was also considered one of the seven most important letters of the *Beth-luis-nion* alphabet, and its calendrical month began on August 5. The runic name for C was *cen*, meaning "torch."

Tory relates the letter to Calliope—the Muse of music. It is thus perhaps appropriate that C is the name of the first note, or key note, of the natural major scale—one of its few high honors. Taking advantage of this musical opening, Frederic Goudy claimed that an individual letter—like a musical note—has no meaning; it acquires its significance in association. Goudy did concede that theoretically letters can be

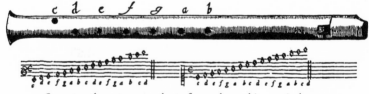

Seventeenth century woodcut of recorder and its musical range

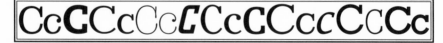

studied individually: each has a long history and manifold associations, and finally becomes a classic sign from which the original meaning and associations may have been lost. With that concession I shall continue my salvage operation…or search-and-rescue mission, if you will.

In his "man of letters" Tory relates the left eye to our current subject—again, seemingly appropriate … if you like puns. C represents the third element in a serial order; and in algebra it is a known quantity—more especially used to denote a constant, as distinguished from a variable quantity. In physics, c represents one of the most famous constants—the speed of light, thus easily becoming our fastest letter. In chemistry, C stands for Carbon. C is also used to represent centigrade degrees on the Celsius scale.

The form of C was also employed by the Romans to represent the number 100. Some say this Roman numeral is an abbreviation of the Latin word for one hundred: *centum*. But others maintain that it developed from the Greek letter *theta* (Θ), which was used by the Romans in their numbering system because they had no need for the letter in their alphabet. Through the years the form of *theta* is thought to have altered until it came to closely approximate that of C, after which time (facilitated by the word *centum*) the two forms became indistinguishable. The medieval mystic Hugo von St. Victor found symbolic significance in Roman numerals having both letter and number applications. He called C a "broad" letter, symbolic of the width of God's love.

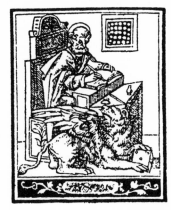

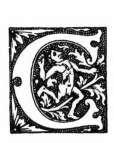

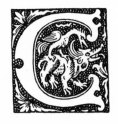

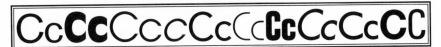

As a symbol of quality, C is commonly the sign of the average. (Does that somehow relate to its confused history?) Not the best, not the worst—certainly, as Tory indicated, not a perfect construct—but one of the most commonly used letters in the English language. Charitably, I shall refer to the last statement to account for James Thurber's comment in his essay "The Tyranny of Trivia" that "C is the letter of catcall, curse, calumny, and contumely," although some readers may consider using Thurber's citations to comment upon my efforts. I am less certain what to make of Wallace Stevens's poem "The Comedian as the Letter C" and will leave detailed interpretation and exegesis to poets and scholars. For my purposes, the poem serves as a fine illustration of the confusion associated with the letter C. Stevens also wrote of "murderous," "fustry," and "ferocious" alphabets. Those notions seem to me much easier to comprehend, and I could quite happily find a place for C in any of them.

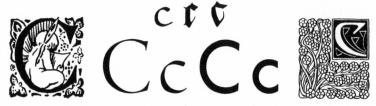

Various letter Cs, including an uncial and two black letter versions (center, top)

There is a charming twelfth century story by Marie de France paraphrased by T.H. White: "Once upon a time there was a wolf who had heard great things about the clergy in monasteries, and how they did very little work, lived easy and had lamb for dinner. So he decided to be a religious. His friends told him that he would have to go through the proper training for this, which would mean going to the abbey school for his education. He did so, and there was a schoolmaster there who had to teach him his alphabet....They got over A, and they got over B. It was hard going. Then they arrived at the third letter. 'What does that stand for?' asked the master. Poor wolf, who thought that this might surely be it at last, cried out enthusiastically: 'Lamb!' But they only turned him out, on the score that he was a humbug." The moral applied to the tale

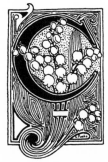
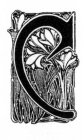

is that secret thoughts can be revealed by one's speech; but we may also find an implied lesson—it's not easy to learn the ABCs.

The philosopher Leibniz stated that "the man who has taught the ABC to his pupils has accomplished a greater deed than a general who has won a battle." I heartily agree; but we may find important ramifications to this statement. We may now fairly claim to know our ABCs; rather than elation, however, a feeling of being "lost at C" would hardly be surprising at this point. Happily, we need not feel becalmed—the alphabet doesn't end here.

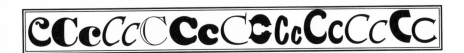

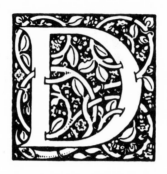

THE LETTER D IS THE FOURTH letter of both the Roman and English alphabets, and in modern times has been used euphemistically for "damn"—as, for example, in the sentence: "D., but it is nice to move on past the letter C."

D corresponds to the Phoenician *daleth* and the Greek *delta*. The ancient Hebrew-Phoenician *daleth* meant "door," and at least one scholar has claimed a relation between it and an ancient Assyrian symbol for the "gate of heaven." Zolar, the modern mystic, says that the Hebrew *daleth* signifies the breast or bosom (which seems appropriate considering modern classifications of bra sizes, the D-cup generally considered the largest—although I have heard mentioned a Z-bra!). Zolar also claims that this letter relates to the origins of all physical existence, "symbolically, every nourishing substance and abundance of possessions." It also expresses the idea of division, and its number is four.

The Egyptian hieroglyph for the [d] sound was a man's hand. Geofroy Tory—seldom at a loss—was able to find a relation between Egypt and the Greek form of the letter. He claimed that the Greeks made *delta* triangular "in memory of the beauty of the island—also triangular—which the Nile, the miracle-working river of Egypt, makes at the place where Memphis lies; and of the shape of Sicily, which is called by the Greeks Triquetra....And, in like manner, because of the division of the World, which was divided by very ancient writers into three parts, Asia, Africa, and Europe." Now that is a rather heavy load of

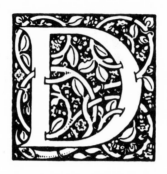

referents for the form of one letter to carry—and perhaps especially improbable is the influence of fond memories of an area that few Greeks had visited by the tenth century B.C., when the Greek alphabet was being formed. Still, our word "delta" has one related meaning and, if we can write of Tory's "man of letters," it seems a bit ungracious to be overly critical regarding his other speculations. Since I have broached the subject, D signifies the right ear of our developing literate man, and also relates to the Muse of sacred song, oratory, lyric, singing, and rhetoric—Polymnia.

A devil trap with a spiral inscription in Hebrew letters

Many ancient Eastern peoples considered their writing systems "holy"—closely connected with deity. Ancient Hebrews—especially those of the Babylonian Captivity—created "devil traps" by inscribing letters according to various formulae in a concentric spiral on a circular dish. This would serve either to drive evil spirits away or else trap them so they could do no harm. Gary Jennings relates a charming Korean legend in which a wise king realized that his people needed a simple phonetic alphabet to replace the cumbersome and difficult Chinese writing system they were using. He created an alphabet but realized it would not be accepted unless the people believed that it came from heaven. So he devised a plan. He drew the new letters with honey on leaves from the garden. That night insects ate the honeyed portions, leaving etched letters in the leaves which the king's advisor found on his morning stroll in the garden. The advisor finally deduced that it was an alphabet—a gift from God—and the people joyously accepted it.

Although the Greeks had some myths that concerned the alphabet, they generally did not consider their alphabet sacred in the same way that many Eastern peoples did theirs. Yet there did exist an active Grecian magical and mystical tradition relating to the letters—especially in the Pythagorean school of thought. Both the shapes of the letters and the sounds they represented were important in Greek mysticism. Some ancient Greek scholars speculated that Pythagoras was the one who gave strict and regular geometric form and proportion to the letters; and many professed to see something transcendent in the shapes of the letters.

The Greek *delta* was a very important letter in Pythagorean mystical circles because of its triangular form. In a Coptic book, *On the Mysteries of the Greek Letters*, attributed to the Palestinian mystic Sabas of Talas in the first centuries of the Christian era, it is claimed that *delta* signifies the creation of the cosmos—its three sides symbolizing the Trinity and the Six Days of Creation. As the fourth letter, it is also a symbol of the four elements and other tetrads important in Pythagorean mysticism.

Among ancient Greeks, D (*delta*) was considered the letter of Demeter. It was the symbol of the vulva (the procreative element), and its triangular form represented the three aspects of the goddess—Demeter, Persephone, and Kore. Many ancient and medieval writers found other correspondences for the letters of the alphabets (Hebrew, Greek, and Roman), relating them to deities, heavenly bodies, astrological houses, phases of the moon, etc. Plutarch compared the nine voiced consonants to the Muses and the vowels to Apollo, thus somewhat anticipating Tory.

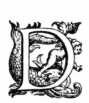 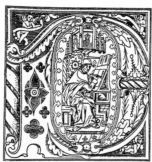 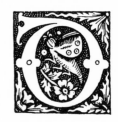

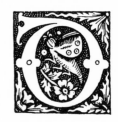

In her study *The Old English Rune Poem*, Maureen Halsell reports that "the notion that letters can be something more than a script for direct communication is as ancient as the first recorded riddles and gnomic utterances. A vast body of poetry from as early as the Sibylline Books used the acrostic device to convey messages additional to those of the main text." This practice was especially widespread in Christian Latin literature of the Middle Ages. Even earlier, Church Fathers as well as Jewish rabbis formulated edifying etymological meanings for the letters, often using acrostic-type sections from the Psalms and Jeremiah, or finding a connection between the beginning letter of a verse and the verse's content; for example, A representing Abraham, who—according to one Father—was the inventor of the alphabet.

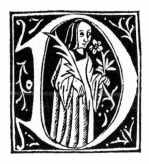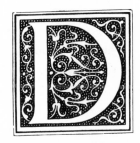

Mystic, cosmic significance was attached to many letter groupings in some societies, where the alphabet was learned forwards, backwards and in various combinations. Rabelais mentions this in *Gargantua and Pantagruel*, when he reports on the education of the young giant by his schoolmaster who "taught Gargantua his ABC so thoroughly that he could say it by heart backwards. This took five years and three months." (Gargantua did almost everything on an exaggerated scale.) A character in *Penguin Island* by Anatole France described a rather unpleasant alphabet instructor: "As I did not easily attain to a knowledge of my letters, he beat me violently with rods so that I can say that he printed the alphabet in strokes on my back." It is quite possible that a hornbook was also used in such a manner by frustrated or impatient teachers. Hornbooks are known from at least late medieval times. One was usually the

DdDDdDDDdDdDddDd

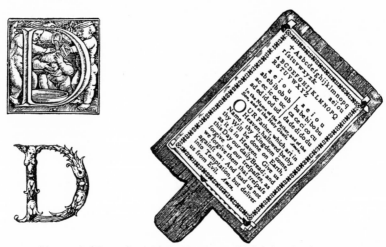

Two capital Ds and an eighteenth century English hornbook

first "book" of an English schoolboy or schoolgirl. Covered by a thin sheet of translucent horn to prevent it from being soiled, it consisted of a thin board of oak about nine inches high and six long on which was printed the alphabet, the ten digits, and sometimes the Lord's Prayer. The horn and board were secured together by a narrow brass frame. As hornbooks were used well into the nineteenth century, the word became synonymous with a primer of any sort.

Learning the alphabet was considered very important in many societies. Ancient and medieval writers (including Horace and Erasmus) mention various alphabet learning aids and rewards, such as letter-shaped pastries that were given to children. Goldsmith and Smollett mention similar teaching methods in their works. Alphabet-shaped soup noodles are a modern example of a centuries-old pedagogical practice. No mention is made of abecedaries in Gargantua's education. Perhaps with such a learning aid he would have mastered the alphabet more quickly. "Abecedarium" is one of the Latin names ("abecedarius" is the other) for the books that get their name from the first four letters, and that since the eighteenth century have been especially popular tools for teaching young children the alphabet. (In the Middle Ages reading and writing were taught from the Psalter, which pupils learned by heart.

Dd*Dd***DDDdDd***D***Dd***d***Dd**

Because there were no abecedaries or other alphabet books, individual letters were picked out from words in the Psalter.) Usually extremely simple, but sometimes quite witty and ingenious, abecedaries link the letters with common objects whose names they begin: "A is for ant; B is for baby," etc. The illustrations of the objects usually are the main charm of such books. One thing probably never illustrated, however, is a flower named Abecedary. It is occasionally mentioned in books concerned with the "language" of flowers in which various flowers are assigned meanings, such as the Rose signifying love, the Nettle cruelty, and so forth. The Abecedary means volubility; yet I have never found a reference to its scientific name nor a description of its appearance. Perhaps this can serve as a reminder how much more ephemeral is speech than writing.

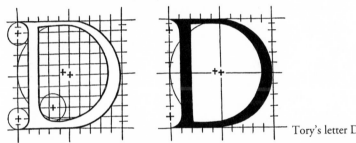

Tory's letter D

The Romans structurally altered the Greek letter *delta* by substituting an arc for two of the angled lines. According to Tory, the Romans made the letter "as they pleased," not out of reverential memory and symbolic association as did the Greeks. Yet other commentators have seen a most happy result in this Roman design characteristic echoing the invention of the Roman arch and dome in architecture. It helped give the Roman alphabet a greater sense of grandeur as well as visual variety and seems appropriate to our idea of Imperial Rome; while the much more angular Greek alphabet agrees with our notions of Grecian order and the aesthetic of post-and-beam architecture. Many authorities claim that as Romans changed from writing with a stylus on wax to using a

ΑΒΓΔΕΖΗΘΙΚ

Greek letters

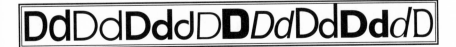

broad pen and ink on parchment, the stiff angles of many letters developed more graceful curves, and thick and thin lines replaced the more uniform and angular lines of the Greeks. Actually, however, many authorities believe that even the Roman stone inscription letters were first drawn with a brush before being carved, and this helped them achieve linear grace and variety similar to pen and ink written letters.

Uncial, semi-uncial, two Insular, and two black letter variant Ds

Through time, Roman letterforms underwent further changes. The classic pen capitals were very formal in appearance; the Rustic script seemed more pastoral, less elegant, and allowed more variation in how the letters were formed by individual scribes, a development that continued with uncial and other more cursive scripts. D underwent further rounding with the uncial script. It was one of the most distinctively altered letters of that style, forming a tail or ascender that curled back above the bowl of the letter. Certain early forms of the letter seem to fit Thomas Pynchon's image in *Gravity's Rainbow*: "comical curly *d*s marched along like hunchbacks." And Dostoevsky (in my opinion one of the greatest D-words), speaking through Prince Myshkin in *The Idiot*, talked of the forms and flourishes of calligraphy: how one can see the soul of the scribe peeping out from his writing and "simply fall in love" with a beautiful flourish or tail of a letter (such as our d, for instance). With

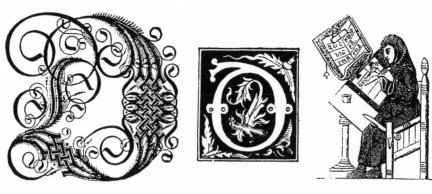

the semi-uncial and later forms, the ascender of d became vertical. This form was later codified as the basic lower-case d.

In the Irish tree-alphabet, D (*duir*) was associated with the oak, which has been called the Tree of Royalty and the Tree of Zeus. Robert Graves relates that D was connected with the lunar month beginning June 10 and with the mid-summer sacrifice. This was the beginning of the Celtic year. The letters D and T were considered twins. D (the oak) ruled the waxing part of the year and was sacred to the Druids. It was also one of the seven most important letters of the *Beth-luis-nion* and was associated with the planet Jupiter and with Thursday. The runic sign for the [d] sound was named *daeg* (meaning "day") and, according to Halsell, was equated with light—the first and least tangible, yet most desired, gift of God.

Plato wrote in *Cratylus* that D expressed the concept of "binding and rest in a place" because of the closing and pressure of the tongue in pronouncing it. More recently, Noah Jacobs called D the "altruistic letter par excellence" because "defensive d's…being formed in front of the mouth by the extended tongue, express assent and gratitude." Both D and T are known phonetically as "dentals" (they are pronounced with the tongue pressed against the teeth) and have been thought to denote "firmness." In modern technical phonetic terminology D is called "the sonant dental mute, or point-voice-stop consonant, which in English is alveolar rather than dental." I certainly hope and trust that is self-explanatory.

D commonly represents the fourth of a series. In music it is the name of the second note of the natural major scale. In higher mathematics, D is the sign of derivation and d the sign of differentiation. (And, in the interests of accuracy and differentiation, it was these kind of *d*s on a burning piece of paper that Pynchon was referring to in the passage cited

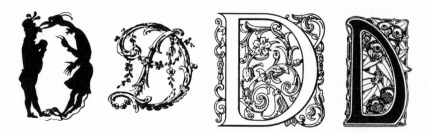

from his great novel.) The sign D is used as the Roman numeral for 500; but, as with C, some scholars maintain that this sign gradually developed out of forms of the Greek letter *phi* (Φ) for which the Romans had no other use. In time, half of this symbol came to closely resemble the letter D, after which time that letter was used to represent the number. (See M for more on this development.)

Like the strong and uncomplaining workhorse, Boxer, of George Orwell's *Animal Farm*, we have progressed beyond some in having learned the alphabet up to D; and, to paraphrase his resolution, we can now devote our time to learning about the remaining twenty-two letters.

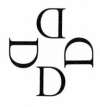

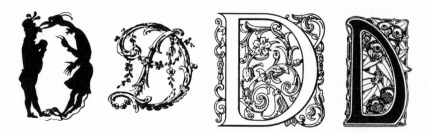

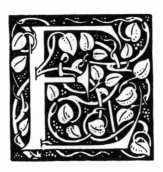

WITH E, WE ENCOUNTER OUR SECOND VOWEL and the fifth letter of both the Roman and English alphabets. We also encounter the most frequently employed letter in English as well as in most other languages using the basic Roman alphabet.

Our fifth letter is descended in a somewhat roundabout way from two different Semitic-Phoenician and Greek letters. Most basically, E is derived from the Phoenician letter *he*, which represented an aspirate (or breathing sound) in the Semitic languages. According to some scholars, the Semitic word *he* possibly meant "window," although most are somewhat in doubt about its exact meaning; ... so we can fairly conclude that this window was not too clear. Donald Anderson relates the sign to an early pictograph of a "man with raised arms." Due to a later development of the Greek alphabet, E sprouted an additional root to its family tree with the Semitic letter *kheth* (also known as *cheth* or *heth*), also an aspirate, meaning a fence or enclosure. As one might well guess from these meanings, the early forms of these letters were quite different from the classic Roman capital E.

When the Greeks adapted the Phoenician script to their language they added signs for vowel sounds, and the Semitic *he* became the Greek vowel *epsilon*, which had a short [e] sound. In time, the Greeks realized that their alphabet lacked signs for some important language sounds and so they created a new vowel, *eta* (long [e] sound) from the Semitic *kheth*. This occurred before the Athenians adopted the classic Greek alphabet

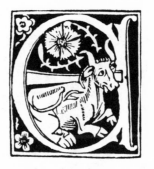

in 403 B.C. but happened too late to affect the Roman alphabet, which had begun developing a few centuries earlier from the western Greek alphabet variant. Thus, the Romans had only one sign for vowel [e] sounds, a limitation that has been passed on to the English alphabet. English, which has many more vowel sounds than signs to cover them, distinguishes them by their specific pronunciation in the words of the language. English usage differentiates many sounds all represented by the sign E—the *Oxford English Dictionary* lists at least fourteen; also, E is often silent in pronunciation and is the first letter of many digraphs, which even further expands its range.

By the time their classic alphabet was codified, the Greeks had seven signs for vowels, and they were adept at finding correspondences for them. The Greeks (and later commentators) related the vowels to the seven major heavenly bodies and the seven strings of Apollo's lyre (which brought harmony to existence). Seven was an extremely significant number in Pythagorean and much other mystical thought, and the seven Greek vowels gained a great number of associations because of this. Consonants were thought to give words their bodies, while vowels put soul or spirit into them. Some saw the letters as symbolic keys to the meaning of existence, and the vowels were considered especially important in unlocking the mysteries.

$$\text{A E H I O Y } \Omega \quad \text{The seven Greek vowels}$$

According to Plato's dialogue *Cratylus*, *eta* is one of the "great" letters and expresses the idea of length. *Cratylus* is concerned with the distinc-

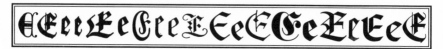

tion between the names of things and things themselves. The participants begin by discussing the letters to see if they represent or denote simple things or qualities. Socrates declares himself incompetent for the task yet for the sake of furthering understanding says he will make some attempt. He then puts forward a few of his first notions but calls them "truly wild and ridiculous" (an apt description of the various citations from *Cratylus* I present). No conclusions are explicitly reached in the dialogue from this attempt; but since the disputants later agree that names and things are not the same, nor is the name fully expressive of the thing, it seems best to take Socrates's notions as merely interesting ideas. Others, such as Rimbaud and Jünger, may appear to take their letter relations more seriously, but then they are also more explicitly poetic. Those of a religious or mystic bent often seek other "true believers" to applaud the letter correspondences they find—if you smile or scoff at them you do so at your peril in their realm of darkness. Tory, delightfully, seems to be in a class by himself most of the time.

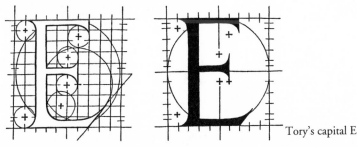

Tory's capital E

E is an important letter in Pythagorean mysticism. Plutarch mentioned that an E was inscribed over the famous oracle at Delphi. Because E has five points and was the fifth letter, the Greeks considered it equal to five. It was also thought to be the letter of light. As the fifth letter, it comes in the middle of the series one to nine. The Greek letter *theta* (Θ) was the symbol for the number nine, and when it is represented as a divided rectangle ⊟ (which also is an early Semitic form of *kheth* and Greek form of *eta*), half of that is E. It is all rather neat in a complicated way, and, if you are a Pythagorean, more meaningful than manipulative. E was thus representative of the Pythagorean Way—which was balance

EeEeEeEeEEeEeeEeEEeEe

and justice—something not to be overstepped. (*Theta*, by the way, also corresponded to an Egyptian representation of the cosmos: the circle represented the world; the line the good Dämon holding it together.)

Our travels along the mystic way seem to have led us a bit from our fifth letter; but the mystical path does not commonly lead to the expected. And, being so important to human civilization, it should not be too surprising that over the centuries the various alphabet signs have been invested with a great number of very curious, interesting, and sometimes profound associations. Victor Hugo, for example, wrote that "E is the foundation, the pillar and the roof—all architecture contained in a single letter."

In the Irish *Beth-luis-nion* alphabet, E was called *eadha* and was related to the white poplar, or aspen; it was associated with the autumnal equinox and old age. Robert Graves also informs us that E was one of the letters created by the goddess Carmenta. The runic sign for [e] was named *eh*, meaning "horse." Tory relates the letter to the cardinal virtue Fortitudo (fortitude, courage, endurance), and it forms the left hand of his man of letters. According to Zolar, in modern mystical circles E signifies hearing. "It represents the ear of man and its interior parts. It is the symbol of all noises and indistinguishable sounds. Everything that is devoid of harmony....It stands for the material sense, the image of emptiness and nothingness. It is used to denote everything crooked, low, and perverse." Its number is 70. (With a list like that, I half expected E to be the sign of a heavy metal rock band and its number to be 666!)

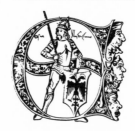

E also designates the first sound uttered by female infants, according to the medieval English scholar Richard Rolle. By no coincidence, this letter is the first in the name of our great progenitress, Eve. And,

Ee*Ee*EeEEeeEe*eEE*EeE

although some writers of a mischievous or chauvinistic bent may relate the ideas of Zolar and Rolle, I myself would certainly strive to resist such a base temptation. Many writers have succumbed to the temptation of constructing works in which E is the only vowel used, however—a task made easier due to its predominance in the language. One anonymous verse concerns Eve and begins: "Eve, Eden's Empress, needs defended be; / The Serpent greets her when she seeks the tree. / Serene, she sees the speckled tempter creep; / Gentle he seems, perversest schemer deep, …" etc., etc. (Elegy: Even Eden's ever esteemed excellent Eve erred; emerged expert except expelled; engendered endless emergency.)

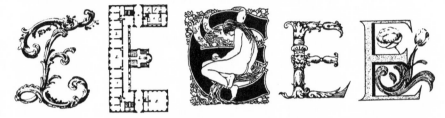

Since ancient times, others have periodically taken on the challenge of composing literary works without using the letter E—perhaps the most ambitious being a 50,000 word novel (*Gadsby*) by E.V. Wright published in 1939 and listed in Martin Gardner's annotated update of C.C. Bombaugh's very delightful book of literary curiosities. Ingenious accomplishments of a sort all these must be; but I know of none celebrated for pure literary excellence. Thus, I am reminded of a remark attributed to the great Persian critic Jami, who listened unmoved when a poet recited a composition in which one letter was omitted. When the poet asked to at least be commended for his ingenuity, the critic replied: "It would have been better if you had left out all the letters."

In Roman square or monumental capitals, the E was considerably condensed in width. It was also one of the letters that in the uncial script

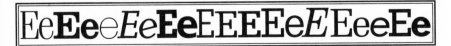

Roman monumental capitals (left), uncial, semi-uncial, four Insular and three black letter E's

became most noticeably rounded, essentially achieving its minuscule form. The transformation could be considered complete with semi-uncial forms of the letter and was firmly established with the first roman printing types, although there had been a number of interesting experiments with the sign during the Middle Ages and have been many more typographic manipulations of both upper- and lower-case forms of the letter, especially since the nineteenth century. Even its more traditional forms vary: Walter Tracy maintains that "in capital E it is the length of the three arms in relation to the stem and to each other that gives the letter its character." He also claims that the design of the lower-case e produces (or should produce) strong feelings, particularly whether the bar is slanting or not. (Drinkers share the typophile's reaction when they notice a slanting bar.)

E e E e

E commonly represents the fifth item in a series, and in music is the name of the third note of the diatonic scale of C major. In chemistry, E (sometimes Er) represents the element Erbium; in physics, E represents energy (which also, according to Einstein, relates it to both m and c—and, if we can accept that type of relation, the Pythagorean connection of E and Θ should not appear too far-fetched, should it?). Even somewhat more abstrusely, in mathematics e equals 2.71828—which is the base of Napier's system of logarithms—and which, it must be admitted, makes the Roman numerals seem quite simple.

In a more poetic vein, Rimbaud linked E with the color white—the "whiteness of vapors and tents." Ernst Jünger says that E pertains to the even, the level. And, in what must by now seem to be surprising agreement among poetic and mystic interpretations, Jünger also relates E to the color white and the quality of "shimmering." He claims that [e] is the one sound with which one can portray the vowel content of entire sentences—it mixes easily with the other vowel sounds. However, Noah Jacobs finds e to be darker than a in their lower-case forms, as illustrated

EeEeeEEeEEeEEeEeEeE

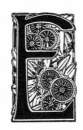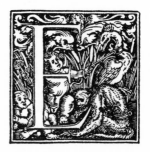

in the variant spellings of a common color: "*grey* is a shade greyer than *gray* because the *a* admits more light than the *e*." E is the mathematical vowel, the vowel of abstract thought. In combination with it, most consonants receive their sound. It is the "constructive" vowel that builds and strengthens languages. And, somewhat paradoxically, in our intricate world of the alphabet, it relates to both emptiness and fullness or grandeur. Those in school, at least, can easily appreciate the relation to emptiness: E is the modern academic mark of emptiness—failure.

Jünger's essay "*Lob der Vokale*" ("In Praise of the Vowels") is often rhapsodic but also attempts a more sober reflection on the letters and especially their sounds in language. He considers the consonants to be the enduring, little-changing structure, while the vowels are the flesh on the bones—that which flavors, colors, and is more transitory in language. Earlier, Jacob Grimm had compared vowels to the feminine and consonants to the masculine principle. Jünger essentially discerns the relations between letters and things from their sounds in certain German words. An obvious problem with this approach is that when translated into another language the same words can be represented by different sounds. For example, the [i] and [e] sounds of the German *Ich liebe dich* become [o] and [u] sounds in the English translation "I love you." Thus, we hardly seem to have the study of eternal vowel associations Jünger would like to claim.

Jünger does mention Rimbaud's poem on the colors of vowels, but concludes he and Rimbaud can reach different understandings of the vowels due to the inherent richness of their sounds and contexts as well as to the deep differences between French and German. He admits that

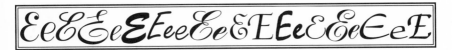

there are discrepancies between words and the sound-meanings he claims; but he maintains that the sound is the base, the fountainhead, the pure picture that language more or less closely approximates or reflects. Further, Jünger claims that all vowels have a two-fold, often opposed, character and connotation—thus many seeming inconsistencies are eliminated. The "idea" of the "pure" basic sounds of the vowels expressing something beyond the meaning of the words they may compose is somewhat analagous to "tone" in speech or the crooning of a mother to her child—a comforting or meaning beyond the words expressed.

Jünger concludes that in the five vowel sounds in their purity and combinations we hear the basic sounds of matter and its movement in existence—an idea similar to the Kabbalistic notion of the letters in their mystical combinations reflecting the structure and meaning of existence. Sounds are also keys to the mysteries of the universe. Jünger claims that if the primal ideas relating to the sounds are kept in mind in writing and speaking, and corresponding words are sought for and chosen in composition, our ideas and words will gain in subconscious power, resonance, and harmony.

It seems appropriate to take leave of our fifth letter by presenting a riddle or enigma concerned with some of the great mysteries of the universe:

"The beginning of eternity; the end of time and space;
The beginning of every end; the end of every place."

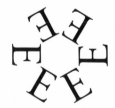

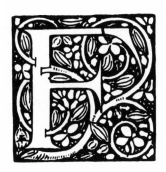

F IS THE SIXTH LETTER of both the Roman and English alphabet; but it is another letter whose history is not simple. It is descended from the Phoenician *vau* (or *waw*), which possibly meant a nail or hook, although scholars disagree. At least one has identified it as an early sign for the cleft or branching Tree of Life, and another believed it derived from an Egyptian hieroglyph of a horned serpent—the bars are the horns, the vertical stroke the body.

The Greeks adopted the sign from the Phoenicians, but it soon disappeared from Greek alphabets—early in the seventh century B.C. The letter originally represented the consonantal [w] and vowel [u] sounds. The Greeks called the letter *digamma* because its form was that of two *gamma*s placed one above the other: F. Before being dropped from the alphabet, it came to represent a [v] or [w] sound; but some scholars claim that this sound was not really needed for Greek speech and so the letter fell into disuse and was finally discontinued. Robert Graves, however, advances another theory. He claims that F was removed from the Greek alphabet for religious reasons: it was associated with the holy name of the Universal God, JHVH, in its pronunciation as [v] and perhaps was considered too sacred for common use.

Graves's rather complicated and obscure idea possibly receives some support from later instances of religious groups changing their script or direction of writing to emphasize the fact that they had altered their beliefs. As Sir Wallis Budge reports of the Coptic Christians, Egyptians

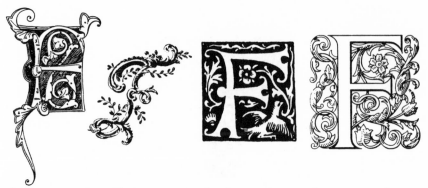

who converted to Christianity in the first and second centuries: "Once their conversion was effected, they determined to break absolutely with the old pagan religion and its cults. They discarded the hieroglyphic, hieratic, and demotic scripts, and formulated an alphabet for themselves."

Also, the holy, secret names (there were many) of God were considered very potent by many religious groups. According to Jewish mysticism, one who knows the correct letters and order of God's most secret name can create man-like creatures (or golems) out of earth, as legend says that Rabbi Low did in Prague in the eleventh century. But it is not easy. According to Gustav Meyrink in his 1915 novel, *The Golem*: "The procedures involved cover some twenty-three folio columns and require knowledge of the 'alphabets of the 221 gates.'" In Pythagorean and Jewish mystical traditions, F stood for the last day of creation—the day of rest. And rest it did … for many centuries. For whatever reason, the letter disappeared from the Greek alphabet without ever having been associated with its modern sound.

The Etruscan alphabet is generally thought to have derived from a western Greek variant, although some scholars feel that it may have developed directly from a Semitic source, as did the Greek. In any case, its later developed form had a sign similar to our number 8, which the Etruscans used to represent the [f] sound. The earliest Latin inscriptions used the digraph F8 (wh) to express [f]. The Romans later simplified this by using only the first of the signs to represent the sound. They kept the sign in the sixth place of the alphabetic order; and at last we had the F sign for the [f] sound, where it has remained in the Roman and English alphabets ever since.

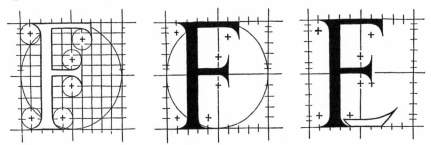

Tory's design of the letter F; also a drawing of its relation to E

F, following the lead of E, was often condensed in classical inscriptions and square capital pen-written forms. It also developed an elongated form in the Rustic script, becoming one of the first letters to be written above the line of most of the other letters. In time this development influenced the lower-case form of the letter. F had a slightly unusual positioning in uncial and semi-uncial scripts. Those forms (especially the latter) were very close to the modern minuscule letter except that they featured a prominent descender and projected only slightly above the line. In modern type forms, f has been raised to be an ascending letter only; however, modern cursive handwriting echoes the past in that this letter—although very different in form—commonly extends both above and below the normal body lines of the letters. An old practice of using ff to represent a capital F can still be found in certain surnames.

Rustic script example (above); uncial, semi-uncial, six Insular versions, two black letter versions, and a 15th century initial letter F (from left to right, below)

Ligatures, or joined letters, are seldom used in this day and age; those most commonly seen are f in combination with i or l. This is not just an arbitrary linkage, as were most of the dozens of ligatures used in earlier times; instead it reflects a solution to a problem found with metal type where the top of the lower-case f would need to overhang its type body in order to fit properly with other letters. This was called kerning. When the following letter had an ascender the two would conflict, so the combination was redesigned and the two letters cast as one. Since this practice generally improved the look of the page it has continued in fine typography even though the technology no longer necessitates it.

fi fi fl fl ff ffi ffl

Regular fi and fl letters and their ligatures, plus three other ff combination ligatures

The letter F (*fearn*) was one of the seven most important in the *Beth-luis-nion* alphabet and was associated with the planet Saturn and the day of the week, Saturday. It related to the vernal equinox, and its month began on March 18. Its tree was the alder, known as the tree of fire, which was a token of the resurrection, being a release from the power of water. In the runic alphabet, the first letter was the [f] sign, *feoh*, which meant "wealth"; it originally referred specifically to cattle (once again we find an alphabet's first letter linked with bovines) but later was generalized to other forms of wealth. The alphabet itself was called "futharc," named after the letters that begin it, just as is our alphabet. F was considered one of the most powerful signs in runic (meaning "secret," "mysterious") writing, a script revered for its potency among northern European people.

Being considered signs of such great power in the human imagination, the letters have tempted many to use them for unsanctified purposes—black magic, in common parlance. I mentioned that ancient Jews used the letters to trap devils; in *Doctor Faustus*, Christopher Marlowe reports their being used to invoke devils—"characters of signs and erring stars by which the spirits are enforced to rise"—when they are used in the proper (i.e., improper) combinations. This is what Faustus wants. "These metaphysics of magicians and necromantic books are heavenly. Lines, circles, signs, letters, and characters—Ay, these are

FfFfFFFfFfFFffFfFFFfF

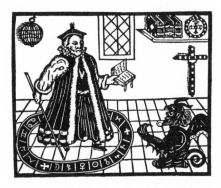

Faustus invoking the devil, from an early edition of Marlowe's *Doctor Faustus*

those that Faustus most desires. O, what a world of profit and delight, of power, of honor, of omnipotence is promised to the studious artisan!" The Faustian drive—human beings' unquenchable desire for knowledge, which is pursued at any price—is naturally associated with the letters, those signs that unlock mysteries and bring us knowledge even in their mundane use. And, though Doctor Faustus may have come to an unfortunate end, his spirit lives on,...and many others have willingly tried to make use of the power of the letters with methods and purposes both sacred and profane.

The power of written signs has been appreciated from their inception. Writing was generally the preserve of a priestly or elite class in ancient societies. The idea that the letters had magical or mystical powers persisted in many forms at least well through medieval times. According to many, however—including Dr. Faustus, I presume—writing was not by any means an unmixed blessing. Claude Lévi-Strauss maintains that

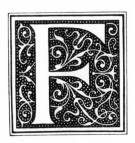
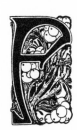
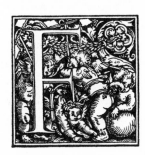

FfFFFfFFfFfFFFfFfFFFfFfFFfFFFF

writing "seems to have favored the exploitation of human beings rather than their enlightenment." In the beginning, as the creation of the few, written laws possessed the aura of Holy Writ for the illiterate masses. Then, as the masses became increasingly literate, they were confronted with difficult and subtle rules and regulations and then told that ignorance of the law was no excuse. Now, with tons of print published daily, Lévi-Strauss feels that writing has become devalued and has lost its power. Yet the media's power still remains concentrated in the hands of a few, who now use means other than literacy to maintain it.

Of course, the idea of knowledge as a type of power persists; but the advantages of literacy are not as dramatic as they once were. In England the legal protection of "benefit of clergy," or exemption from trial for criminal offenses before secular courts, was extended in the reign of Edward I (1272–1307) not only to ecclesiastics but to any man who could read. A prisoner might be claimed by the bishop of a diocese and given a book in Latin to read a few lines. If it was declared, *legit ut clericus* ("he reads like a clerk," that is, like a cleric, or scholar, generally the only literates of the time, and thus potentially able to take Holy Orders), the offender was only (!) branded with a letter signifying his crime and then set free. The statute was not wholly abolished until 1827, and was an instance of the ancient conflict between civil and religious powers. According to E.C. Brewer, F was branded near the nose on the left cheek of felons admitted to the benefit of clergy and was also used on those convicted of brawling in church. Barbara Tuchman reports that after the Great Plague of 1348, when there were far fewer laborers than before, F was branded on the foreheads of fugitive laborers who tried to charge more for their services than the official rate.

The power of the alphabet even in its daily, ordinary use of facilitating understanding between humans has always been extremely impressive—especially to the ancients, non-literate people, and those who have not unreflectingly taken the alphabet and writing for granted. Jean-Paul Sartre, for example, wrote movingly in his novel *The Reprieve* of an illiterate man bewildered by events and holding in his hands that great source of information, a newspaper: "He unfolded the paper and

FfFfFFffFfFfFFfFFfFFf

inspected it. What he saw were thousands of black specks, ... he felt quite dizzy if he looked at them for long. There was also a photograph of a spruce and smiling man with plastered hair. He dropped the paper and burst into tears." There are also many modern accounts of non-literate peoples' astonishment at the ability of literate individuals to exchange or discern information through the medium of marks on paper. Edward Clodd reported a story from the *Smithsonian Reports* of 1864 in which a missionary sent an illiterate native to deliver four loaves of bread along with a note that stated the number to a colleague. Along the way, the messenger ate one of the loaves and was of course discovered. When he was later sent on a similar errand and again stole a loaf, before he ate the bread he first took the precaution of placing the accompanying note under a stone so that it would not see him.

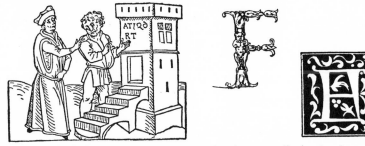

Left: an illustration from William Caxton's *Aesop* (1484), supposedly showing Aesop being put in prison (perhaps because he couldn't decipher the inscription on the building!).

This amazement at the simple power of writing has ancient antecedents. But Pythagoreans, ancient astrologers, and other mystics have endeavored to link the letters to even greater "realities"; and thus conjunctions between the letters and heavenly bodies developed and proliferated. These attempts to find astral correspondences for the letters are but variants of the very ancient practice of "reading in the stars," which was especially popular in ancient Babylonia. The Hebrew prophet Isaiah spoke of the heavens as a scroll filled with mysterious writing. In the sixteenth century, Guillaume Postel, a noted Hebrew scholar, presented his Celestial Alphabet, which he claimed to have received by divine revelation. He maintained that eternal laws were written upon the

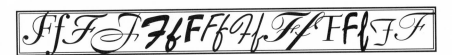

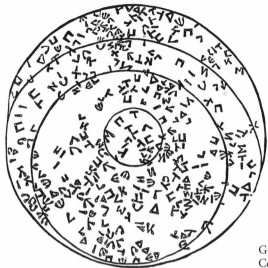

Guillaume Postel's
Celestial Alphabet

heavenly vault in archaic Hebrew letters, which could be revealed by drawing lines between the stars. The idea is said to have found favor later with Cardinal Richelieu's librarian, Gaffarel. In his poem *Hyperion*, Friedrich Hölderlin also speaks of the stars as "only letters, with which the name of the brotherhood of heroes is written." And, more recently, the poet Galway Kinnell wrote in *The Book of Nightmares* of reading "the cosmos spelling itself, the huge broken letters shuddering across the black sky." With the ancient idea of the heavens as a book, it is possible that the letters and their order may have originated in correspondence to a star pattern, as Moran maintains. However, this notion seems to be of quite recent origin; classical speculations on alphabet order generally seem to be based on phonetic considerations.

Well, it may seem that, like the ancient Greeks, we have left out F in our recent discussion; so let us return to it before it drops completely from sight. In music, F is the name of the fourth note of the scale of C major. In chemistry, it stands for the element Flourine; and it also signifies degrees on the Fahrenheit thermometer scale. The sound [f] is technically known as the "voiceless labiodental spirant." Although not as highly placed in English as in the runic alphabet, F still stands for the sixth of a series, a rather high position; but as a scholastic mark of quality it ranks the lowest among the letters so used, being the traditional mark of failure. However, in modern times it has shared the fate of its Greek ancestor, having commonly been dropped as a grade, most grading systems having found E to adequately represent failure. F is still commonly used as an abbreviation for "False" in many types of examinations, however.

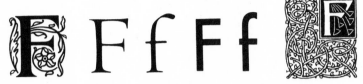

When we consider the troubles related to our letter, it may be appropriate here to mention that Geofroy Tory relates F to Melpomene —the Muse of tragedy. And, F represents the left ear of his man of letters who, had he been an early Greek, could have fittingly (if somewhat strangely) had the name of Vincent. Fortunately, his man seems to be of Roman ancestry, and so thus far we have a healthy model and a full-fledged alphabet.

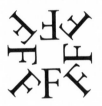

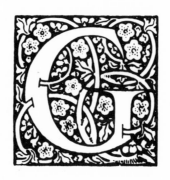

WITH G, THE SEVENTH LETTER of the Roman and English alphabets, we pick up a tale that we left with C. And this is just what G did—pick up a tail when it was at C. Both letters are descended from the Phoenician *gimel* and the Greek *gamma* (and yes, yes, I would ask the reader to see C for more information). Moran relates the Semitic third letter *gimel* to the constellation Gemini, and also to the idea of emptiness, which he somewhat surprisingly relates to birth—that is, the empty vessel waiting to be filled. Thus, it corresponds to the "child" principle, the natural outgrowth of the dualism established by the first two letters. Nerdinger relates the early Semitic sign to a symbol of division or equality of day and night. And, in Plato's *Cratylus*, *gamma* is called a "heavy" sound expressive of detention or slowing. All are interesting ideas,…and if the reader thinks (s)he can relate them to one another, (s)he has my best wishes.

Originally the Romans had no letters to differentiate the [g] and [k] sounds, and the letter C was used to represent both. In the course of time, the Romans realized that it was important to distinguish those sounds, so they modified the letter C by adding a stroke to it and thus invented the letter G to express the [g] sound. Tradition ascribes this added stroke to Spurius Ruga about 230 B.C. (and it appears that he derived some immediate benefit from it). The Romans put their new letter G in the seventh place in the alphabet, where it took the place of the previous seventh letter—Z—which the Romans considered unnec-

11)《《ΓΓGGᏮᏮᏜᏝᎢᏃᏃᏒᏒᏃᏃᏒᏒᏃᏃᏃᏒᏃᏃ

essary for ordinary Latin pronunciation. Besides signifying the [g] sound, the new letter also represented the later Roman softer [j] sound.

ꝼ ꝼ ꝼ ꝼ ꝼꝼ ꞅꞇꞇꞇ Various Insular forms of the letter G

Insular scripts had a form of G called *yogh*, which resembled a modern cursive z; for a time it existed side by side with the Roman G introduced after the Norman Conquest. It was gradually replaced by the Roman letter y in its initial uses and by gh in the interiors of words. Some dialects replaced it with a z or s when it was used at the ends of words. In Middle English, the letter G had both a [g] and a [dz] sound —a somewhat unusual coincidence, but unrelated to the fact that G had taken the place of Z in the alphabet. About the year 1200, Ormin, an Augustinian monk and spelling reformer, tried to differentiate g (the minuscule at that time being the common form of the letter) into two separate symbols: g representing the [dz] sound, and ᵹ symbolizing the [g] sound. As the reader probably realizes, his example was not widely followed—one added stroke to a letter no doubt being considered plenty. In modern English the letter G represents many subtle sounds but is phonetically characterized as the voiced guttural stop.

G being established as a variant form of C serves as an analogy of sorts to the alphabet itself: the letters as a set of variations on geometrical themes of line, square, circle, and triangle which, set together, become a dynamic frieze of spatial forms and rhythms. Writing is then seen not only as repeated letters but also as repeated letter forms with slight variations—C and G, E and F, P and R, among others, serving as

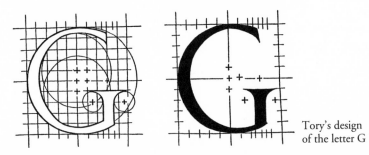

Tory's design of the letter G

excellent examples. Patterns and rhythms are established by words, letters, and letter elements, and they are accentuated or diminished by the various typefaces or writing styles employed.

With the uncial style of the fourth through seventh centuries, the distinguishing stroke or tail of the G began to descend below the line of the letters, and it became one of the most notably altered letters of the style. However, the modern lower-case g developed from more everyday Roman cursive forms rather than from the more formal uncial and semi-uncial scripts, in which the upper part (or bowl) of the letter was not closed except when most hastily or sloppily written. Lower-case g, like a, has two common typographical forms—one with two closed bowls (found in most serif faces), and a more cursive single closed bowl and stem form usually found in typewriter and sans serif fonts.

Uncial, semi-uncial, two black letter, and serif and sans serif forms of G

Having touched on the subject of cursive handwriting, and since G is the first letter of the name Gutenberg, this seems a grand opportunity to develop those subjects further. First, it should be made clear that Johann Gutenberg did not invent printing nor even printed books—wooden blocks, in which all the material on a page was carved in a piece of wood, had been used before his time to print broadsides, playing cards, and even booklets. The contribution of Gutenberg—a goldsmith by trade—was the casting of reuseable metal type forms or letters and then (in about the year 1452) developing a method of using them with a printing press. It was an immense achievement. Also, his solutions to both problems were so good that they have been used throughout the history of letterpress printing. His greatest triumph, the magnificent 42-line per page Bible of 1455, is probably the world's most celebrated book. Gutenberg, however, died in relative poverty a few years after his invention was realized; at the moment of triumph his banker foreclosed on him and took over the operation of his printing press.

uiri ei̊. Et addiderunt adhuc philisti=
im ut alcenderent:et diffulli lūt i valle
raphaim. Colúluit autē dauid dūm.
Þi alcendā cōtra philisteos:₹ trada⸗
tos in manus meas⸗Qui rūdit. Mō
alcendas cōtra cos led gira post tergū
torū:₹ uenics ad cos ₢adūlo pirorū.
Et rū audieris lonitū clamoris gra⸗

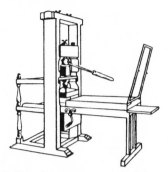

Part of a column of the 42-line Gutenberg Bible (left); early printing press (right)

Although the cynical Ambrose Bierce defined type as "pestilent bits of metal suspected of destroying civilization and enlightenment," virtually all cultural historians agree that printing from moveable type is one of the most important inventions in human history. Some, including Marshall McLuhan, have developed theses on the subject involving controversial and far-reaching conclusions (some of which I will mention later). Yet even if one does not accept all of the ideas associated with this technological watershed, it can be fairly claimed that printing magnified many of the psychic and social changes begun by the development of writing. McLuhan, for example, maintains that typing and

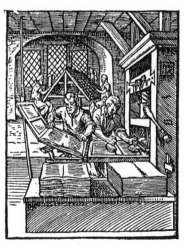
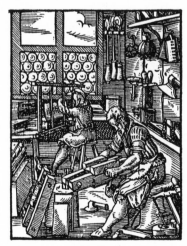

Woodcuts of printers and book binders by Jost Amman from his *Book of Trades* (1568)

GgGgGGgGGGGggGgG

typesetting reduced written expression from an art to a technique, from the personal to the impersonal. These mechanical writing extensions became a means of transcribing thought, not of expressing it. S.H. Steinberg also observes that "one of the long-term results of Gutenberg's invention was the irretrievable separation of formal book-hand and informal business-hand. The former was absorbed by the printed type while the latter degenerated into the illegibility of every man's hand worse than his neighbor's."

Examples of rather poor handwriting, including signature of King Richard III (left)

In the interest of fair play, it should be noted that other authorities find different culprits for the poor state of modern handwriting. Charles Anderson names the ornate script letterforms of seventeenth and eighteenth century engravers: "Because of the difficulties it presented for the layman; because of its poor legibility in the hands of the common individual; and because of the extreme license taken in its rendition, the script is often credited with a major role in the general decline of beautiful, readable handwriting." Alexander Nesbitt also finds fault with the pointed-nib pen, which ruined personal writing because it did not allow the variation of letter stroke widths and other subtleties possible with the flat-nib pen, thus leaving us with scrawling, scratching writing "as illegible as it is unlovely."

Not all people feel that illegible handwriting is bad; many studies have shown that often a person's writing degenerates in legibility as he or she assumes more influential or powerful positions in society. Many writers have been noted for their poor handwriting. While a student, Nathaniel Hawthorne wrote that he thought he could become a writer since he considered his rather poor handwriting very "author-like." Carlyle's "calligraphical summersaults" were noted by a friend, who continued: "Some letters slope in one way and some another, some are halt, maimed, and crippled, and all are blind." Horace Greeley was

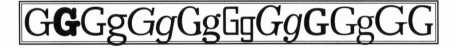

especially notorious for his execrable penmanship. Many of his contemporaries commented on the difficulty of deciphering his missives (Mark Twain's hilarious section on Greeley's writing in *Roughing It* is perhaps the best known). In his *Handybook of Literary Curiosities*, William Walsh also seemed to find Greeley delightful copy. He wrote that upon first seeing Greeley's scrawl, another person exclaimed: "Good God! If Belshazzar had seen this writing on the wall, he would have been more terrified than he was." To add to Twain's treasure, I cannot resist relating one brief portion of a Greeley letter and its recipients' "translation" as reported by Walsh. Greeley: "I find so many cares and duties pressing on me that, with the weight of years, I feel obliged to decline any invitation that takes me away a day's journey from home." This was deciphered by a committee to read: "I have hominy, carrots, and R.R. ties more than I could move with eight steers. If eels are blighted, dig them early. Any insinuation that brick ovens are dangerous to hams gives me the horrors."

Such observations bring to mind Ruskin's statement that "all letters are frightful things, and to be endured only upon occasion"—although, strictly speaking, he was referring to the use of inscriptional letters on buildings, not advocating a standard of bare literacy. And in defense of script lettering we might enlist one of the greatest of the sixteenth-century writing masters, Wolfgang Fugger: "When written in the right manner and order, it surpasses all others. However well it may be written, it may be done yet better. I am almost tempted to say that there is no end to the study of this letter." In any case, it seems that there is one

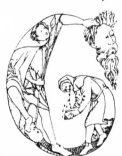
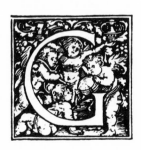

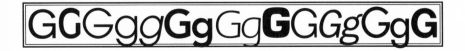

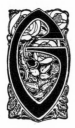
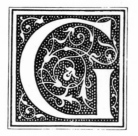
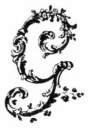
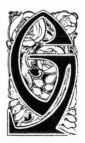

point of agreement about cursive handwriting: "it may be done yet better." And we should note that the quality of letterforms (both type and handwritten) is not necessarily a function of knowledge or technology—even with general improvements in both, few periods since the fifteenth century have produced work of comparable quality. It is more a matter of *caring* about the letter forms.

Percy Smith was one who cared a great deal about the forms of the letters, and he had a decidedly different opinion than John Ruskin regarding Roman inscriptional lettering in particular and the roman letters in general. In the influential typographic journal of the 1920s, *The Fleuron*, he wrote: "The classic roman letter can be as perfect and entirely beautiful a form as any evolved by the mind and skill of man. At its best it possesses intellectual symbolism, organic construction, and the strength emerges, always new, from the only test that matters, the test of time. It is as modern now as when a Roman carver carved it on the Trajan column and on the Arch of Constantine; its rank among the crafts for satisfying completeness and dignity is as that of the human body among natural forms. And while it is true that beautiful letters, beautifully used, are difficult to attain and therefore rarely seen, it must be remembered that a Venus de Milo and an Apollo by Phidias are also rare."

Although they can be distinguished by their respective excellence and components, it must be conceded that type forms are standard and impersonal when compared to handwriting, where we shape the letters on impulse, each letter varying from its textbook form according to our individual manner of making it. Another of our G-words—Graphology—is based on the idea that a person's handwriting reveals something

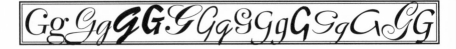

about his or her personality and character. Many books have been written which claim that the way we form our letters—from line density to slant to ways of making loops—reveals our nature and perhaps even our destiny. The books don't all agree on what means what, however; and many people suspect that a belief in graphology reveals one's density rather than one's destiny. But there is an aspect of the distinctiveness of individual letterforms that is accepted by our most august institutions as a basis of responsibility in modern society. I am referring to a person's handwritten signature, which is considered to be unique and serves as the guarantee for legal contracts. And many a destiny has been altered by those particular handwritten letters!

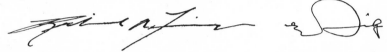

Destiny, God, and the problem of evil have all been related to the alphabet at various times and in many cultures. In his novel *The Portage to San Cristóbal of A.H.*, George Steiner presents a Judaic version. "When to Rabbi Jehudah Ben Levi, God, hallowed be His name, dictated the Torah,…might there have been an error made? Because the stylus slipped or the wax of the tablet flaked in the bronze heat of the Babylonian day. Because a gnat had lodged in Jehudah's ear. Because, for a millionth of a second, the Master had drowsed. Because God, may He forgive the libel of my thought, chose to plant one tare in the harvest of His giving, one false accent, one letter wrong, one word out of place, out of which speck has grown till it smothers man the black tree of our hurts.…But *which* word? Which letter or vowel sign or number?… Which *iod* has been omitted, which *gimel* misplaced in the three million and eleven characters of Torah?" Unfortunately, no one knows, and so evil exists among us, … but, happily, so too does good—one of our finer G-words.

The runic alphabet had two letters for variant [g] sounds. One, an X (primitive signature) form, was named *gyfu*, meaning generosity or gift. The other was named *ger*, meaning year—especially the idea of a fruitful year or harvest. In the Irish *Beth-luis-nion* alphabet, G—*gort*—was

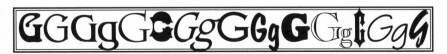

related to ivy and to the lunar month beginning September 30. It was associated with Dionysus and with the idea of resurrection. The Greek letter *gamma*, with its richly symbolic right-angled form, was often used in combination to make other signs. One was the "gammadion," or swastika, formed by radiating four *gamma*s from a central point. Although now a notorious symbol for Nazi Germany, the sign is an ancient one, which formerly connoted good fortune and well-being. Four *gamma*s with their angles facing toward each other form a symbol often used in medieval church architectural decoration, the Greek cross.

Geofroy Tory related the letter G to Clio, the Muse of history, and it formed the right nostril of his man of letters. G commonly represents the seventh item of a series, and in music is the fifth note of the scale of C major. In physics, g is the sign for the force of gravity.

As we have seen, the letters G and C are closely related in both their histories and their forms, one small stroke the beginning of the differentiation. Speaking of this letter G, the American type designer Frederic Goudy said: "If I were to plead trouble with any letter it would probably be the *g*, a mere 'twiddle' of the pen at best, but a delightful twiddle nevertheless." One further observation: Robert Louis Stevenson wrote that as a child he saw the capital G as a genie swooping down to drink out of a handsome cup or chalice. With this taste, let us move on to other delights (or twiddles, if you prefer).

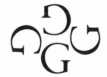

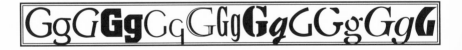

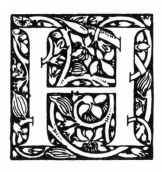

H IS THE EIGHTH LETTER of the modern English alphabet and was also the eighth letter of the Roman; but through many centuries its status as a legitimate letter was repeatedly called into question. It is descended from the Phoenician letter *kheth* (or *heth*), whose meaning is uncertain but was possibly fence, as the early sign was a figure enclosed on all sides (目), perhaps signifying an enclosure. Donald Anderson believes that the sign and related sound were of Egyptian origin and originally denoted a twisted string or bundle. In Greek, as we have seen, the Semitic *kheth* was at first dropped from use but later became *eta*, used to represent the long [e] vowel sound. The modern open form of the letter developed in Greece about 550 B.C.

The Romans inherited the letter from the western Greek alphabet in which the sign symbolized the [h] sound only. It was thus well established in the Roman alphabet when the Greeks later assigned the vowel sound to the letter form, and so the Romans did not follow suit. They basically used the letter as an aspirate—as it is also generally used in modern English. It is its use as a breathing sound rather than as a pronounced sound that brought the status of the letter into question. The Roman writer Priscian stated that "H is the symbol of the breathing, and has nothing else pertaining to a letter save the figure of one and that by custom it is written among the other letters." H has little effect on the sound of the vowels, but when placed with certain consonants, particularly C, P, S, and T, it becomes conspicuous. Tory quotes another early

ㅐㅐ日HHHHㅐ(bbbカ丸hhbh

writer, Aulus Gellius, who observed that "H was inserted by the ancient writers in certain words to give them a firmer and stronger sound."

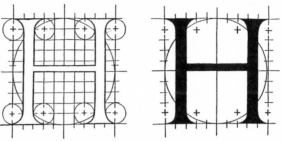

Tory's letter H

The controversy over the legitimacy of H continued into Renaissance and Elizabethan times. Tory himself claimed that H "is not a letter; none the less it is, by poetic license, given place as a letter." One of our finer poets, Ben Jonson, took the license to comment on H: "Whether it be a Letter or no, hath been much examined by the Ancients, and by some, too much of the *Greeke* partie, condemned, and throwne out of the *Alphabet*, as an *Aspirate* meerely....But, be it a Letter, or Spirit; we have great use of it in our tongue....And though I dare not say, she is (as I have heard one call her) the *Queene mother of Consonants*: yet she is the life, and quickening of them." Zolar, the contemporary mystic, reaches similar conclusions regarding the symbolic meaning of H (which he links with the Hebrew letter *he*): "Everything that vitalizes, i.e., air, life, and being. It ... represents the breath of man, the spirit, and the soul. Everything that vivifies." Its number is 5. Although most scholars would feel that he should be relating all this to E, mystics seem to have their own ways of seeing things. And Zolar comes around to the more common view by also relating H to *kheth*, which he says "signifies the principle of vital aspiration and is the symbol of elementary existence. It represents the field of man, his labor, and everything that requires an effort on his part." Its number is 8.

It is certainly an effort to make a coherent narrative around the various meanings and interpretations associated with the rather ethereal letter H. In the ancient Irish tree-alphabet, H (*uath*) corresponded to the lunar month beginning May 13, and its tree was the hawthorn. The

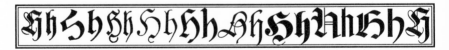

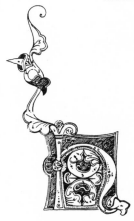
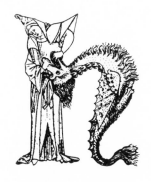
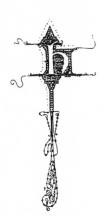

Three medieval decorative H initials

hawthorn was linked to May because of its tendency to blossom then; but in pre-Christian times it was also considered an "unlucky" tree—a tree of enforced chastity—so May was not deemed a good time for marriages. About the first century B.C. in Britain antithetical associations began to develop, perhaps in reaction, and by medieval times orgiastic celebrations around a May-pole were part of the fertility rites of Spring. Students of American literature may see a surprising conjunction of these ideas, names, and themes in the somewhat ambiguous works of Nathaniel Hawthorne—especially the story entitled "The May-Pole of Merry Mount."

According to Robert Graves, H (not B) was originally Sunday's letter in both the ancient Hebrew and *Beth-luis-nion* alphabets. He also reports that the Hebrew equivalent of the hawthorn—the wild acacia— was the timber used in the arks of both Osiris and Noah, as well as the

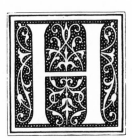
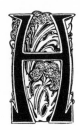
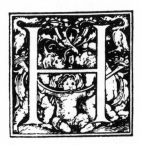

HH*H*h*H*h*H*h*H*h*Hh*h*HhH

Ark of the Covenant, and it was the combustible of Jehovah's "burning bush" recorded in the Book of Exodus. Graves claims that H was removed from the Greek alphabet for religious reasons—it was part of the holy name of the new Universal God. In Pythagorean and Jewish mystical traditions H stood for the first day of Creation. The runic sign for the [h] sound was named *haegl*, meaning "hail," and may have originally been the first of a triad of potentially threatening runes in Germanic divination (N and I were the next letters of this triad).

By A.D. 80 the Roman capital H was beginning its transformation into what became its lower-case form. With the uncial script, the left stem of the H began to grow. Soon the right stem also began to contract, finally becoming a continuation of the stroke of the (now rounded) bar, so that by the sixth century the letter could be said to have attained its modern minuscule form.

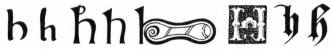

Uncial, semi-uncial, three Insular, one decorative, and two black letter versions of H

The English-American name of the letter H is perhaps the most unusual or least systematic of any in the alphabet. There has been a great deal of scholarly disagreement regarding the names of the Latin letters, though all agree that the names are meaningless as words. Some say that they were Roman adaptations from the Greek, others say from Etruscan, while still others claim that they originated from old syllabic forms. According to the noted authority Hans Jensen, one plausible explanation is that at an early stage all consonant names (except *ha, ka,* and *eks*— that is, H, K, and X) ended in e. But with the great Roman scholar Varro (116–27 B.C.), two groups of consonants—mutes and semi-vowels— were distinguished. According to tradition, Varro ordained that the mutes were to retain their old names, while the semi-vowels were to have an e (with a short sound) preceding them—thus *ef, el, em, en, er,* and *es.* The exceptions: K was linked with A, and Q with U (as we shall see), while H (*ha*) stood alone as merely a breathing sound or aspirate. X (*eks*) was expressly regarded as a semi-vowel; Y and Z were strangers to Latin

HhHHhHHHhHHHhHhH

and thus retained their Greek names, *ypsilon* and *zeta*. Vowels, of course, were named by their own sounds. The English pronunciations of the letter names are very similar, although some authorities feel that they come through Old French rather than directly from Latin. This idea is supported by our pronunciation of H—aitch—which, it has been claimed, comes from the French *la hache* ("the hatchet"—an object the lower-case letter somewhat resembles), not the Latin *ha*. It seems that we thus lost a good opportunity to laugh about the names of our letters; but some wits have tried to make up for it by using the otherwise meaningless names as words, derived from their pronounced homophones. One recent example is a popular little book, *C D B*, by William Steig. If you have a hard time visualizing that, consider I Y Q, which is definitely more pleasant than a combination featuring this chapter's subject: I H U. Another example I learned in my childhood should more than suffice to illustrate the genre (note: the first two letters constitute a proper name): "'ABCD puppies?' 'LMNO puppies!' 'OSMR puppies. CMPN?'" At this point, it might be instructive to recall the pride Lewis Carroll's White Queen took in her related reading expertise.

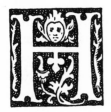   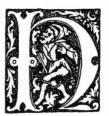

Although it was used as an aspirate in classical Latin, H was usually mute in late Latin, the Romance languages, and Middle English. It gradually regained its usage as an aspirate in English, and in recent times this use has been a mark of a speaker's education—particularly in the British Isles and Commonwealth. Many writers have commented upon or characterized common, uneducated folk by their tendency to drop the H in their speech. William Walsh wrote that "in the dialect of the London cockney a rule seems to have finally emerged that h is to be dropped wherever it should be pronounced, and inserted wherever it is

HhhHHhHhHhhHHHhH

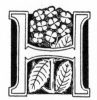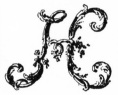

superfluous." In an anonymous verse, the letter H laments that the Cockneys have driven him "from 'ouse, from 'ome, from 'ope, from 'eaven; and placed by your most learned society in Hexile, Hanguish, and Hanxiety." One mocking wag recorded the written equivalent of a welcoming address given to King William III: "Future ages, recording your Majesty's exploits, will pronounce you to have been *a Nero*!" British and American grammarians, pedagogues, and editors still find H to be an incredibly rich mine to develop; others consider it to be more a dangerous minefield. Controversy periodically rages as to whether the article "a" or "an" should be used preceding an (a?) H-word because, if the H is considered mute, the following vowel sound seems to require the "an"; if an aspirate, "a" is sufficient. It is easier to handle in speech than it is in writing where the eye rebels against using "an" before a consonant—whether or not it is pronounced. Conventions change; consult your local pedant if in doubt; ... or, better yet, when possible, use plural forms of H-words. Historians won't mind.

H is used to denote the eighth place in a serial order, and is well known as the symbol of Hydrogen in chemistry. It also has a couple of symbolic uses that are not as well known. In German musical notation, H is the symbol for B natural; and h denotes a small increment in differential calculus. Though some question its place as a letter, it is found in earth, heaven, and hell, in lightning and thunder, birth, death, health and wealth—much to the delight of riddle-makers; although it must be confessed you will never find it in riddles.

H is a good letter to illustrate certain facets of type design, such as the problems of inner space. As Donald Anderson points out: "Within an alphabet the spaces inside the letters must be consistent....If the two strokes of *n* are closer than the two strokes of *h*, more black appears in *n*

HhH*Hh*HH Hh**Hh***Hh*HHhHHH

than *h*, and this will upset the balance of the line. Letters are nothing more than strokes of black and areas of white." H has been considered by some to be more a "spirit" than a letter, as we have seen. Interestingly, a large part of the page of type or written matter that we read consists of what has been called "invisible type"—the spaces within and between letters, words, and lines—spaces that are as important to legibility and beauty as the characters themselves. The leading, or spacing between lines of type, is essential to legibility, giving the eye channels of white to follow in reading. Type designs that feature short ascenders or descenders thus can sometimes be hard to read; the letters h and l, especially, need a definite ascender to be legible.

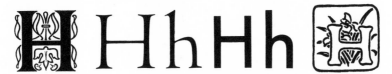

Letter forms must not only be individually pleasing but also combine well with others on the printed page. Type designers continually struggle with this problem; calligraphers have more freedom. Donald Anderson counsels calligraphers: "Above all, the form of the letter as taught is not sacred....Sacrifice the form of the letter to produce the word, and sacrifice the word to produce a tranquil line." Variety of letter shapes and widths is important for legibility and was one of the features lacking in black letter scripts and type. Edward Johnson wrote: "The essential or structural forms are the simplest forms which preserve the characteristic structure, distinctiveness, and proportions of each individual letter....The beauty of a letter depends very much on its inside shape—i.e. the shape of the space enclosed by the letter form."

Though Geofroy Tory personally did not consider H to be a proper letter, he accepted it; and he did consider it to be a model form for most letters with a cross-stroke—which was placed slightly above the vertical mathematical mid-point "to show us that our said Attic letters need to be so logically made that they may be conscious in themselves, instinctively, of all due proportion and of the art of architecture, which requires

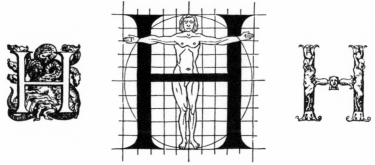

Tory's drawing showing the placement of the transverse stroke of the letter H (center)

that the body of a palace or a house shall be higher from its foundation to its roof than is the roof itself…to avoid the violence of high winds and earthquakes. So, too, our letters do not choose to fear the wind of envious backbiters, desiring to be built stoutly." Since Tory does not elucidate his reasons for assigning particular correspondences between the letters and the parts of the body, we can only speculate if there is a relation between the above statement and the correspondence he assigns between H and one of the Graces—Euphrosyne (Joy)—finding the letter's counterpart in the body of his man of letters to be the rump! Yet we may fairly conclude that it is a rather stoutly built and joyous rump, with very little that is insubstantial about it and no fear of the wind of others.

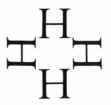

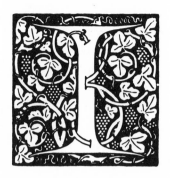

THE LETTER I IS THE NINTH LETTER and third vowel of both the English and Roman alphabets, and is descended from the Semitic consonant *yod* and the Greek vowel *iota*. Many scholars claim that in the ancient Phoenician language *yod* was the word for "hand." Eugen Nerdinger believes that I originally came from an early sign of bisection, in which a vertical line cut through a circle—ϕ—which would make it resemble the Greek letter *phi*. To make things appear even more complicated, in early Semitic and Greek alphabets *yod* and *iota* had angular, zig-zag forms similar to a modern Z. The letter was straightened out in the later and classical Greek alphabets, however; and it was the vertical straight-line form which the Romans inherited and adopted.

A vertical line is one of the oldest and simplest human signs. Referring to it (not necessarily the letter I) Rudolf Koch writes that it represents the oneness of God and also symbolizes power descending to man from on high and man's yearning towards higher things. Perhaps the straight form of the letter influenced Socrates to speculate in *Cratylus* that *iota* was expressive of penetration—"the subtle elements which pass through all things." *Iota* has been called the Lacedaemonian (Spartan) letter, perhaps because of its very simple or spearlike form. It is the smallest letter of the Greek alphabet (as its counterparts I and i are of the Roman), which is the origin of the use of "iota" to mean a tiny bit or the least quantity possible, as in the phrase, "not one iota." As a personal pronoun in English, however, I is quite commonly considered to be one of the greatest of all things. In the words of Ambrose Bierce, "I is the first letter of the alphabet, the first word of the language, the first thought of the mind, the first object of affection."

Geofroy Tory was able to muster considerable ingenuity in discussing the letter I, which he considered (along with O) one of the two foundation letters of the alphabet. Basically, these two letters were seminal because their forms are the line and the circle, from which all other letters can be constructed; but, of course, Tory was able to find many other curious and delightful reasons to justify their importance. I will mention some of them but refer the reader to *Champ Fleury* for the full account.

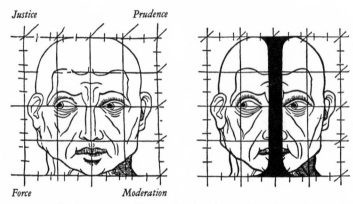

Tory's drawings of human head and capital I on his grid

The capital I establishes both the height of all the capital letters and the thickness of a particular script's vertical strokes or lines. Letter designers have disagreed about the ideal proportions of the letters established by the height-to-width ratio of the letter I and, of course, many interesting type designs can be created by changing the ratio; but from Renaissance times most scholars and designers have claimed that the ideal alphabet has a ratio of about 9:1 or 10:1. Tory accepted the 10:1 ratio, and he established a grid for designing the letters that was ten units high—a number he then related to the nine Muses of antiquity plus their chief, the god Apollo. This suggested many interesting analogies and commentaries throughout his work which, farfetched though they may

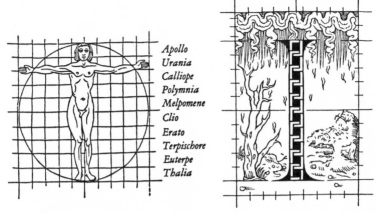

Apollo
Urania
Calliope
Polymnia
Melpomene
Clio
Erato
Terpischore
Euterpe
Thalia

Tory's drawings relating grid to Apollo and Muses, and I to the chain of Zeus and the grid

sometimes appear to modern readers, are fascinating and occasionally quite thought-provoking. Nevertheless, with the letter I, Tory at times seems to stretch his analogical method too far: "I would fain show that it is not without good cause that I have heretofore adapted the nine Muses to the proportions of the I; and to that end I say that the ancient fathers, Greek and Latin alike, to indicate the ideas I have set down above concerning the said I, made it the ninth letter in the order of letters in the alphabet." It is a nice conjunction in regard to the order of the letters, but somewhat manipulative regarding proportions since Tory's letter I is ten units high—the Muses plus Apollo—not nine. In continuing to extol the letter, Tory does make much of the number ten, however. He draws an I consisting of ten links (10 being the noblest and most perfect number, for it "contains all the others"—"that is to say, all good qualities and perfection"), the links symbolizing the golden chain of Zeus which Homer mentioned in *The Iliad* and which Macrobius said were the links of inspiration between heaven and earth. This helps Tory illustrate that I is one of the two "divine" letters.

The letter I was associated by Tory with the cardinal virtue Prudentia (Prudence), and it corresponded to the right foot of his man of letters. Our ingenious author, who may have put his foot in his mouth once with this letter, prudently gets it back on the ground in discussing the

IiⅡiⅡⅡⅡⅡⅡⅡⅡiⅡiⅡⅡⅡⅡⅡⅡⅡⅡiiiⅡII

basic form of the Roman capital I. In its ideal form the top serif is three units wide on his grid, while the bottom serif is four. "And the reason therefor is derived from the natural posture of the human body, which, when it is on its feet, has its feet spread out over more space than the breadth of the head covers. A man stands more firmly when his feet are half-way apart, than when they are close together. So, then, our I must be broader at the foot than at the head."

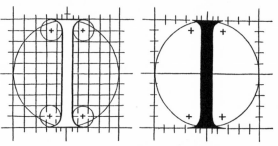

Tory's design of the I, including the proportions of its serifs

Tory's beautiful and precisely drawn capital I, which he constructed as a model base for the complete alphabet, although basically simple is full of subtle nuances. For hundreds of years designers have developed their own variants of this and all the other letters, often disagreeing passionately about just what combination of elements makes for a beautiful version of the letter. But versions and nuances are what is being discussed—the basic form of each letter is a "given," although, as Karl Gerstner points out, one that cannot really be defined: "There is a basic form of each letter which is codified nowhere except in a common convention among literates. The vagueness of this convention affords scope for the typographer, who has never ceased to design endlessly new versions of the basic form as style, fashion and mood dictated." And, speaking of one of our I-words, Nicolete Gray adds: "In the history of lettering, invention, in the sense of inventing a completely new form, is almost unknown; it is not indeed in the nature of this particular art. A letter is a sign: to be recognizable is of its essence, and it cannot be recognized unless it has some minimum connexion with previous known examples. Letters may change over the centuries, ... we know that the forms have some sort of historical continuity, that we can trace

Ii*Ii*IiIiIiII I*Ii*iIiIIiIi I1/Iii IIiI I/iIiiI I

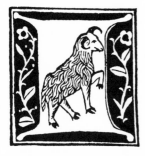  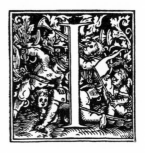

them back, see how at certain points, owing to change of tool, purpose, or taste, they changed this way or that, and so learn to read them." Aside from conscious stylistic design choices, there are three main influences that tend to modify letter shapes at all times and places: 1) the instrument with which the letter is made; 2) the material on or in which the letter is made; and 3) the speed at which the letter is made.

In the course of time, the form of I found in early Roman inscriptions underwent a couple of changes. During the first centuries of the Christian era, I was sometimes written or carved above the level of the other letters. This elongated form—called *I-longa*—continued in occasional use in uncial as well as some medieval script hands, especially at the beginning of words. Some scholars think that it originally designated the long [i] sound, but the idea failed to become established in Latin writing. Although this form became obsolete, it probably influenced the development of ascenders and descenders in later minuscule alphabet forms, and it may have helped influence the development of the consonantal form of I as a descending letter in its lower-case form. Consonantal I? Yes. The Romans used I as both a vowel and a consonant. The consonantal I originally had a sound value close to modern [y]; gradually it acquired a soft [g] sound. This will be discussed more fully when we come to our next letter, for J is the sign that came to denote the consonantal form of I.

In its uncial form the letter I closely resembled its modern lower-case form, except that it was lacking its most noteworthy feature—the dot. Unfortunately, there does not seem to be a universally accepted explana-

IiIiIIi i I Ii i IiIiIIIi i i III

Uncial, semi-uncial, two Insular, two black letter, with serif and sans serif versions of I

tion for the dot's appearance. According to Frederic Goudy, it was introduced in the fifth or sixth century, beginning as merely an accent mark to denote double I (II), single I being written without accent. Other scholars claim that it developed with the highly pointed black letter script of the twelfth century—a script in which there was little difference between the letters and sometimes even actual fusion, where two letters shared a common member. As the script name *Textura* indicates, the letters were virtually woven together into a texture. When two I's occurred together, faint slanting marks were placed above them to distinguish them from U. These accent strokes later became conventionalized as a dot, which was used to designate the minuscule i in all type variants. To "dot your i's" is a phrase meaning to be meticulous and precise even about very small things of little apparent consequence. Precise design came to characterize the lower-case forms just as it did the capitals. One such example is that the dot of the i must not be placed exactly above the stem in order optically to appear centered. (It is also worth mentioning that many modern typographic fonts feature a dotless i so that various accents can be floated over it.)

Medieval scribe's amusing use of black letter script, creating a verse in which it is even harder than usual to distinguish the words and letters from each other; initial I (right)

An interesting feature of medieval manuscripts is their use of often highly ornate decorative initials. The strongly vertical letters I and L were sometimes decorated with climbing figures, which some claim was meant to be symbolic of the soul's upward striving and journey (akin to

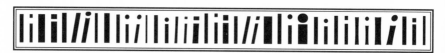

the claim of Rudolf Koch). Others, more skeptical, feel that it has nothing to do with any inherent symbolism of those letters and is due solely to their affording the necessary shape for such drawings.

Large initial letters did not necessarily have to be embellished. In the late Roman and early medieval periods, square capitals much larger than the other text letters began to be used at the beginning of major sections of some manuscript books, and they have been given the name Initial letters. Since these letters were too large to be made with simple pen strokes, a new method evolved: they became drawn letters—the form was outlined and then the space filled in. As Donald Anderson says: "This seemingly simple change from a calligraphic letter to a drawn letter was one of the developments that led to the separation of minuscule and majuscule letters in our alphabetic signs and to the preservation of Roman inscription letters in the Middle Ages." The classic capital letters continued to be used in texts where the majority of the letters were written in one of the many unusual styles of the medieval period. A related development was the coloring of the large Initials (whether gothic or Roman capitals) to embellish the texts. A special scribe called a Rubricator would hand draw and color the Initial letters of manuscript books and even of some of the first printed books—such as the Mainz

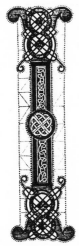
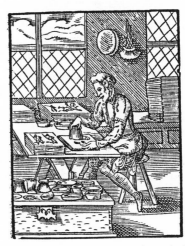

Tenth century initial I (left); and illuminator from Jost Amman's *Book of Trades*

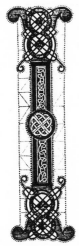

Psalter, for example. "Rubricator" derives from the Latin word for red, which was the color most often used in the specially designated Initials and headings (or rubrics). The phrase "red letter day" derives from the practice of marking holy days in red letters on church calendars.

In the Irish tree-alphabet, the letter I did not have anything near the pleasant connotations that it did for Tory or medieval scribes in the Roman. In the *Beth-luis-nion* its name was *idho*, and it shared the winter solstice with A. Its corresponding tree was the yew, which was known as the death tree and was sacred to the witch goddess, Hecate. Its corresponding metal was lead. In the somewhat related ancient Ogham alphabet of the British Isles, it was the last letter and was dedicated to Death. The runic letter was a vertical stroke like the Roman and was named *is*, meaning "ice." However, according to Norse mythology (*The Prose Edda*), ice was the primal material from which life emerged. The sound [i] has been called "the universal sound of woe." The contrasts of the symbolic associations of this letter are striking and somewhat unusual; but it must be remembered that we are dealing here with one of the most basic and powerful human signs and sounds, which has correspondingly important associations.

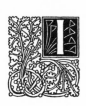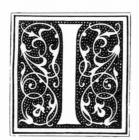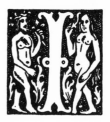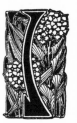

I was used as the Roman numeral for one; however, most authorities believe that this was due to its resemblance to a raised finger—a most basic and ancient numerical designation. To the contemporary mystic Zolar, *yod* "signifies all manifested power. It represents the hand of man, his pointing finger." Its mystical numerical value is 10. The letter I represents the ninth place in a serial order, and in logic is the symbol of a particular affirmative. In mathematics, i is the symbol of the imaginary

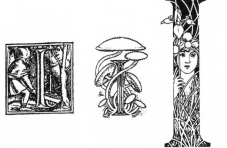
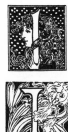

number, the square root of minus one; while in chemistry I represents the element Iodine. The *Oxford English Dictionary* reports that this vowel signifies at least eight separate sounds in modern English usage.

The poet Rimbaud associated I with the color red—"spit blood, laughter of beautiful lips." In his essay "In Praise of the Vowels," Ernst Jünger claims that I has a feminine, motherly character. We hear it in the living sounds of growth and decay. It is also the sound of unity at the source of all things, and has a magnetic, democratic connotation. He agrees with Rimbaud that its color is a deep red. As opposed to the abstract E, it relates to the living, the actual, the concrete and particular. But even here—as we have so often found elsewhere—this seemingly simple, straightforward letter has two ends: Jünger maintains that the world of madness is also contained in its sound. Psychiatrists treating egomaniacs would probably agree.

Let us leave the letter proper and its sound before we fall any further into its hidden world, and move on to our next letter, which is historically only a variant of I, made independent by a simple twist of shape.

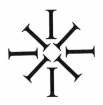

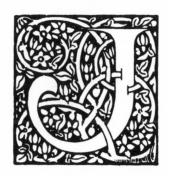

WITH J WE COME TO THE TENTH LETTER of the modern English alphabet but the first of our letters that was not in the ancient Roman alphabet. For that matter, J was not even considered by many people to be a proper letter of the English alphabet until the nineteenth century. Yet, although of quite recent origin, its antecedents go back to ancient times.

J is descended from I, and thus comes from the Greek vowel *iota* and the Semitic consonant *yod*. *Yod* is the smallest letter of the Hebrew alphabet, and it is said to show that he who makes himself small will inherit the world to come, since it is used as the prefix to the future conjugation and tense. The historical and mystical associations of the Greek and Phoenician letters are discussed in the previous section on the letter I; and I will only add here the specification Zolar makes concerning the consonantal form of *yod* (I-J): "As a consonant it is of inferior value and means only material duration." This notion of J as somewhat inferior is found both expressed and implied through the centuries. Its mystical number of 10 does seem to be more appropriate from the modern position of the letter in the alphabetic order than it does for I.

As we have seen, in Roman times the letter I was used to represent both a vowel and a consonant sound. The early Roman consonantal I had a sound value—like *yod*—close to that of modern Y; in time the usage changed, however, and the letter commonly came to represent a soft [g] sound. Later, in medieval times, the J sign was developed to represent the consonantal form of I. As the reader might expect by now, there are

ꝛꝛ||III1J]ıɩ]|ɾıɩJ]I]ıɩíȷδı

differing accounts of how this came to be. A small hook is found at the bottom of some uncial forms of I, which possibly influenced the later J form. According to Frederic Goudy, in the fifteenth century I was occasionally lengthened and hooked to the left at its tail in the margins of book pages as a decorative elaboration. In time, this form was used in more regular contexts and, as the consonantal I often occurred at the beginning of words, J became regularly used as its representative sign.

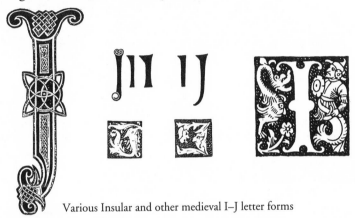

Various Insular and other medieval I–J letter forms

Others have found a J form used as early as the twelfth century in gothic or black letter scripts where ij was occasionally used to distinguish a double i from the very similar u. In the *Chronology of Books and Printing* by Helen Gentry and David Greenhood, "Spain 1485–7" is given as the place and date where lower-case i and j were first differentiated. I discussed some of the ideas regarding how lower-case i came to have the dot added above it. As a natural extension (or variant form) of i, lower-case j similarly acquired one. The word "jot," meaning a tiny amount, is a variant consonantal form of the Greek letter name *iota*; and in the biblical phrase "jot or tittle," "jot" refers to the i and "tittle" (from the Latin *titulus*) to the mark or dot over the i.

Although some claim that the J form was used prior to 1500, Geofroy Tory, for one, did not seem to be aware of it when writing *Champ Fleury* in the 1520s. He made no mention of J either as a letter or variant form of I; he only referred to the fact that I was used as both a vowel and a consonant. Yet, lest the lacuna caused by the lack of commentary on the letter by Tory seem too immense and disheartening, I will devote some space to what people have said of Tory and other Renaissance type designers. Frederic Goudy called *Champ Fleury* (which translates as *Field of Flowers*), "the most useless and most curious work on lettering in existence." Joseph Blumenthal, however, wrote that *Champ Fleury* "was an important factor in the more widespread use of the roman letter and in greater respect for its design." Harry Carter claimed that Tory's book has probably greatly influenced typography, "more, perhaps, than a more level-headed approach would have done"; while D.B. Updike called Tory "a kind of divine jack-of-all-trades," for he was also a noted scholar, grammarian, printer, and book designer. William Dana Orcutt felt that the average student of the art of the book knows far too little about Tory, who "was of supreme importance in determining the basic principles upon which the Book has rested ever since."

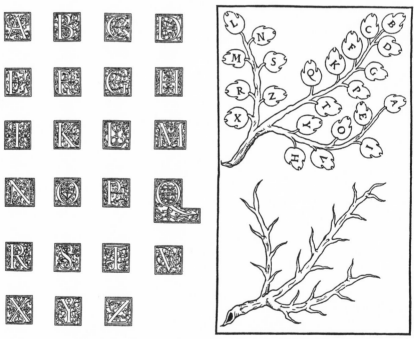

Tory's "Floriated Letters" (left), and his "Branches of knowledge and of ignorance" (right)

There were many Renaissance theories and systems of letter design besides Tory's. The first was probably that of Feliciano in the mid-fifteenth century; but others soon followed, including those of Albrecht Dürer and Luca Pacioli. As Donald Anderson writes: "Certain curious people began to investigate the Roman capitals on a theoretical basis and to impute to the ancient letters an origin of correct or divine proportion. Thus began an international game of reconstructing the Roman capitals with rulers, straight-edges, and compasses, and an international dialogue on proper ratios of letter parts. Woven into the fabric of the studies...are these several Renaissance preoccupations: antiquarianism, an interest in ideal form, and geometry." The geometrical proportioning of letters probably reached its apotheosis in the late 1600s with the system of the French official Jacques Jaugeon (cut into type by Philippe Grandjean), who designed each of the Roman capitals on a grid of 2304 squares—a vast increase over Tory's grid of 100 squares. (The pixel-by-pixel construction of some computer alphabets, though often more complex, has a completely different intent: adaptation rather than creation.)

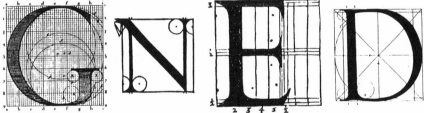

Renaissance letter designs of Jaugeon–Grandjean, Yciar, Ruano, and Rossi (left to right)

Modern scholars and designers have not looked too favorably upon that whole enterprise. Donald Anderson credits it to a Renaissance need to rationalize and systematize a human endeavor, thereby creating a type of Procrustean bed, since the original Roman capitals were handmade—not mechanical—forms and never fit a strict, uniform theory. Concerning the theoreticians, Goudy adds that "almost invariably their rules or principles are so burdened with artistically worthless and impossible geometrical calculations as to be of little real use to a designer of types." According to Nicolete Gray, modern Western lettering has primarily

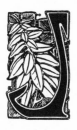  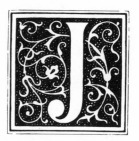 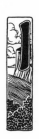

been training in typography, the arranging of already made formal types rather than the more expressive manipulation (or drawing) of the letter forms. The calligraphic tradition and interest has filled the gap in some ways; but the Renaissance theorists had an opposite intention and a more dominant influence: "They sought to restrict and confine the art by arriving at perfect, that is, immutable forms."

Contemporary type designers have generally modified the Renaissance approach to letter design. Warren Chappell writes: "The great monumental Roman letters can be thought of as having simple geometric bones, so fleshed-out that the straights and curves relate organically. A letter should seem to be of one piece, not a sum of parts. But despite many efforts to develop formulae for the construction of the alphabet ... no set of rules can be slavishly held to. The subtleties of the great Roman forms have always eluded the compass and square. The perfect expression of a letter remains in the mind of an artist as a pure concept of form, essentially abstract in nature." Ms. Gray points out that though there is some relation between the classic Roman letters and geometrical forms and rules, it is a flexible, not a doctrinaire relation, "and it is surely this flexibility which has made for the permanent value" of the Roman letters. Seán Jennett adds that "perfection of form is something that might conceivably be fatal in a type-design; the humanity of imperfection, of divergence from the ideal, appears essential.... We are more comfortable with a type that is human and warm; harmony is all." And, as I opened this side-door excursion with Frederic Goudy, let me close it with him: "When a type design is good it is not because each individual letter of the alphabet is perfect in form, but because there is a feeling of harmony and unbroken rhythm that runs through the whole design, each letter kin to every other and to all."

We seem to have reached a fine and high note of harmony, but one that for a long time J had no part in before finally being admitted to the select company. The Italian author and spelling reformer Gian Giorgio Trissino has been credited as the first to require the use of J as a consonant, about 1525. Despite their wranglings over proportional ratios, the Renaissance theorists generally interpreted a whole set of letters—B, E, F, K, L, P, S—as being much more narrow than the forms developed for early printing types that have come down to us (I, of course, is narrow in both classes; J eventually came to be designed in both wide and narrow forms). And, it is an interesting fact about J that when it finally was included in the alphabet and designed into various type fonts, it was the tallest capital letter form in many of them, being one of only two capitals that commonly descend below the base line of all the others. Designers seem often to have adopted the extended form in order to achieve greater differentiation between the I and J and to seek that optical rhythm and harmony distinct from mathematical regularity.

LETRAS CAVDINALES

A.B.C.D. E.F. G.Ib.J. Ik.L.M. .A.O.P. Q. R.S.T. U.X.Y.Z.Z.

Self-portrait of Renaissance designer Juan de Yciar, and one of his alphabets from *Arte subtilissima* (1548)

J really came into English as the consonantal I with the Norman Conquest of 1066 and the resulting influx of French words into the language. Modern English can be said to have begun about 1400 as a rich and developed amalgam of Anglo-Saxon and Norman root words. As late as the sixteenth century there were fewer than five million speakers of English—a situation that has changed dramatically in the last 400 years (that is, if you don't ask English teachers their opinion), English currently being the most broadly disseminated and probably the most widely used language in the world. J was not used as an independent letter in the English Bible of 1611 or in Shakespeare's Folio of 1623; but it was gradually added to all fonts of type beginning about 1625. By 1630, J had come to be used only for the consonant sound, and soon was in common use. In Ben Jonson's *English Grammar* of 1640 it was used as a consonant with the [j] (more accurately [dzh]) sound. And, as William Walsh wrote 250 years later, it has been used with a consistency that makes it a "rare jewel in our orthography." Still, for a long time it was considered by many to be just a form of I—as, for example, in Dr. Johnson's dictionary of the eighteenth century. This continued to be the opinion of some up until the beginning of the nineteenth century when J was regularly assigned its own place in the dictionaries—a sure sign that it had fully arrived.

The English pronunciation of the name of the letter employs a long [a] sound instead of the long [e] used following most other consonants. This may have originated to help distinguish the letter from the quite similar sound of G. It might also be influenced by the name of its neighbor K, of which more will be said in the next section. Although a recent addition to the alphabet, J assumed the tenth place in the order due to its natural connection and long historical association with the ninth—I. Until the twentieth century it was rarely used to express the tenth place in a serial order; but today it is accorded full letter rank and is the initial letter of a large number of English words, as well as the names of James Joyce—a writer deeply concerned with letters. In his semi-autobiographical early work, *Stephen Hero*, Joyce gave an account of his own methods of composition: "He sought in his verses to fix the most elusive of his moods and he put his lines together not word by word but letter by letter." Being a man of many moods and great talent, Joyce, no doubt, was thankful that J was available at the time of his writing.

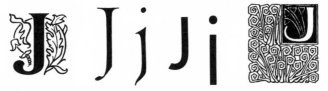

Robert Graves reports some very interesting things about J in his stimulating book *The White Goddess*. He claims that the new letter J is really one of the three consonants of the *Logos*—the Creative Word. It is the letter of new life and sovereignty. In Kabbalistic lore, J (*yod*), as the first letter of the Tetragrammaton, JHVH (Jehovah), was considered to be the active principle in Creation. According to Graves's account, J is actually a double I and is associated with the "Day of Liberation," set apart from the other 364 days of the year. In mystical religious lore, II was occasionally considered a sort of "super" vowel (much like *omega*) relating to Creation. It is this II that is transcribed J in "Jehovah"; while A, as the first letter, also shared many of its connotations—for example, the designation of God: "I am Alpha and Omega...." Graves further associates J with amber and calls it the "royal consonant"—the letter of the Divine Child born on the Day of Liberation. Although his thesis is not explicitly linked with Christianity, the basic idea would meet with the approval of millions; and one of the most prominent and well known uses of the letter is as an abbreviation for Jesus.

J's rise from nothing to the "royal" consonant and initial of the Christian messiah would have to be considered quite a success story. Perhaps it makes one wish that Tory and some of the ancients were more involved in the telling; but, patience, ... we will next encounter a letter with an ancient lineage and controversial (some might say, konfused) story.

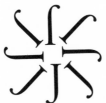

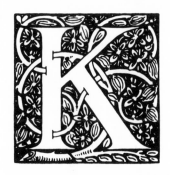

IN K WE ENCOUNTER THE ELEVENTH LETTER of the modern English alphabet and the tenth in the ancient Roman order of the letters. And, in tracing its history, we once again touch upon the C story. Unlike the relatively new form of G, however, K is a letter of ancient lineage, a descendant of the Semitic *kaph* and the Greek *kappa*. The Phoenician letter *kaph* is generally thought to mean the palm of the hand, although some scholars believe that it derived from a pictograph for "branch." Eugen Nerdinger takes this idea even further in his claim that the early pictograph from which K descended depicts a fissure or cleft in the Tree of Life.

The Etruscans also used K as one of their letters, and the early Romans, borrowing and mixing signs and sounds from both the Greeks and the Etruscans, found themselves with three separate letters—C, K, and Q—all essentially representing the same [k] sound: a superabundance, as one scholar says, that was foisted on the world by the Etruscans. The Romans recognized this overabundance of signs for one sound and gradually modified the usage of certain letters. K was virtually (though never completely or officially) dropped from the alphabet, C taking on most of the responsibility for representing the [k] sound. K was essentially used only in the spelling of foreign (especially Greek) words.

The specialized use of the Roman letter was not without a precedent. The Etruscans had used K only before the vowel sound [a]—a practice the Romans basically followed. This usage may well have affected the pronounced name of the letter—that is, joining the consonantal sound [k] with the long [a] vowel sound rather than the customary long [e] sound. It is rather obvious that using the [e] sound would have led to confusion with our name for C, but there are three other vowel sounds that could have been used; further on we will see that one of them was used to differentiate and name the closely related letter Q. In any case, the [a] sound was chosen and possibly was then also attached to the preceding (but later accepted) letter J, according to the traditional practice of relating the names of adjacent letters.

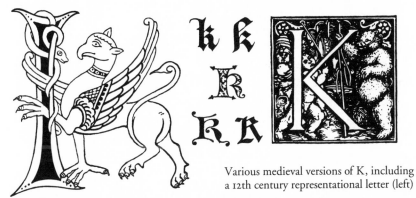

Various medieval versions of K, including a 12th century representational letter (left)

Continuing from and expanding upon the ancient practice, Latin scribes from the sixth to eighth centuries considered K to be a variant form of C and used it in some medieval manuscripts, especially in foreign words. It gradually came into common usage preceding certain vowels—usually I and E in English. In modern English, many words beginning with K—especially when followed by A, O, or U—are of foreign origin. Yet K is rather commonly used in the bodies of English words and is very common in German. Both of these languages share Germanic roots, unlike the Romance languages of Europe (including French, Spanish, and Italian) which have their roots in classical Latin.

The Frenchman Geofroy Tory devoted a long discussion to the differences between the Greek use of K and the corresponding Latin use of C, and he quoted a Roman writer to the effect that in Latin K is a "useless and superfluous" letter. Tory assigned it to Erato, the Muse of

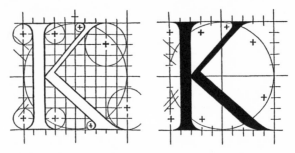

Tory's design
of the letter K

lyric and love poetry and marriage songs, whose symbol was the lyre—
perhaps indicating that Tory considered such things somewhat useless
or superfluous. "And perhaps not!" the indignant poet or lover may well
respond. Granted; … however, the fact that Tory also assigned the letter
to the left nostril of his man of letters does not seem to be overly
romantic or lyrical.

Tory was very interested in the letter K from the design standpoint,
since it is a rather striking and unusual letter. Carrying forward his
architectural imagery for the letters, he likens K to a stairway: "The K,

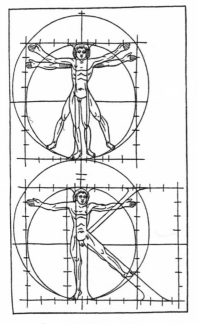

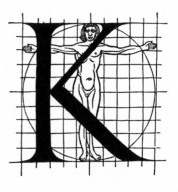

Additional drawings of K by Tory

KKkKKkKkKkKKkkKKkK

because of its joint signifies stairs to ascend in a straight line to the first floor, and thence to ascend, also in a straight line, to another floor." In discussing the Greek and Latin uses of the letter, Tory mentions two Greek proverbs. One, from Erasmus, maintains that double K—KK— "signifies two evil things essentially opposed to a good one; as if we imagine a lamb in the fields between a lion and a wolf." This seems to derive from the fact that *kakon* was the Greek word for "bad" or "evil." The second proverb is that three Ks are very bad, referring to three ancient nations "full of guile and given to every sort of deceit." (The spellings don't hold for Latin, where K could be said to have been "cleaned up" to the point of being almost "wiped out.")

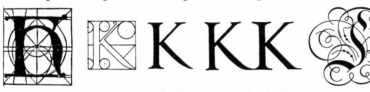

Various Ks, including one by Yciar (left) and four by Dürer (center)

The fact that three letters share the same basic [k] sound, and that certain languages often employ one to the exclusion of the others, can have some interesting consequences. For example, in the English-speaking world during the protest years of the 1960s, the substitution of k for c in the spelling of "America" served to designate that nation as a fascist, repressive, and war-mongering state, thereby revealing the symbolic power of the letters: a simple orthographic substitution can carry an immense weight of meaning. As Frank Budgen points out, James Joyce worked with similar ideas, especially in *Finnegans Wake*: "A letter added or left out—the sound of a vowel or consonant modified—and a host of associations is admitted within the gates. And one letter may stand pregnant with meaning as a rune."

K is such a letter. De Lamartine said that "letters are symbols which turn matter into spirit," and that power seems to be most evident to poets and mystics. George Steiner observes that children and poets especially bear witness that even individual letters "can assume particular symbolic values and associations." Steiner continues: "To a literate

KkKKkkKkKKkKKkKKk

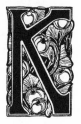

member of Western culture in the mid-twentieth century, the capital letter K is nearly an ideogram, invoking the presence of Kafka or of his eponymous doubles. 'I find the letter K offensive, almost nauseating,' noted Kafka mordantly in his diary, 'and yet I write it down, it must be characteristic of me.'" As W.H. Auden said, Kafka seems to represent the modern age and temper more than any other writer; and Steiner points out that Kafka has almost appropriated the letter K as his own, something no other writer in any language has done.

With several letters representing the same or similar sounds, the spelling of new, foreign, and little-known words can vary widely even in this day and age of standardized orthography. An example is the "Kabbalah" (also spelled "Cabala" and "Quabbalah," among other variants), the occult Jewish system of lore and ritual based on a mystical interpretation of the Scriptures, through which initiates can hope to understand the mysteries of the universe. This is not the place to seriously discuss the Kabbalah, but, as letter mysticism is an important part of the system, I will note a few things and leave it to the interested reader to pursue the subject. Essentially a mass of esoteric writings, the Kabbalah—which means "tradition"—is not a systematic, canonical set of works or doctrines. It flourished in the Middle Ages from supposedly ancient antecedents, and has continued to be studied in mystic and occult circles up to the present day.

In Jewish mysticism each letter is thought to embody a fragment of the design of creation. We have already noted Ben Shahn's retelling of one of the legends involving the Hebrew letters from the thirteenth century *Sefer Ha-Zohar*. Sir Wallis Budge reported that the Hebrews

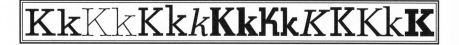

"attributed greater powers to some letters than to others, and a proper knowledge of the use of these formed a separate branch of the study of magic. Each letter had its special powers." K and P, signifying "holiness and deliverance," were often used on amulets. Again, in *After Babel*, George Steiner speaks clearly on the subject: "All human experience, no less than all human discourse unto the end of time, is graphically latent in the letters of the alphabet. Those numinous letters whose combinations make up the seventy-two names of God may, if they are probed to the hidden core of meaning, reveal the cipher, the configuration of the cosmos. Accordingly, prophetic Kabbalism developed its science of the combination of letters....But although Hebrew may have a privileged immediacy, the Kabbalist knows that all languages are a mystery and ultimately related to the holy tongue."

ו נ כ י מ ח ז ד ה ו ח ד ג ב א

ץ צ ף פ ע ס ן כ ם מ ל

. ת ש   ר ק פ

Hebrew alphabet by Geofroy Tory

The Hebrew alphabet has long been linked to the occult system of the Tarot and to other Kabbalistic ideas, including the Sephiroth or paths of the mystical Tree of Life with which we have seen the K sign specifically related. More recently, many commentators on the subject have tried to relate the letters of the English alphabet to these older forms and mystic doctrines. The subject (and claimed correspondences) is too involved, esoteric, and (to be honest) contradictory to develop here; but, from ancient times to the present, the relation of the occult to the letters does have a long and complex history relating to secret doctrines and the "meaning" of life. And we do get a taste of this in the notions of Zolar, who provides an English equivalent of the Hebrew letters whose mystical significance he discusses.

Alphabet oracles (similar in idea to modern ouija boards) have been used since ancient times. In one form—called alectryomancy—a bird

KkKkKkKkKkKkKkKkKkKkKkK

(usually a rooster) was allowed to eat grain covering a circle of letters, thus supposedly revealing words with prophetic significance. Another method mentioned by Zolar was to recite the letters of the alphabet, taking note of those at which the cock crowed. In the form called gyromancy, people moved around in a circle marked with letters until they became dizzy and stumbled at different points, thus spelling out significant or prophetic words. Another practice of ancient and medieval times that has extended to the present is to open the Bible at random and point to a word or letter which is then deemed an oracle or direction from God. In classical times there were also dream interpreters such as Artemidorus who would interpret the significance of a person's dream about the alphabet or a particular letter. (That type of dream seems less common now, although I have overheard people say that they "had a dream about U.")

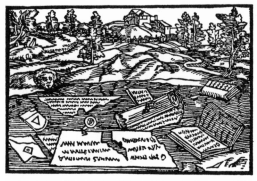

Woodcut of scattered writings from 1536 edition of the prophecies of the mystic Paracelsus

Perhaps our phonetic alphabet has been the subject of so much abstract speculation and poetic association because it replaced both an ideography that was laden with magical referents as well as early writing systems that were themselves considered magical. Such ideas still exist and give an interesting twist of meaning to the biblical phrase, "the letter killeth, but the spirit giveth life." Mystical significance is given readily to the letters which, though few in number, can combine to represent the world of objects, events, ideas, and emotions. The French poet Mallarmé worked towards recreating this mythos. He called the letters "purely

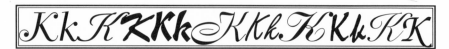

hieroglyphic" characters whose significance is a matter of shape. In his essay "La Musique et les lettres," he called the letters "our ancient heritage from the ancient books of magic." He also said that letters are "gifted with infinity…everything is caught up in their ancient variations." Because of the power of letters, "typography becomes a rite." "The book, which is the total expansion of the letter, must find its mobility in the letter."

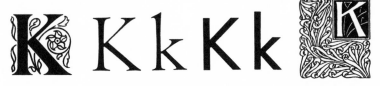

Closing this mystical interlude and returning to K, Zolar says of the Semitic *kaph* (which he spells *kaaw* and gives as its English equivalent Q), that "it is the symbol of reflection and assimilation.…It is a kind of mold, receiving and communicating indifferently all forms. The movement which it expresses is that of similitude and of analogy." The reader will likely agree that it has certainly served to do all of that here!

The reader, however, may remain skeptical about at least a few of the associations made concerning the various letters, finding some of them to be idiosyncratic and arbitrary—or perhaps based on little more than an acrophonic principle characteristic of abecedaries (that is, A is for apple, B is for bird,…when A could as well be for aardvark or airplane, and B for behemoth or badger). Well, that is probably true enough; not all relations are high mystic or poetic truths; yet abecedaries can be entertaining if nothing else, giving an interesting glimpse into a particular cast of mind. So, enjoy. Other associations seem to fall into a type of personal–artistic middle ground. Some obviously have private meaning and significance, yet one can sometimes glimpse the rationale if not the personal force of the association, as, for example, when Michel Leiris writes that the s in "suicide" retains for him the precise shape and whistling sibilance of a kris. In still other cases, we feel that the author has reasons for his associations, but they escape us (although others may find the connection obvious). Thus it is for me with Charles Olson's poem "The K." But perhaps that is an illustration of the ways of art—each individual relates in his or her own way and in some sense brings his or her own meaning to the artist's work—a meaning perhaps different than the author's intention.... ... Kuhrumba!!

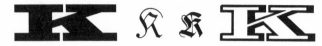

According to Zolar, the mystical numerical value of K is 20. In a serial order K is used for either the tenth or eleventh place; but, because of that confusion, we do not commonly find alphabetical serial orders going past ten items, and if they do it is customary to count which place the letter signifies instead of taking for granted that it must represent a particular place in the order. Most people begin to count after the third or fourth letter anyway, since we generally have not learned to associate the letters with their numerical place in the order.

In chemistry, K is the symbol for Potassium—which may seem strange until one realizes that English is not the sole basis for the abbreviations of the periodic table of the elements. K here comes from the Latin name of the element—*kalium*. K is a symbol of degrees of heat (or cold) on the Kelvin thermometer scale, the 0° point of which is absolute zero, -273.16° centigrade. In astronomy, *k* designates Gauss's Constant, the square of which is a measure for the mass of the sun. If that is not a usage you commonly employ, there is another use of the letter that usually kindles more interest and attention: in assaying, K equals carat—the Midas, not the garden, variety—a measure of precious metals and gems, and an appropriate place where we can leave this letter and go to ...

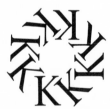

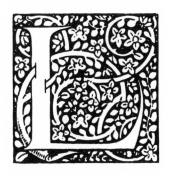

L—THE TWELFTH LETTER of the English and eleventh letter of the Roman alphabet. It is descended from the Semitic *lamed* and the Greek letter *lambda*. Scholars generally believe that *lamed* was the Phoenician word for either an ox goad or a whip lash, although some claim other meanings for the sign—a most basic and ancient one. The Greek letter names, as we have seen, had no other meaning as words in the language; in Plato's *Cratylus*, however, *lambda* is considered expressive of liquidity and smoothness because the tongue "slips" in pronouncing it.

Throughout history, the letters have often been grouped according to the quality of their sounds. The vowels are the best-known group and, according to Tory, are the "greatest" or most valuable letters because they are necessary components of every syllable. Other categories include the mutes, semi-vowels, aspirates, sibilants, and the liquids, among which the letter L is included. Tory calls them "letters which are tractable, and of such easy virtue that they glide along and, becoming as it were invisible, vanish in certain syllables." Sometimes they make the preceding vowel long; at other times they leave it short. In his *English Grammar*, Ben Jonson also considered L to be a liquid, but for a slightly different reason: because "it melteth in the sounding." I shall leave it to the reader's fancy whether to consider the letter a literary banana peel, libertine, spectre, or candy.

Although Tory called this letter one of "easy virtue," he also ascribed to it a position of importance—in this particular case an honor that is

$LJJL\Gamma\Lambda\Lambda LL ILLLLLLLLLLP$

141

difficult to understand, for it seems to have involved a surprising miscalculation rather than manipulation, as we found in his discussion of the letter I. Tory called L the middle letter of the alphabet when, in fact, in the Roman alphabet of twenty-three letters which he was using and considering, the middle letter would be the twelfth Roman letter—M. In any case, whether he miscalculated, which seems unlikely, or based his choice on convoluted reasoning not apparent to this writer, Tory assigned the medial position to L and found good things to say about the letter because of it: "I propose to show here by a figure of Astrology, which is one of the said seven Liberal Arts, the explanation of the horizontal arm of the letter L, and therewith that it is the centre and navel of the Alphabet. The letter L was designed and drawn by the ancient writers in its relation to the human body and to its shadow cast by the Sun when it is in the sign of the Balance,—or, as we say, of Libra,—in the month of September."

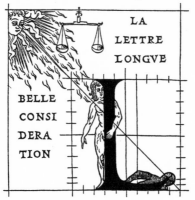 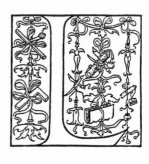

Two of Tory's drawings of the letter L, including one relating it to the sign of Libra (left)

    Tory's explanation hardly proves his point about L being the center of the alphabet: all he has is an L-word—Libra—that is the astrological sign of a balance. The shape of the L is tenuously arrived at by calculating the "proper" length of the horizontal foot of L in relation to its height. It may be charming, but it can hardly be considered much of an explanation. No data was provided to determine the length of a shadow cast by a man standing in the September sun in France or anywhere else;

but I trust that a man of particular height standing in sunshine at a particular time of day could fit the schema. I realize that I am getting mighty particular, but Tory himself complained about those "who go about trying to teach others when they themselves are not taught as they should be." I dislike appearing so critical of a man who has charmed and delighted me so frequently; but it does seem to be a major lapse and forced treatment of L—the more so when one considers that the mathematical central letter of Tory's alphabet is M, a symmetrical letter that would seem to complement his analogical methods ideally had he considered it the navel of his alphabet. Yet he did not, and I do not know why; but I will leave the matter by quoting Tory on another author with whose thoughts he disagreed: "Whether he is stupid in this matter I leave to the judgement of greater and wiser men than I, and I say in his behalf…that there is no man so wise who does not sometimes err."

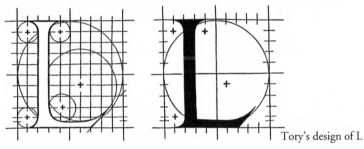

Tory's design of L

Tory does have a few other things of interest to say about the letter L. It relates to a Liberal Art, Music, and corresponds to the brain in his man of letters—both correspondences seeming to give the letter a position of high honor—especially the latter, if his man uses it. L is also called the *literam longam*, or "long letter"; and Tory cites a "right witty passage" by the Roman comic dramatist Plautus that this name signifies "that a man or a woman hanged by the neck represents with his body and his feet the letter L."

Both the ancient and classical Greek forms of *lambda* resemble an inverted V. In the western Greek, Etruscan, and early Roman alphabets the angle began to twist downwards. However, it was in the classical Roman alphabet that the letter gained its perpendicular right-angle

LILILILLLLLILILILILILLLLLIlL

Ս Ս Ĺ Ճ L L Ĺ Ճ ℓ ℓ

Uncial, semi-uncial, six Insular, and two black letter versions of the letter L

shape, which led Tory to say that the Romans created the form of L by turning the form of *gamma* upside down. This seems to be a simple case of concerning oneself only with final forms rather than with evolutionary development. Tory was familiar with the Greek forms, including *lambda*, however; and his explanation was meant to point out the resemblance between the forms of the Greek and Roman letters, not to imply a relation between *gamma* and L. Tory mentioned that the Greek *lambda* was a mark used in ancient times to indicate that there was insufficient evidence to reach a verdict in a criminal trial.

The basic form of the Roman capital L has been quite stable through the centuries, although some minor modifications were made. L and F were the first to go above the basic letter height in the square capital script. This elongated form was subsequently used in various book hands; and in some scripts of the Middle Ages the foot of the letter was shortened. When the dual alphabet became established in the early years after the invention of printing from moveable type, an elongated, footless (and fancy free) form was eventually adopted as the minuscule to accompany the roman capital L. The terms "lower-" and "upper-case"

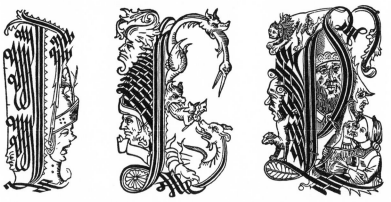

Three elaborate initial Ls from early printed books (late 15th and early 16th centuries)

LLℓLℓLℓ*LℓL*LℓLLℓ*Lℓ*LℓLℓLℓLLℓLL

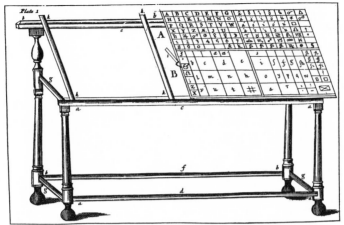

Printer's type cases from Joseph Moxon's *Mechanick Exercises…*(1683)

for the minuscule and capital forms of the letters originally referred to the two-part, compartmented cases that printers used to hold a font of type (all of the metal letters of a particular size and style) from which they took the individual letters in composing lines of type for printing. It is interesting to note that lower-case l is both the narrowest of all the letters in most typefaces and also the least recognizable in typical tests of reading legibility. Perhaps to distinguish the letter, a spurred lower-case l (l) was a design peculiarity of some seventeenth and eighteenth century types (including the highly detailed design of Jaugeon); but it was a feature that never gained wide acceptance and has since disappeared from virtually all typefaces. Lower-case l is most legible in faces where it is relatively tall compared to the body height of its lower-case fellows.

Although l itself may not be highly legible, Beatrice Warde pointed out in her book *The Crystal Goblet* that "the most efficient of all aids to

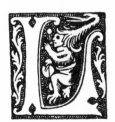 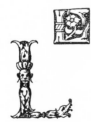 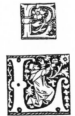 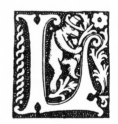

LlLLLlLLlLLLlLlLlLl

legibility [is] the dual alphabet with nearly all the minuscule letters clearly differentiated from the capital forms." John Woodcock elaborated on the idea in *The Calligrapher's Handbook*: "Generally, any amount of Roman lower case letters is more readable than a similar amount of capitals, not because we are unfamiliar with the shape of the capital letter but because we do not normally read it in any quantity. In a way the capital letters are more distinctive as units than the small letters but our normal quick reading habits lead us not to see consciously each letter that we read, but to recognize each word or even sometimes a whole phrase by the peculiar shape given to it by its own unique combination of letter shapes….For similar reasons capitals remain perfectly legible even when widely spaced to form a particular texture in a heading but lower case letters spaced in a similar way become relatively much more illegible than when spaced closely enough for the distinctive word shape to be quickly identified."

A few scholars feel that the evolution of minuscule letter forms was more a stylistic than a radical functional development, but many others (probably including most grade school teachers) strongly disagree. They claim that although adults often assume that making the change from roman to sans serif or from all capitals to a dual alphabet of upper- and lower-case comes naturally, it actually involves learning what are essentially new signs for the familiar sounds. And I would agree. Literate adults have been subconsciously trained by experience in our culture to recognize hundreds of unusual and distorted letter shapes through our exposure to modern advertising; but it is a mistake to assume that children have that facility after brief exposure. For them, new forms are just that—new; and mastering them is a learning experience. Even so, our teaching of the alphabet seems simple in comparison to the exhausting methods of Hellenistic and Roman education. Pupils began by

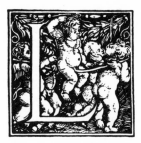

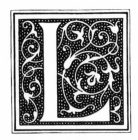

learning the letters, then they moved through syllables until they were finally able to advance to actual words. Each stage required a thorough mastery before advancement to the next; the alphabet was learned forwards, backwards, and in various combinations (A–Z, B–Y, C–X, etc.) before students could even begin with the syllabic combinations, …and then an involved process began again.

In recent times there have been attempts (including one by the noted Bauhaus type designer Herbert Bayer) to combine the dual alphabet into one symbol for each letter; but these efforts have invariably failed due to our established reading habits and conventions. Beatrice Warde called "graphic monkeyishness" the "tedious pretense that English can be written without recourse to capital letters." And she cited as an example the sentence, "where is john brown?" asking, has John been hiding or sunbathing? The poetry of e.e. cummings can be cited as a small but effective counter-example, however. It has been said that his refusal to capitalize his name was in part a renunciation of vanity, and that his struggle was against "manunkind"—the mechanistic, rule-bound establishment, including typography. He flouted conventions of capitalization and word division. His methods at first antagonized many readers but gradually won some of them over to see a new way of looking at

abcdefghi
jklmnopqr
s tuvwxyz

Single character alphabet by Herbert Bayer

things, even a sort of wisdom. And, though in less poetic hands his methods are mainly madness (or even less, affectation), cummings probably wouldn't have minded being a graphic "monkey"—if only it was a living, loving one.

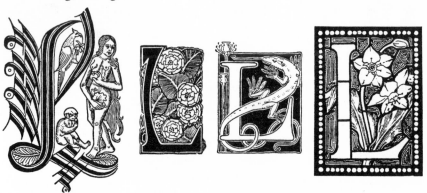

Various decorative Ls, including one from the late 15th century (left)

One of the most familiar uses of the L form is as the Roman numeral for 50, although some say that it is an adaptation of the Greek letter *psi* (Ψ), for which the Romans had no other use. L denotes either the twelfth or (more commonly) the eleventh item of a series. Although still termed a liquid by some, in English the sound normally expressed by this letter is phonetically designated the "point-side" consonant.

The runic sign for the [l] sound resembled an early Greek sign for the letter and was named *lagu*, meaning "water" or "sea." According to Zolar, L (*lamed*) mystically signifies "extension." "As a symbolical image it represents the arm of man and the wing of a bird; everything that extends or elevates itself, displaying its proper nature. It denotes a movement of extension, of direction, expressing reunion, coincidence, dependence, and possession." Doing all that, one would almost expect its mystical value to be more than the 30 Zolar assigns it.

The letter L was very important in the ancient Irish tree-alphabet. In fact, it was the second letter and middle element of the common name of that alphabet—the *Beth-luis-nion*. According to Robert Graves it corresponded to the date of January 21 and also represented the rowan

LLILLLILLLLLLILLILLILLL

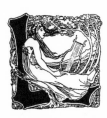 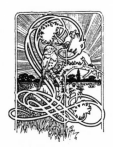 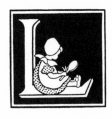

tree. It had powerful oracular uses and was employed in witchcraft to help obtain difficult answers. Perhaps it is unfortunate that ancient Greek jurors and this writer trying to make sense of Tory's constructs were not familiar with that usage—for more answers would be welcome. Yet we should remember that although letters are by definition "literal" facts, the answers given by oracles are not often crystal clear.

LILIILLLLILLIILILLLLILILILL

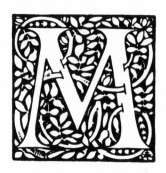

M IS THE THIRTEENTH LETTER of the English alphabet and was the twelfth and central letter of the classic Roman alphabet. It is descended from the Greek letter *mu* and the Semitic letter *mem*. *Mem* was the Phoenician word for "water," and most authorities agree that the sign was originally a pictograph for water. In its original Semitic, Greek, and early Roman forms this letter's legs were of unequal length, creating a form that resembled jagged waves. The capital letter M as we know it is a classical Roman derivation.

According to Greek mythology, Cadmus was responsible for introducing the Phoenician letters to Greece and hence is called the father of the Greek alphabet. Of all the Greek myths that relate somehow to the letters, this accords best with modern scholarship—that is, that the Greeks received their letters from the Phoenicians. Lord Byron alludes to the myth in *Don Juan* when he addresses the modern Greeks:
> "You have the letters Cadmus gave,
> Think you he meant them for a slave?"

Other parts of the Cadmus myth are fascinating and possibly applicable to the study of the alphabet. Cadmus was the founder of the city of Thebes; but in the process of accomplishing this he slew a dragon sacred to the god Ares (Mars). Cadmus sowed the dragon's teeth in the soil, from which armed men sprang up and began fighting amongst themselves. Marshall McLuhan relates the dragon's teeth to the letters of the alphabet and the battle to the alphabet's challenge to and disruption of older, preliterate tribal society. With five survivors (vowels?), Cadmus founded Thebes. After doing penance to Ares for eight years he married Harmonia (daughter of Ares and Aphrodite), but he still seems to have incurred that god's lasting enmity. The House of Thebes was ill-starred and plagued by misfortune despite the fact that Cadmus was a good ruler. In distress, Cadmus and his wife quit the city and according to their wish were later transformed by the gods into serpents—the animal symbolic of eternity. However, all of the members of his house—including Oedipus, Semele, and Pentheus—continued to be ill-fated until the family line finally was destroyed.

Although I have never encountered the idea in any scholarly thesis, it occurs to me that the myth of Jason and the Golden Fleece may also pertain at least in part to the alphabet. Like Cadmus, Jason also sowed a dragon's teeth into a field of earth, although he first plowed the field with wild, fire-breathing oxen. The oxen may refer to the head letter of the alphabet—*aleph*, the ox—and the plowing could relate to the early boustrophedon style of alternating writing direction. Armed men also sprang up from the teeth Jason sowed, but in this case they completely destroyed each other in the subsequent battle. Perhaps Jason's writing system was never accepted. I do not wish to make too much of this, but even if it is no more than a personal conceit, it does find some echoes in the Cadmus myth.

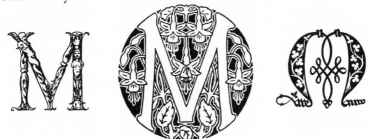

As I have mentioned Marshall McLuhan (whose names begin with the letter under discussion), it seems appropriate to introduce some of his often controversial but usually thought-provoking ideas on the alphabet and printing technology. To begin with, McLuhan takes very

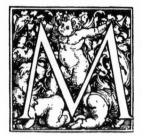 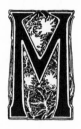 

seriously (and quite literally) the familiar saying that "the alphabet is the tool of thought": "All human tools and technologies, whether house or wrench or clothing, alphabet or wheel, are direct extensions, either of the human body or of our senses …[and] give us new leverage and new intensity of perception and action." In his book *Counterblast* he maintains: "In a pre-literate world words are not signs. They evoke things directly in what psychologists call acoustic space. By being named, the thing is simply there.…Acoustic space is the space-world of primeval man. Even his visual experience is much subordinate to his auditory and magical domain wherein there is neither centre nor margin nor point of view." McLuhan considers writing to be an abstract form of technology, especially writing arising from a phonetic alphabet in which the sound and letter forms are divorced from all meaning. "To abstract sound from meaning and then to enclose that sound in a visual space happened only with the Greek alphabet. The Phoenicians proceeded only so far as to visualize consonantal sounds. And this abstraction achieved by the Greeks and transferred to the Romans created an imperial visual net in which the Western world has captured every oral culture that it has met."

"By the meaningless sign linked to the meaningless sound we have built the shape and meaning of Western man." Such statements from McLuhan's writings often startle the reader at first; but upon reflection one often sees the glimmer of truth behind them and need not necessarily find them to be negative or iconoclastic. To McLuhan, writing with the alphabet has actually affected the way we perceive the world and ourselves. "With writing comes inner speech, the dialogue with one-self—a result of translating the verbal into the visual (writing) and

MMMmMmMmMMMmMM

translating the visual into the verbal (reading)—a complex process for which we pay a heavy psychic and social price—the price, as James Joyce puts it, of ABCED-minded-ness. Literate man experiences an inner psychic withdrawal from his external senses which gives him a heavy psychic and social limp. But the rewards are very rich." Further, he maintains that "only phonetically literate man lives in a 'rational' or 'pictorial' space. The discovery or invention of such space that is uniform, continuous and connected was an environmental effect of the phonetic alphabet in the sensory life of ancient Greece. This form of rational or pictorial space is an environment that results from no other form of writing, Hebrew, Arabic, or Chinese." The alphabet has influenced things as basic as our thought processes and our modes of perceiving the world—such as the artistic development of perspective in drawing, for example.

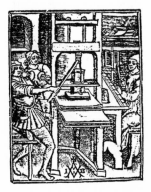 

Woodcut of early printing press operation (left), and a rather unusual form of M

According to McLuhan, not only has the alphabet wrought momentous changes in the life and psyche of literate man, but Gutenberg's invention of printing from moveable type has also decisively altered things. Typographic printing provided the first uniformly repeatable commodity, the first assembly line and mass production. It revolutionized thought by subjecting traditional ideas to wider scrutiny while encouraging and facilitating new intellectual developments built on the foundations of the old. "Print is the extreme phase of alphabet culture

MmMmMm*MM*Mm*m*M

that detribalizes or decollectivizes man....Print is the technology of individualism," he says in *The Gutenberg Galaxy*.

McLuhan also maintains that typing and typesetting are means of transcribing thought, not expressing it. They reduced written expression from an art to a craft, from the personal to the impersonal. This is because even the personal touch of the scribe forming the letters with his own individual style is lost with mechanical letterforms. But with the twentieth century media explosion of instantaneous, nonliterate modes of communication—especially radio and television—he feels that "we experience in reverse, what pre-literate man faced with the advent of writing. Today we are, in a technical if not literary sense, post-literate. Literacy: a brief phase." I have only been concerned here with introducing a few of McLuhan's ideas and will leave it to the interested reader to pursue the subject further. The subject is controversial: McLuhan has many opponents as well as supporters. I will add only that I feel that the study is well worth the effort.

Beyond the "normal" heavy psychic price paid by literate humans is a world illustrated by Sylvia Plath in *The Bell Jar*. To one living on the edge of sanity, the letters can tip the balance—to either side. "I squinted at the page. The letters grew barbs and rams' horns. I watched them separate, each from the other, and jiggle up and down in a silly way. Then they associated themselves in fantastic, untranslatable shapes, like Arabic or Chinese." Reversing the normal childhood pattern, the book's protagonist finally was able to read only mainly pictorial matter: "The little paragraphs between the pictures ended before the letters had a chance to get cocky and wiggle about."

M is another of the liquids, those letters of "easy virtue," according to Geofroy Tory. He relates it to the Liberal Art Astronomy (which he also called astrology), and to the lungs of his man of letters. Throughout

MmᴍMmMm*m*Mᴍ Mm

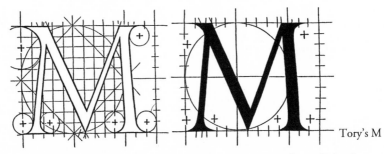

Tory's M

its long history from Phoenician times the phonetic value of the letter has changed very little. In modern phonetic terminology it is called the bilabial nasal consonant. It was called the "half-tone" letter by some ancient writers because of its "imperfect" sound pronounced from the interior of the mouth. George Steiner reports that according to the important modern linguist Roman Jakobson it is one of the easiest sounds for infants to articulate, and this may help account for the common usage of the basic "first" words "mama" and "papa" ([a] and [p] being similarly easy to pronounce) in many different, unrelated languages and cultures.

Uncial and semi-uncial (left), with various Insular and black letter versions of M

With the uncial script of the fourth through sixth centuries, M began to be noticeably rounded, assuming a form resembling the modern lower-case m. This resemblance was virtually achieved with the semi-uncial script and echoed in the humanistic cursive just before the invention of printing. It was then transferred to roman type forms, from whence it came down to us. This rounded form of M probably influenced a medieval notion that the name of man was written (by God) upon his face. The "M" consisted of the brows, nose, and cheekbones; the eyes constituted two O's: ⊙⊙, resulting in OMO (*homo*), Latin for "man." Dante referred to this notion in Canto 23 of *Purgatorio*, speaking

MmMMmMMMmMmMMM

of a group of emaciated sufferers: "Their eye-sockets seemed gemless rings: he who reads 'omo' in the face of man would clearly have recognized there the 'm.'"

The runic alphabet sign for M was named *man*, meaning "man." According to Zolar, however, the modern mystical meaning of the Hebrew *mem* is "woman." "It is the symbolical image of man's mother and companion. Everything that is fruitful and formative." Its number is 40. And, in Kabbalistic thought, *mem* was one of the three "mother" letters, corresponding to the element water and the season of winter. In the Irish tree-alphabet, M—*muin*—was associated with the lunar month beginning September 2 and related to the vine or bramble—with connotations of joy and exhilaration.

Less joyously, M was branded on the brawn of the left thumb of persons convicted of manslaughter and admitted to the benefit of clergy in medieval England. It represents the thirteenth or twelfth position in a serial order. Also, the capital M is used as the Roman numeral for 1000—which some people assume was an abbreviation of the Latin word *mille*, meaning "thousand." However, most scholars now believe that the Romans adopted the Greek letter *phi* (Φ) for the purpose,

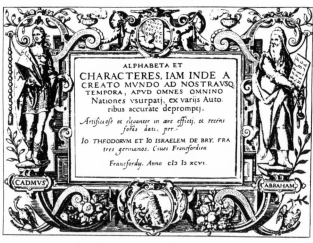

Title page from alphabet book of Theodore and Israel De Bry (1596), with illustrations of Cadmus and Abraham, incidentally showing Roman numerals in developmental form

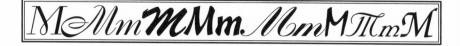

having no use for it in their alphabet. In time the sign came to resemble the M, which then became commonly used to express 1000 (CⅠƆ to ⅭⅠƆ to M). Half of the early sign (ⅠƆ) later became D—used to express half of 1000, which is 500. The fact that Roman numerals were both letters and numbers was very significant to some medieval mystics. Hugo von St. Victor said that as a Roman numeral M symbolized the "height of Hope" (although commonly that letter was no taller than any other), possibly because it signified the largest Roman numeral.

According to the modern scholar S. H. Steinberg, M does have design significance: "The letter which, in upper and lower case, affords the widest facilities for judging any given set of letters, is M and m; it has therefore by general agreement been made the yardstick with which students of incunabula unravel the intricacies of early types and identify them." Being the widest of the ancient letters, and with an interesting shape full of design possibilities, the M is a highly visible and very expressive letter. Nicolete Gray claims that of all the letters it is the most problematic in its structure, having many variants, including an unusual Insular form of three vertical strokes crossed by a horizontal or diagonal bar. Yet it is almost immediately recognizable in most scripts, and it is a natural focal point for the student of writing. It was also the featured letter of the Dormouse's story in *Alice in Wonderland*, where the characters were to draw "everything that begins with an M." "'Why with an M?' said Alice. 'Why not?' said the March Hare. Alice was silent."

Geofroy Tory's version of the ideal capital M is a distinctively wide letter, three units more broad than it is high. "This letter M is like some men, who are so stout that their girth is greater than the height of their body; and, upon this point, let me say that our Attic letters were formerly made by the ancients, some square, others broader than high, and others higher than broad, with covert reference to men's bodies, among which

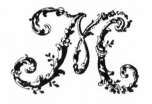

the most perfect and comely are the bodies squarely built." Even allowing for a measurement of circumference rather than diameter, that amounts to some rather heavyset men. (I have not come across any reference to Tory's own size in my research to see if that could have influenced his opinion on the matter.) In any event, the fact that some letters are more broad than they are tall—like M—is to Tory "a sign of abundance, which signifies that they who abound in the knowledge of well-made letters abound in all good things and in surpassing perfection and virtue." (At the Mad Tea-Party it could be called "much of a muchness.") With those proferred rewards beckoning, I suggest that—like Alice—we move onward through the garden.

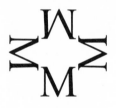

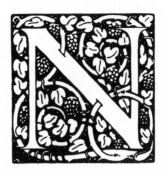

N IS THE FOURTEENTH ENGLISH LETTER and the thirteenth letter of the Roman alphabet. It is descended from the Greek letter *nu* and the Semitic letter *nun*. In the ancient Phoenician language, *nun* was the word for "fish." Donald Anderson thinks that the sign was originally a pictograph for "snake." Eugen Nerdinger believes, however, that the letter descended from an early sign for lightning. His opinion may have been influenced by early forms in which the legs of the letter are not equal, making it form a sort of jagged stroke.

Certain ancient Greeks considered the letters to be elemental, basic things in a very real sense. As Gerald Bruns says: "For the Stoics, it appears that language was not simply modeled after the physical world but belonged to it part and parcel. It was customary among the Greeks to identify the letters of the alphabet (and with them the individual sounds of speech) as *stoichêia*, literally physical particles." Throughout the Classical and Middle Ages—especially in Pythagorean circles—the alphabet was invested with very real mundane significance, and we find an echo of the Greek conception today in our use of the word "literal" (that is, "letter") to mean the objectively ascertainable. Calligraphers and type designers in their concern with the forms of the letters at times make statements seemingly akin to those of the ancients; for example, Eric Gill's assertion: "Letters are things, not pictures of things."

In both the ancient Greek and Hebrew languages each letter had a numeric as well as a phonetic value, and according to some scholars the

numerical use may well have preceded the phonetic use. Until the Christian era, the Hebrews possessed no numerical signs and used their alphabet letters as numbers. The number values commonly followed the order of the letters of the particular system (incidentally affording scholars further corroboration of the standard order of the letters), going from one through ten, with the next letter equaling 20, then 30 up through 100, with the next being 200, and so on. When the letters were exhausted, new signs or doubled letters were used to represent very large numbers. It could be very complex and confusing; the Roman numerals were a great simplification over this system, and, of course, our modern Arabic numerals—developed in the early Middle Ages—have proven immeasurably superior in use to Roman numerals.

An especially important part of alphabet mysticism in many different lands, periods, and cultures is the idea that letters can be transposed into numbers and number codes to reconstruct the "true" meaning of certain writings. Transposition was extensively used by the Greeks (especially the Pythagoreans, to whom numbers were of basic importance), and had even more ancient antecedents among the Assyrians and Semitic peoples. Perhaps the best known of all such beliefs is the Kabbalistic idea that letters and numbers are reservoirs of divine power. According to the late-medieval mystic Cornelius Agrippa: "Immovable numbers and characters breathe forth the harmony of the Godhead, being consecrated by divine assistance. Therefore, the creatures above fear them, those below tremble at them." And it is written in the earliest Kabbalistic treatise, *The Book Yetzirah*, that the twenty-two letters of the Hebrew alphabet and the first ten numbers constitute the uniting bond of creation. "With letters, God has created the soul of every form, in combining them in infinite ways." Magic squares utilizing letters in a grid in both their phonetic and numerical aspects have been used by many mystics including Pythagoreans, Hebrews, and Christians. The letters form meaningful words or formulae, and the sum of their numerical equivalents when combined in prescribed ways is significant. The letters usually add up to the same number either vertically, horizontally, or diagonally. Budge reports that such magic squares were often used as amulets in ancient times and were very important in medieval mystical practices.

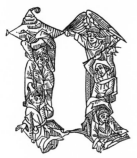 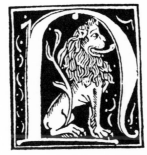 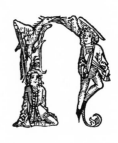

Medieval letters, two of which are composed of animal and human figures

Gematria was the Kabbalistic practice of discovering some of the hidden relations between words by calculating their numerical values—obtained by adding the number values of the constituent letters. Words of the same value were then used to replace others in sacred or important texts to reveal new meanings. Thus, hidden truths or elaborations on a text not meant for the masses were divulged to the spiritual masters or magi. (As John Barth reminds us, when the ancient Jews or Greeks looked at words on a page they also saw a string of numbers, so it is easier to understand the practice of Gematria as well as the importance of numbers for the Pythagoreans.) Of course, the possibilities for new constructions seem virtually endless, but arbitrary or frivolous constructs were supposedly prevented because only highly trained spiritual masters of the art were considered fit to attempt it. However, things could get more interesting if two or more masters disagreed in their interpretations, which occasionally occurred. A good example of this is

NnNnNNnNnNnnNNnN

the later Gematria-like practice of certain Christian sects identifying with their principal opponents the "number of the beast"—666—from the Book of Revelation (13:18). The "beast" has been variously identified as the Pope, Martin Luther, and several Communist leaders, depending on the source of the required letters and the animus of the investigator. In attempting to explain the disagreements I will only suggest that perhaps these "masters" have not sufficiently studied the art, although I am afraid that each can probably find many others who accept his or her particular "wisdom." Macaulay offered what I consider to be ample commentary on the practice: "If I leave out T in Thomas, B in Babington, and M in Macaulay, and then spell my name in Arabic, I have not the slightest doubt that I can prove myself conclusively to be the Beast."

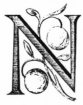

Word substitutions through numerical equivalents have also been used by those trying to prove that Shakespeare was really Francis Bacon (or at least that Bacon wrote the works attributed to Shakespeare), and, more humorously if no less frivolously, by the fictional scholar Walter Shandy in Laurence Sterne's masterpiece, *Tristram Shandy*. Another example of the power of numbers as they relate to letters and names is found in the story "The Farm Laborer and Death," written about 1400 by Johannes von Saaz. In it, Death claims victims whose names in their letter-number equivalences or in their initial letter equal the particular number he happens to have in his control at the time. This idea was not confined to literature; it is found in many cultures, sources, and periods.

Gematria, like much else of Kabbalistic thought, was alien to orthodox Jewish religion. The Kabbalah had Judaic roots but was also greatly influenced by Gnosticism, Christianity, Neo-Platonism, and Pythagorean thought. Pythagoreans built upon the Platonic idea of a transcendent soul and believed that the harmony and order of the cosmos was built

NnNnNNnNNNNnNnNnN

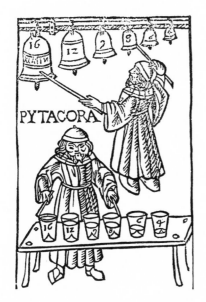

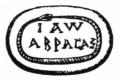

Woodcut of Pythagoras using numbers in relation to music, from a musical theory book of 1492 (left); an ancient talisman of Abraxas (above)

upon a numerical foundation which supported and ordered all earthly manifestations: "All is number. Number is the World Principle." A famous Gnostic talismanic name for the Supreme Being was "Abraxas." He was considered the source of 365 "emanations," and the sum of the numbers represented by the Greek spelling of the name equalled 365. Numbers were the keys to relating the elements of the cosmos and understanding its mysteries. Much of modern science is built upon this idea; but it could also lead to speculations of great fancy when numbers were used to render into language otherwise inarticulate "truths" (usually spiritual) and concepts. Common modern numerology equivalents are: 1=A-J-S; 2=B-K-T; 3=C-L-U; 4=D-M-V; 5=E-N-W; 6=F-O-X; 7=G-P-Y; 8=H-Q-Z; 9=I-R. Many others could of course be devised, and this is basic to the constructing of codes and ciphers. Ancient correspondences also differ in even the simple models due to the differences in alphabets and letter orders. But the basic idea remains popular and powerful when coupled with the notion that "with letters, God has created the soul of every form." Letters have here a basic reality and power that even Geofroy Tory would be hard put to equal.

NnnN*Nn*NnNNn*n*NNn**N**

Juno Jordan, a recent writer on numerology, asserts that the idea of the primal foundation of numbers is still current in mystical circles, and that numerology is based on Pythagorean precepts—that nature geometrizes and that divine law can be computed with mathematical exactitude: "Our modern alphabet is an entirely accurate and exact mathematical arrangement and association of numbers and ideas." But many others are skeptical. In *The Profits of Religion*, Upton Sinclair satirized what he considered the pretensions of numerology: "Would you like, for example, to understand why America entered the War? Nothing easier. The vowels of the words United States of America are UIEAEOAEIA which are numbered 3951561591 which added make 45, or 4 plus 5 equals 9. You might not at first see what that has to do with the War—until the Philosopher points out that '9 is the number of Completion, indicating the end of a cosmic cycle.' That, of course, explains everything."

Three sets of mystic letters by the 17th-century Kabbalist Athanasius Kircher

Plato expressed differing views of writing, a couple of which I mentioned earlier. But he also called writing "the divine art," and in another place speculated that it had existed for all time. He discussed the letter *nu* in his dialogue *Cratylus*, in which it was affirmed that as the [n] sound was made from within, the letter therefore expressed notions and concepts of inwardness. The sound of the letter N has changed little through millenia of use in different languages and is known in modern phonetic terminology as the voiced nasal consonant. It is also considered one of the four liquids because a vowel preceding it does not have a

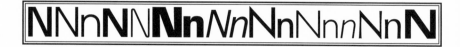

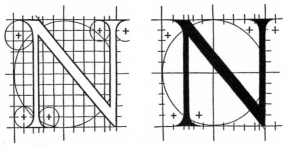

Tory's letter N

standard sound. To Geofroy Tory, this is a rather dishonorable quality, indicating a fickle nature. In Tory's design of the alphabet, virtually all Roman capital letters had the same basic height, but their widths differed greatly. All of the capitals, however, had a width equal to or less than their height with the exceptions of M and N (the broad letter W was not part of the classical Roman alphabet)—so I guess one could say that Tory considered those two to be "broads" of easy virtue! To Tory, the extra width of these two letters was a sign of abundance; and, coming directly after what he considered the middle of the alphabet, he claimed that they presented "covertly a symbol of good fortune and felicity to those who persevere in the knowledge of letters and learning."

Uncial, semi-uncial, four Insular, and three black letter forms of N

N underwent some rounding but essentially retained its basic capital form through both uncial and semi-uncial book scripts—longer than virtually all the other letters that evolved forms resembling modern lower-case letters. Not until after A.D. 800 did the lower-case N begin to develop. The letter possibly retained the capital form longer to minimize confusion with R, which had developed its rounded lower-case form

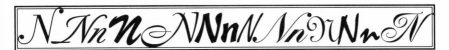

N n 𝒩 N n

with semi-uncial scripts. Cursive writing was the prime mover in alphabet letter changes. Book hands tended to become more rounded in the effort to write them more rapidly. Each script generally evolved as a simpler, more rapidly executed set of forms than its predecessor. It was then gradually improved and refined until it took much more time to write than it had initially,…and then a faster script again evolved. As Marc Drogin says: "As we follow the history of scripts, we find that most came into prominence to fill a need for functionality, flourished, became ever more calligraphic, and died of a surfeit of scribal exuberance."

In the ancient tree-alphabet, N, called *nion*, was the last part of that alphabet's tripartite name and was obviously an important letter. It corresponded to the lunar month beginning February 18 and was associated with the ash, a tree (in turn associated with water) which is usually found isolated since its roots are said to strangle those of other trees. Thus, the northern European runic alphabet—said to have been invented by the god Odin—was also said to have originally been constructed of ash twigs as a symbol of its power. The runic name for N was *nyd*, meaning "need, hardship, or constraint."

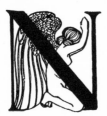 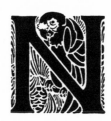 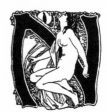

According to Zolar, N mystically "signifies the son of man, every being that is individualized and distinctive.…It has the double virtue of recoiling upon itself and of spreading out." Its number is 50. In his book, Tory related N (most conveniently) to the Liberal Art Arithmetica and

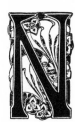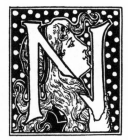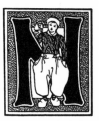

also to the liver in his perfect man of letters and learning. In chemistry, N is the symbol of the element nitrogen; and in a series it designates the fourteenth or (more commonly) the thirteenth place. In mathematics, n is used to indicate an indefinite number and hence can mean "to any extent, to the utmost"—as in raising something to the exponential n^{th} power, or "to the nth degree."

And, now that I have introduced the concept of the limitless, the utmost, let us move on to the letter that has been most frequently associated with that concept.

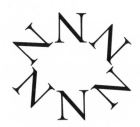

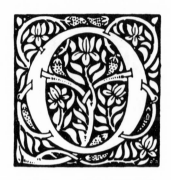

O, ONE OF THE MOST CELEBRATED LETTERS, is the fifteenth of the English and fourteenth of the Roman alphabet. In a burst of enthusiasm Tory called it "O Triumphant." He considered it to be (along with I) one of the two basic and "divine" letters of the alphabet, since the I presents the basic straight line and the O the curved form from which all the other letters can be constructed. But Tory goes further and interprets the Greek myth of Io as an allegory setting forth the divine inspiration of the Greek letters.

To briefly summarize Tory's retelling of the myth: Io was one of the many loves of Zeus, who, after receiving the amorous attention of the chief of the gods was transformed by him into a cow in a vain attempt to deceive his jealous wife, Hera. Still suspicious, Hera asked for the cow as a gift, which Zeus reluctantly had to give. Hera placed her prize under the watchful care of Argus, who would be an effective guard against even the wiles of Zeus. Argus mistreated Io, and Zeus witnessing this asked Hermes, the cleverest of the gods, to find a way to release the poor creature. Hermes, a master musician, played his shepherd's pipes so soothingly that Argus fell asleep—all one hundred eyes closed in slumber. Hermes immediately cut off Argus's head, and Io was freed from her tormentor. But Hera immediately sent another—a gadfly which stung the poor creature so mercilessly that Io began roaming the earth seeking to escape the insect. After great wandering and tribulation, Io was at last recognized by her father because her hoof prints on the

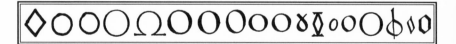

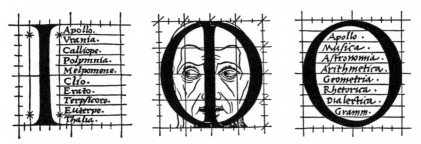

Tory's drawings illustrating the importance of the letters I and O

ground (Ω) formed an I and Ω (*omega*—a later Greek sign for the long [o] sound), spelling out her name. Io's troubles then ceased, the land became known as Ionia, and its people the Ionian Greeks (the dominant Grecians of Classical times).

As we have seen before, here again Tory had to manipulate his facts somewhat (as well as distort the myth) to make the point of his story. The curious can read about the myth in any number of books and will note that among other things Io ended her travels in Egypt, not Greece;

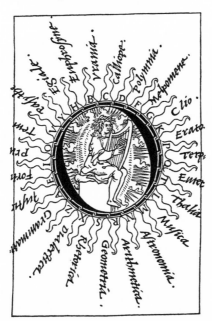

Tory's drawing of Apollo with his lyre within the "divine" letter O

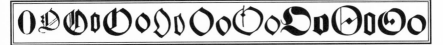

nor need we concern ourselves in Tory's retelling of the story with the many cows Io's father might have mistakenly claimed for his daughter before finally finding the right one. Tory seems alone in considering this myth related to the alphabet; but he was using it as an allegorical vehicle: Io representing knowledge; Argus, the rude contempt of the unlearned; Hermes, "the man who is diligent in seeking the purity of all goodly letters and true knowledge," etc. Tory's purpose was to illustrate that I and O were the foundation letters of the alphabet, and to him the myth of Io served the allegorical purpose, for he believed that the ancients consciously cloaked their truths in legends.

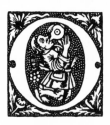 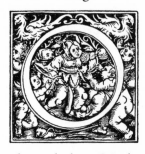 

According to most modern scholars, O is descended from the ancient Semitic letter *ayin*, which meant "eye" in the Phoenician language. Donald Anderson believes that the Phoenician letter developed from a pictograph of an eye. Nerdinger believes, however, that the form—one of the most ancient and basic—came originally from an early sign for the sun. Rudolf Koch, speaking of O as a form (not a letter), says that it is a sign of God or Eternity—without beginning or end. An analogous idea in many early cultures was that the symbol of a serpent with its tail in its mouth signified eternity. In time this notion was associated with the letter O.

The Greeks adapted the Phoenician symbols to their own language needs and in the process created the vowel signs. The O form came to symbolize the [o] vowel sound, and the resulting letter was known as *omicron* in the early Greek alphabet. In the discussion of the Greek letters in Plato's dialogue *Cratylus*, since *omicron* is circular it was said to express "roundness," based on the "imitation of things" in the scheme of

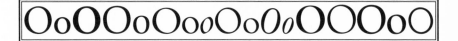

the "original imposer" of letter names. As there were many rival Greek city-states, so too there existed many Greek alphabet variants, which have come to be grouped into two categories—the western or Chalcidian Greek alphabet, which became the basis of the Roman, and the eastern or Ionian Greek alphabet, which in time became the classical Greek alphabet. Both alphabets used the name *omicron* and the symbol O for the basic [o] vowel sound; but between 800 and 500 B.C. (authorities differ) the Ionians added another symbol—Ω, *omega*—to represent the long [o] sound, and placed it at the end of their alphabet. From this practice came the biblical phrase, "I am Alpha and Omega; the beginning and the end." Both the western Greek and the Roman alphabets were essentially formed before the eastern addition of *omega*, and thus they used the O (*omicron*) to represent both the long and short [o] sounds. Tory used both the O and Ω shapes as it suited him in retelling the legend, but his references to Ionia and *omega* are surprisingly apt.

Although the Roman and English alphabets use only the O symbol to represent the sounds of the vowel, they have incorporated all literary uses of the letter *omega* into the domain of the letter O, which has been greatly enriched in the process. So, in this regard, Tory was merely helping establish a precedent that later writers, scholars, and translators willingly followed. I shall continue the tradition, including all references to *omega* with those of O. *Omega* had many mystical uses but basically represented the essentially inexpressible in its fullness. Oceanus—the source of all the Hellenic gods—was often spelled with an initial *omega* instead of *omicron*. Among the Greeks, *omega* was commonly considered a "greater" letter—it was sometimes known as "big O" whereas *omicron* was "little O." Robert Graves makes an interesting distinction between the two forms of O when he says that *omega* seems to signify the world-egg of the Orphic mysteries which was split open by the Demiurge

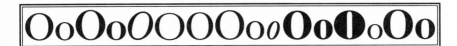

to make the universe, while *omicron* shows the egg of the year waiting to hatch. He says further that "Omega must be regarded as an intensification of Alpha, and as symbolizing the birth of birth"—thus effectively bringing things full-circle, as it were, being both beginning and end.

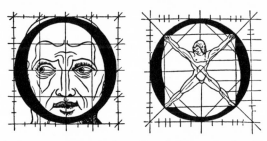

Tory's drawings relating the letter O to the human head and body

In analyzing the shape of the Roman capital O, Geofroy Tory was able to find further reason to honor the letter. He superimposed a human face on his square grid and added the form of the letter. He then went on to say that "the human face and the O are so in accord that we can see therein how the worthy Ancients conceived the idea that, as the circle is the most comprehensive and perfect of all figures, so the head of man, which is almost circular, is more capable of reasoning and imagination than all the rest of the natural body." It is pretty hard to disagree with that last part, even if one is tempted to think that Tory's head wasn't much more capable of thought than was the rest of his body when he wrote it. It might seem somewhat strange, however, that Tory proceeded to relate the letter to the left foot of his ideal man of letters unless one knows that he associated the first four vowels with the hands and feet,

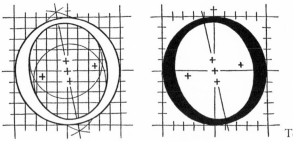

Tory's letter O

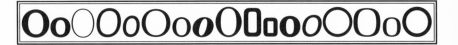

these being particularly important in man's mobility and excellence. Also, there is no letter related to the head itself, but only to its various parts. Tory also associated the vowels with the cardinal virtues; O was related to Temperantia, or Temperance.

Many scholars have agreed with Tory in considering the letter O to be important—especially as a key to the form of the other letters in a particular type design. O has been called the "mother" of the alphabet— as it becomes compressed, rounded, elongated, etc., so too do all the other letters with curved forms that are based on it. Edward Johnston, considered by many to be the most important figure in the development of fine English lettering in the twentieth century, said that O "may be regarded the key letter of an alphabet. Given an O and an I of any alphabet, we can make a very good guess at the forms of the other letters."

O has generally remained unchanged in its basic form from Roman times to the present through all scripts except the black letter (in which it was closer to a square). For the lower-case form, a smaller version of the capital was used. In many typefaces and calligraphic forms, O, among other letters, is made slightly larger than the uniform character height in order to overcome an optical illusion. It has been found that when all letters are made exactly equal in height, pointed and round letters actually appear to be shorter.

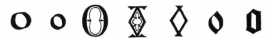

Uncial, semi-uncial, three Insular and two black letter versions of O

O has attracted the attention of many writers and has been featured (to rather opposite conclusions) in stories by Edgar Allen Poe and James Thurber. Thurber's "The Wonderful O" has been called part spoof on lipogrammatists, those who drop a particular letter from a literary work, and part political fable. It tells the tale of the unhappy consequences that arise when the letter O is banished from an island. To give one example: "A swain who praised his sweetheart's thrat, and said she sang like a chir of riles or a chrus of vices, was slapped." Such problems led to the following exchange between two of the characters: "'Taking a single

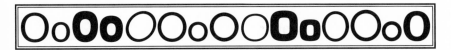

letter from the alphabet,' he said, 'should make life simpler.' 'I don't see why. Take the F from life and you have lie. It's adding a letter to simple that makes it simpler.'" Yet, if we can conclude from that the need for the fourth vowel, we should heed Poe's tale of an editor's overfondness for the letter, "X-ing a Paragrab," which warns against its overuse. Poe himself could have been guilty of such a practice, for in his essay "The Philosophy of Composition" he called O the "most sonorous" vowel.

Thurber's example notwithstanding, and despite all of the honors showered upon the vowels, modern linguists have pointed out that consonants actually convey more information to us than do vowels, and, once a language has been learned, we could better afford to do without the vowels than the consonants. In Yuen Ren Chao's words: "All items in a list of symbols do not have the same information value, since they do not occur with the same *frequency*. Since there are fewer vowels (i.e. the letters) than consonants, and vowels occur much more frequently than consonants, each of the latter gives much more information than the former; hence it is much easier to g++ss +t th+ w+rds wr+tt+n w+th++t v+w+ls than to +ue++ a+ ++e +o+++ ++i++e+ +i++ou+ +o++o+a+++." Scrabble players should be aware of all this, but it helps us understand more clearly how Semitic scripts such as Hebrew could be workable even though they did not have written vowel signs. Yet it also helps us understand the great improvement of the full alphabet developed by the Greeks. It is interesting to note that whereas the Jews used only consonants to name their god, JHVH, certain Greek Gnostics and Christians wrote the name of this same diety IAO (usually *omega*), thus honoring the "three-form god" with their more important vowel signs.

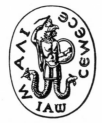

Ancient representation of the "three-form god," IAΩ (left); decorative versions of O (right)

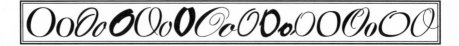

In Bell's "visible speech scale" of the nineteenth century, O was known as the "mid-back-round-vowel." And although the Greeks used two different letters to express the sounds of O, according to the *O.E.D.* our modern sign expresses at least seven different sounds. Like all the vowels, however, in English it is named after its basic long sound. Speaking of the sound, Rimbaud called O the "Supreme Clarion," imagining it a brilliant blue or violet.

In the Irish tree-alphabet, the letter O—*orin*—was associated with the vernal equinox and also with the gorse, or furze—a shrub that traditionally produced the first flowers of the year and was said to be effective against the powers of witches. The runic sign for O was named *os*, meaning "mouth," from the Latin word of the same meaning; however, originally it was the name of an Icelandic pagan god. The letter O indicates the fifteenth (or fourteenth) place in a serial order. In logic, it is the symbol of a particular negative, and, in chemistry, it represents one of the most basic and essential elements—Oxygen.

Outside of logic, one of the few less than positive things that can be said about the letter O is that it closely resembles the Arabic character zero, or cipher (o), although it is only a resemblance of form, there being no other relation between them. This has led to some conflation of the two in passages of literature, one notable instance being the Fool's speech in *King Lear*: "Now thou art an O, without a figure. I am better than thou art now; I am a Foole, thou art nothing."

Ernst Jünger also waxes poetic—and a bit more positive—about the letter. In his essay "In Praise of the Vowels" he claims that O is the sound of the aristocratic; its color is yellow, its metal is gold. Its form is that of an open eye. It is the falcon in the world of sound, and it is fitting for the

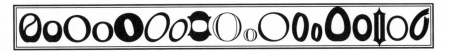

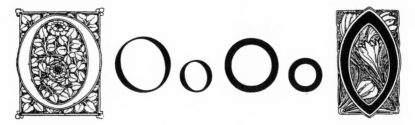

idea of Apollo. Like A, it has a masculine connotation and is a sound of wonderment. To Jünger it is suggestive of a scornful and defiant laughter, or mockery, and of the rhythmic sound of the clock. Finally, it pertains to both the high and the deep.

Well now, what more could be said about this letter—thought of as mother and masculine, high, deep, birth of birth and end of all, nothing and everything? Probably, knowing writers, quite a bit. But I shall take leave of the letter by quoting a line of Rimbaud's: "O, the Omega, violet beam from His eyes."

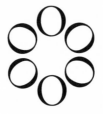

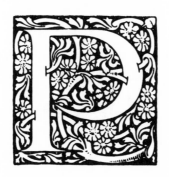

P IS THE SIXTEENTH LETTER of the English alphabet and the fifteenth of the Roman. It is descended from the Greek letter *pi* and the Semitic *pe*. The Phoenician *pe* is generally thought to have meant "mouth," and one scholar sees its sign as a pictograph of the lower lip. Nerdinger believes that it originated from an early bisected sun sign. Still another theory has it depicting a human head, from which the R sign was also derived. The Phoenician letter *pe* was much like the letter *gimel* in form, but more rounded. Similarly, the early Greek form of *pi* resembled a cursive *gamma*. In time, the Greek letter began to curve downwards, eventually becoming an inverted U or arch form which developed into the classical Greek form of *pi* (π) familiar to students of mathematics (in which it denotes the ratio of the circumference of a circle to its diameter, that ratio being a transcendental number having a value to five decimal places of 3.14159). In the western Greek alphabet—adapted by the Romans—a more hooked form (9) was accepted instead of the inverted U form; and with the development of strictly left-to-right writing (superseding boustrophedon writing, in which the lines alternated direction), the letter faced to the right as it has continued to do. Some scholars believe, however, that for reasons unknown the Romans simply took the form directly from the Greek letter *rho* and then created a new form for their R (which we shall examine more fully when we come to that letter).

The letter in all its forms has always represented the same sound—technically known as the lip unvoiced stop—which is considered one of

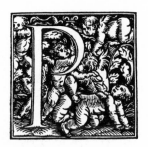

the easiest and most natural for human infants to pronounce. In English, however, many words beginning with PH are descended from the Greek letter *phi*, which is pronounced with an [f] sound. Similarly, a few P-words are descended from the Greek letter *psi*, which the Romans also excluded from their alphabet. Words beginning with P were among the least common in the Anglo-Saxon language; but in modern English it is the third most frequent initial letter (following S and C); approximately one-third of all English words begin with one of these three letters. P's prevalence is mainly attributable to the great number of prefixes that begin with it, but there also has been a great influx of P-words of foreign or unknown origin. According to the *Oxford English Dictionary*, P "presents probably a greater number of unsolved etymological problems than any other letter."

Problems of phonetics, pronunciation and orthography are also prominent in English. For hundreds of years, right up to the present, linguistic reformers have lamented the inconsistency between the spelling of words and their pronunciation. No rules seem to apply here: letters are pronounced now one way, now another … and yet another. Also, similar sounds are spelled with maddeningly different letters in seemingly arbitrary disregard. In 1603, in his *Olive Leafe: or Universal Abce*, Alexander Top called English spelling and pronunciation absurd, and said that children who have to try to learn it "as it were enter Purgatorie before their time." Among the many recorded attempts to improve the situation was that of Charles Butler, who in his *English Grammar* of 1634 introduced new alphabet signs to help standardize the spelling of sounds. Among his creations were double O and double E vowels, as well as signs for some of the common digraphs including ph, which became Ᵽ in his system. Similarly, ch was Ꞓ, wh was ꟽ, and sh was Ꞩ. Obviously, the idea never caught the popular fancy—which was the fate of all such systems, some of which will be mentioned later. However, as Beverly Boyd points out, before Butler the idea of placing a stroke through letters to indicate abbreviations did have some use in Middle English manuscripts: "The letter *p* was especially subject to signs of abbreviation: a curve through the stem indicating *pro*; a horizontal bar through the stem indicating *per, par, por*; a horizontal or waved stroke or curve above it (in nonterminal positions) indicating *pre*."

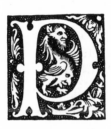
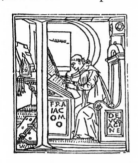

The runic alphabet had two different signs for P, whose name was *peord*, the meaning of which is unknown but, according to some scholars, perhaps was a kind of game. And, taking advantage of that opening, games, puzzles, and problem exercises have been devised with the letters since ancient times. A literary diversion of antiquity was to write a piece in which each word began with the same letter. One example was a poem by Petrus Placentius entitled "Pugna Porcurum" ("Battle of the Pigs"), in which all words began with—you guessed it!— the letter P. Another favored letter was C. Latin seems to lend itself more easily to such enterprises; but similar things have been attempted in English—for example, the first and final chapters of *Alphabetical Africa* by Walter Abish. The lipogrammatist's literary pursuit—dropping a particular letter from a literary work—is somewhat similar. In ancient times, Tryphiodorus was said to have composed an epic poem on the adventures of Ulysses in twenty-four books, each banishing a different

PpPP**Pp***P*PpPpPpPPp*P*PpP

letter of the alphabet. The Greek poet Pindar was credited with writing an ode in which the letter *sigma* was omitted; and many others have tried their hand at the practice since.

Anagrams—another literary exercise of great antiquity—are transpositions of the letters of a word or phrase which at their best comment upon the original: for example, lawyers—sly ware, or French Revolution—Violence Run Forth. Pangrammatists are those who try to place all the letters of the alphabet into a single sentence—usually the shortest one possible. A familiar example is "the quick brown fox jumps over a lazy dog," which consists of 33 letters. A more concise effort is "Waltz, nymph, for quick jigs vex Bud," which uses only 28 letters. The ideal is to produce an intelligible sentence of 26 letters without resorting to strange words and proper names. A successful effort is thus far unknown to this writer. Palindromes—another of our fancy-full P-words—are sentences which read the same forwards or backwards. A very familiar one is "Madam, I'm Adam." Examples less well known include: "Step on no pets"; "Draw pupil's lip upward"; and "No, it is open on one position." And, while it is open, I should mention puns, those often delightful and inciteful plays on words favored by many writers, among whom James Joyce (especially in *Finnegans Wake*) is preeminent. One further note, somewhat related to palindromes: Addison mentioned an epigram (most likely in Latin) called the "Witches Prayer," which could be read backwards or forwards; however, read one way it offered a blessing, read the other way, a curse.

According to James Thurber, "no other letter is quite so addicted to the vice of alliteration" as is P. "Peter Piper picked a peck of pickled

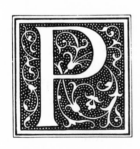
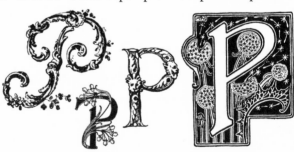

peppers…" is one of our best-known alliterative sentences or tongue-twisters—so named because of the difficulty in reciting them rapidly. Although this example seems to have no deep or profound meanings, in certain mystical systems each letter was thought to have a special power which could be released through the correct combination of letters in words. "Abracadabra" is one famous (if often misused) example. Some folk tales, fairy tales, verses, and tongue-twisters are vestiges of this type of thinking; and though Peter Piper may have little to do with this, it is quite possible that Rumpelstiltskin does. Many alphabetical games, exercises, charms, and riddles had serious as well as lighthearted applications. Serious variants have been considered magically potent in mystic circles from ancient times through the medieval period and claim a few believers even now. To Zolar, the Hebrew letter *pe* "signifies the open mouth. It is the symbol of expression through which man makes himself known in the outer world.…The outlet. The outward and visible means for the Spirit's manifestation." Its number is 80.

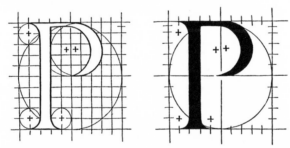

Tory's letter P

Geofroy Tory had comparatively little to say about P, although it also represented the mouth of his man of letters. He related it to the Muse Terpsichore, the inventor and patron of dancing as well as the mother of the Sirens. Although O represented fullness, Tory was able to continue his commentary by maintaining that "the idea of prosperity is denoted by the P following the O"; though I think he was influenced by the fact that P is the initial letter of that word in Latin (and French)—*prosperitas*.

With the door of P-words again open, it seems proper to mention James Thurber's comments on the subject. In his essay "The Watchers of the Night," he suggests a ramble through the letters of the alphabet for

PPp**P**PPp*p*P*P*p**P**PPp**P**pp**P**

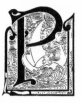

insomniacs; commenting upon our present subject, he observes: "The letter 'P,' that broad, provocative expanse between 'O' and 'Q,' is one of the most ambivalent of all the twenty-six, for in it one finds pleasure and pain, peace and pandemonium, prosperity and poverty." Centuries before Thurber, Sir Robert Burton in his *Anatomy of Melancholy* suggested other pleasures for insomniacs (or anyone else). To Burton, mathematical calculations—including permutations—were among the greatest worldly delights. "By this art you may contemplate the variation of the twenty-three letters, which may be so infinitely varied, that the words complicated and deduced thence will not be contained within the compass of the firmament; ten words may be varied 40,320 several ways." (Actually eight letters could be varied that many ways; ten would have 3,628,800 permutations.) It is to be expected that no insomniac could work out all the possibilities before falling into a deep sleep of one kind or another. A somewhat easier mathematical calculation is that in a serial order P designates the sixteenth (or fifteenth) place. In chemistry, P is the symbol for Phosphorus.

P is also the initial letter of papyrus, parchment, and paper—those three materials so important in the history of writing which helped influence the forms of the letters as they were written with pen and ink. Papyrus was first used by the ancient Egyptians; it consists of a series of split reeds of the papyrus plant laid in layers, each alternating layer at right angles. It is then beaten, the natural juices of the plant holding the

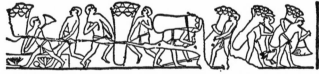

Papyrus being harvested in ancient Egypt (from a tomb at Memphis)

sheet together. Parchment is the scraped and treated hide of animals—generally sheep and goats. Vellum is a finer grade of hide that comes from younger (sometimes unborn) calves and sheep. Both papyrus and parchment were costly; the former was used by the ancient Egyptians, Greeks, and Romans, the latter was more extensively used in medieval Europe, where it was the material of the great manuscript books. It has been estimated that the thirty vellum copies of the Gutenberg Bible alone required the slaughter of over 5,000 calves. Add to that the hundreds of other books—both printed and manuscript—being produced, and it is easy to imagine how expensive they could be. It is also easy to suppose, as Ruari McLean says, that veal became a regular part of many people's diet during that period. Like papyrus, parchment was also reused after scraping the surface to remove the ink. Since the scraping rarely if ever removed all the earlier writing, scholars often have been able to reconstruct the earlier writings, thus getting two (or even more) manuscripts from the same parchment surface, which is then called a palimpsest.

Paper—formed from the pulp of beaten plant materials which is pressed and dried into a mat of interwoven fibers—was invented in China. The traditional date is given as A.D. 105. It journeyed from East

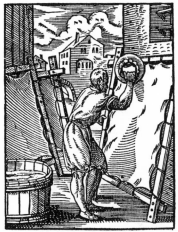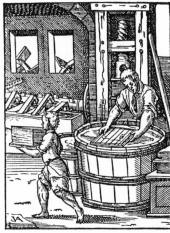

Illustrations of parchment preparer and papermakers from J. Amman's *Book of Trades* (1568)

to West by way of the Arabs, who are said to have captured Oriental papermakers (and their secret) in the year 751. The Arabians made paper in North Africa before the tenth century and carried the art to Spain, where the first European paper mill was established in about 1100. From there, paper made its way to Italy by the thirteenth century and to England, France, and Germany by the fourteenth. That it could be produced plentifully and economically was key to the expansion of the new printing technology, since an abundance of material was available for the rapid printing processes.

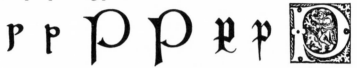

Uncial, semi-uncial, two Insular, two black letter, and a decorative version of P

The stem of the P began to descend below the line in uncial and semi-uncial scripts, presaging and closely resembling the modern lower-case form of the letter. In most respects, P has changed very little through the centuries, being easily recognizable in most book hands and typefaces. In medieval times, however, although readily recognized, the letters could still be considered somewhat fluid things. In his *Bestiary*, T.H. White mentions a medieval etymological practice of finding relationships between words by interchanging or linking key letters. He cites an example involving the letters P and F in discussing *Aper* (a wild boar) to account for that animal's ferocity (*a feritate*). Similarly, *canities* (hoary age) was linked with *candor* (pure whiteness) as though the T were a D.

To continue with the theme of substitutions, Robert Graves finds a rather unusual relative of the letter P. Named *pathboc*, it was an uncommon letter in Anglo-Saxon but was used as a substitute for an ancient "ng" letter and sound for which the Brythons had no use. Ng had stood for the reed in the *Beth-luis-nion* alphabet, and its lunar month began October 28. P took over these associations in early English usage and was also linked to other flora—whitten, guelder-rose, and water elder.

It all gets a bit confusing at times, so before we get too perplexed I will remind the reader of the famous cautionary phrase—"mind your p's and

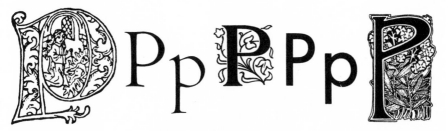

q's." This has many possible derivations, including the tally kept by the barkeeper of the pints (p) and quarts (q) of ale consumed by a patron at the local pub; but I favor the likelier reference to the similar forms of the lower-case p and q, especially when reversed in printers' type cases. A young apprentice—also called a printer's devil—could easily select the wrong one if he did not pay close attention to what he was doing, thus creating considerable havoc with the printed words and leaving many authors and printers of past centuries believing (and claiming) that there was a composing spirit or "imp of the perverse" corrupting their work under the direction of the arch-fiend himself! (In our own time, the use of computers—which seem to be packaged with at least one such imp— could promote a religious renaissance!) The alphabet effects great changes in meaning through rather minor distinctions of form.

Great changes can also be effected by a P-word, according to L. Frank Baum in *The Magic of Oz*. That word is "Pyrzqxgl." Pronounce it properly and you can transform yourself or other things into whatever you wish. Try it. I predict that, even if not quite what you desired, your attempt, coinciding with a shift of your attention to the next page, will at least take you from the world of P to a quite different one.

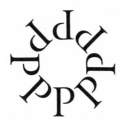

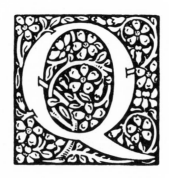

Q is the seventeenth letter of the English alphabet and the sixteenth of the Roman. It is descended from the Greek letter *koppa* and the older Semitic letter *koph* (or *qoph*). Nerdinger believes that, like P, it originated as an early bisected sun sign. Scholars are uncertain of the meaning of the Phoenician word *koph*: various interpretations include "monkey," a "knot," or "the back of the head." Although the Greeks adopted the Phoenician letter and its sound (a guttural [k] sound), it was soon dropped from the eastern Greek alphabet, those Greeks considering that the sound was already well covered by *kappa*. It was retained only as a numerical symbol equal to 90.

The Romans adopted Q from the western Greek alphabet but only used it in front of a consonantal U—that is, when U was followed by a vowel. This usage also has been adopted in English (for example, "queen," "quick," and "quote"). This restricted use of Q (analagous to that of K) was probably a response to the multiplicity of [k] sound letters (C, K, and Q) that the Romans inherited from the Greeks and Etruscans. Some Romans favored eliminating the letter from the alphabet altogether. The famed orator Calvus, a contemporary of Cicero, refused to use Q because he considered it superfluous. The Etruscans did not use Q in their language; however, they kept the Greek sign in their alphabet lists.

Although the English alphabet followed the Roman in retaining Q but restricting its use, some Englishmen also favored dropping the letter.

ᵠΦΡꝖΡQQQ Q꜀ꝗꝗꝗꝗꝗꝗꝗ꜀꜀ꝗꝗ

In his *Grammar*, Ben Jonson said that Q "is a letter we might very well spare in our *Alphabet*, if we would but use the serviceable *K* as he should be, and restore him to the right of reputation he had with our Fore-fathers." I trust that the forefathers he was referring to were Greek rather than Roman; but, in any case, Q has been retained even if restricted in use. The pronounced name of the English letter Q—*kyu*—follows naturally from its standard usage. The few exceptions to the paired Q and U are found in foreign words with variant spellings, such as "Qabbala," one of the variations of the word I have written "Kabbalah." "Qran" or "Quran" are also occasionally used for "Koran"; but in both these cases the K form of the word is currently the common spelling— which would no doubt please Ben Jonson. It should also be noted that because in English Q is always followed by U, it never occurs at the end of a word.

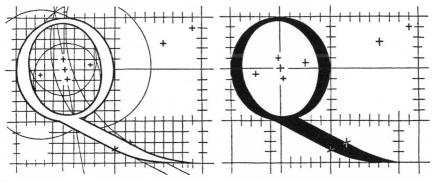

Tory's letter Q

A distinctive feature of the capital Q is its tail, which has assumed hundreds of variations through the centuries. It was quite long in the classic Roman inscriptional forms that Tory used as the models for his ideal alphabet. The tail of his Q descended below the base line of all the other capital letters, making it the only letter that deviated from the standard height. (J also descends below the line in some forms, but was not considered a letter in Tory's time.) Tory commented upon this peculiarity as well as upon Q's constant association with U: "I have discovered that the Q extends below the line because he does not allow

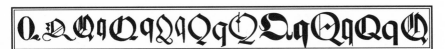

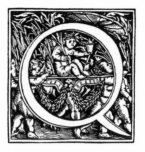

himself to be written in a complete word without his trusty comrade and brother V (U), and to show that he wishes always to have him by his side, he embraces him with his tail from below."

There is further significance to be found in Q and its comrade. "Those who persevere in well-made letters add a tail to their knowledge over and above its perfection; that is to say, they acquire worldly goods by their virtue, which the V, the first letter of the word Virtue, signifies covertly." The fact that V and U were not considered independent letters at that time explains why Tory was able to conflate the two; but the coupling of virtue with worldly gain may seem odd to idealists who believe that "virtue is its own reward," and quixotic to hardened realists who reject Horatio Alger plot scenarios, having learned from experience that the practice of virtue does not often lead to gain in a cutthroat world. But, although few calligraphers, scribes or type designers ever become wealthy from their work, Tory's linking of knowledge and wealth may not seem so crass or even metaphorical when we realize that the percentage of literate individuals was much lower in his day than it is in ours, and that many high positions and privileges were available to those who could read and write. For example, we have seen that even literate felons were spared harsher punishment for their misdeeds if they were admitted to the benefit of clergy.

French Cannon.

Quouſque tan-
dem abutere,
Catilina, pati-

Quouſque tandem
abutere, Catilina,
patientia noſtra?

Two Lines Great Primer.

Quouſque tandem
abutere, Catilina,
patientia noſtra?
quamdiu nos etiam

Quouſque tandem a-
butere, Catilina, pa-
tientia noſtra? quam-
diu nos etiam furor

Type specimens of William Caslon featuring "Quousque…"

Others have also commented (often not nearly as admiringly) upon the peculiarities of Q which Tory found to be so significant. Ben Jonson noted that the Anglo-Saxons used K instead of Q, "for the *English-Saxons* knew not this halting Q with her waiting-woman U after her." Also, the important American printer and typographer D.B. Updike may have wished that Cicero had followed the example of Calvus. Commenting upon the tail of the capital Q in its many and lengthy forms, he found much to deplore aesthetically; he placed the blame for the situation on type designers' practice of following the example of the great eighteenth century English printer and type designer William Caslon, who used the opening lines of Cicero's oration "Quousque tandem abutere, Catilina" to illustrate his type designs. Others followed suit, and, although those particular letters were not the most representative, the phrase soon became the classic type specimen—a practice that has continued to the present day. Updike reasoned that in order to outdo each other, type designers kept further elongating the tail of the Q. Had Caslon (or Cicero) begun his quotation with another letter, the tails of some typographic Qs would not be so long and ungainly. Eric Gill agreed that "a Q which were all queue and no Q would be 'past a joke,'" but felt that still "it is difficult to say exactly where a tail should end."

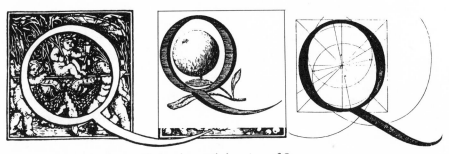

Various long-tailed versions of Q

There are of course many people who do not consider such letter embellishments as a long tail on the Q ungainly; in fact, calligraphers often draw highly ornate letters, many of which feature elaborate flourishes. And decorative letters have had a long and colorful history. In Western writing, the idea of lettering as a moving, expressive line (as distinct from a formal, more static, shape) was first expressed in Roman cursive forms. Cursive writing had a definite effect on almost all of the letters, especially influencing the development of minuscule forms. In the case of Q, with the uncial and semi-uncial scripts, the tail became more of a vertical descender, creating a form closely resembling and ultimately leading to the modern lower-case letter.

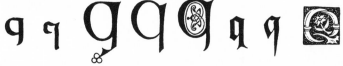

Uncial, semi-uncial, three Insular, two black letter, and one medieval decorative Q

Since the time of the Romans, elaborate scripts have been created in almost every historical period, with scribal exuberance, ingenuity and artistry often creating letter variants outside the accepted norm. (In fact, some samples of medieval writing show a Q with an interior tail.) In his important book *Anatomy of a Typeface*, Alexander Lawson states: "Ever since people gave shape to letters, they have rarely been content to allow their creations to remain pure in form. The urge for personal embellishment is eternally irresistible....Indeed, the survival of many of the ancient texts has depended at least as much on the appeal of their decoration as on their content."

The development of decorated initials in early medieval times had a great influence on the increasingly popular idea of lettering as art. J.J.G. Alexander explains: "As the text came to be considered as something

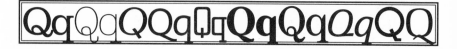

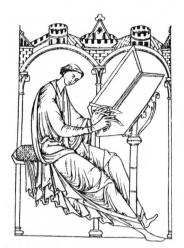

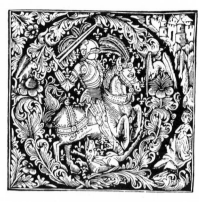

Illustration of scribe from 12th century Bestiary (left), with highly ornate decorative Q

revealed visually to the understanding through the written word (a development that may have had something to do with the spread and triumph of Christianity and its emphasis on a revealed truth recorded in the written text of the Gospels), so did the appearance of the text become a matter of concern. It could be decorated and embellished." Decorated initials were extensively used from the seventh through twelfth centuries, even though in theory decorated letters were at odds with the medieval scribes' striving for regularity. The scribes often became more personally involved—as artists—in their work. T. H. White has written of the medieval scribal monks and "their blunt, patient, holy fingers carefully forming the magic of letters." Occasionally, however, their fingers were not very careful or created a more obscure magic than they intended, as letter forms were often confused or distorted by being decorated. More commonplace errors of transcription can also be found in medieval (and classical) manuscripts, generally due to the eye confusing the letters—common examples being E and F, c and e, etc. Also, scribes often were not truly literate and would transcribe texts whose sense they did not fully understand, thus facilitating the transmission of errors if their letters were not perfectly legible. Writing for hours each day was very difficult—especially when copying unintelligible words—

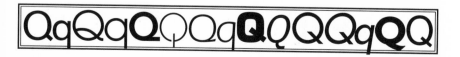

and many scribes recorded that fact in the margins of their work. Wrote one: "The sailor is not more glad to reach harbor than the weary scribe to arrive at the last line of his manuscript."

The Merovingian scribes of the Rhine area from the sixth through the ninth centuries turned letters into birds, fish, and other representational forms, which led to a great proliferation of the art form in the Middle Ages. In representational lettering, letters are primarily drawings of things rather than abstract forms. This differs in spirit and intention, however, from many other alphabet curiosities which are drawings of men or other objects in contorted or unusual positions representing letter shapes. These whimsical alphabets have also existed for centuries; Tory included one (which he called a "fantastic alphabet") in *Champ Fleury* that featured common tools such as a compass for A and an open pair of scissors for X. These alphabets are extremely popular at the present time, new examples being regularly published in typographic magazines and books; however, they are almost always lighthearted conceits, exercises in ingenuity for amusement even when exquisitely rendered and highly imaginative. The early medieval letters had a more serious decorative purpose: either through pattern, theme, or shape to complement a space and text. Both sorts of letter have a validity and delight; but whereas one might be compared to a painting, the other is more akin to a cartoon or caricature which, even though it is beautifully executed, evokes a different type of response in the viewer.

L ṁ ꓵ ꙩ ꟼ ꙩ ꓘ ʃ T

Letters (including Q) from Tory's "fantastic alphabet"

The most accomplished examples of lettering as art are found in the great Insular manuscripts—for example, *The Book of Kells*—from the early medieval period. As representational lettering became more common, its seriousness and significance dwindled. Framed initials, in which a regular capital letterform is placed in a highly decorated or pictorial square, did develop as a less elaborate variant, however, and they have been popular from the late medieval period to the present.

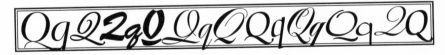

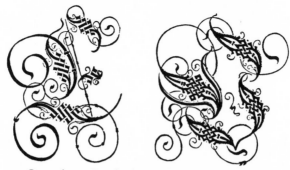

Ornate letters E and V by Wolfgang Fugger (1555)

Gothic initials of great variety were also developed in the medieval period. They were based mainly on uncial modifications of the Roman capitals. Many became very florid, in marked contrast to the uniformity of the basic black letter texts they embellished. They revealed great ingenuity, some beauty, and little legibility. Writing masters of the Renaissance and Baroque periods developed medieval ideas of letter construction and decoration to their fullest elaboration, often creating fantastic embellishments that overwhelmed the basic letter and, in fact, at times left it completely unrecognizable. William Gardner cautions us against viewing these creations as analagous to some of the silly typefaces created in our own time—typefaces composed of drawings of cats, neckties, logs, or daisies, for example—which are meant to amuse or to fit a very specific use. The earlier embellished letters were exuberant (if sometimes misguided) expressions of the writing masters' skill and were

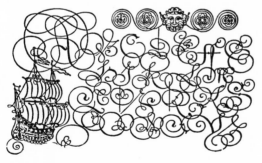 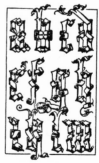

Writing sample of 1657 by Edward Cocker (left); with ribbon letters by L. Vicentino (1533)

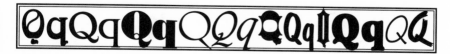

executed in all seriousness. Geofroy Tory raised his voice against all such practices, admonishing designers not to change the basic shapes and proportions of the letters: "If one mutilates a letter in any way whatsoever, it is no longer a letter, but a counterfeit, or a thing so evil that one could not give it a fitting name, unless he should say that it was a monster." Tory took letters seriously!

One of the greatest writing masters, however, had a more tolerant attitude. Although his work would likely have been condemned by Tory, Wolfgang Fugger, writing some twenty-five years later, obviously felt that he constructed letters quite properly: "I have made them as the pen, in its rightful manner, shapes them. Whoever is able to write them well may, hereafter, if he so desires, bend them, twist them, break them on the wheel, hang them, behead them, make them walk on stilts—in short—do with them what he likes. But I leave it to you to judge what good that will do them." I do not know if Fugger would be pleased to learn that virtually all of those things have indeed been done to the letters in the service of nineteenth and twentieth century advertising.

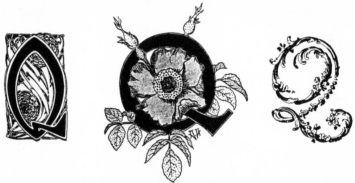

Tory himself made a somewhat uncongenial association regarding the letter Q—although I feel certain he had nothing disrespectful in mind—when he related it to the anus of his man of letters. Since in his scheme the letters represented the vital channels and parts of the body, one would obviously be assigned that particular representation. It was Q, separated from its otherwise constant companion. Perhaps to Tory the representation was quite apt, Q having the most distinctive tail of any

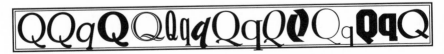

Q q Q q

letter, and that the closest to a tail he could find in man. In any event, Tory also related Q to Euterpe, the Muse of lyric poetry, whose symbol was the flute. No comment.

Robert Graves comments that Q—in a variant form, CC—was one of the seven most important letters in the *Beth-luis-nion* alphabet. It was associated with the planet Venus and with Friday, and it was also related to August 5 (as was C) and to the apple, sorb, or quince trees. According to Zolar, Q as the Hebrew letter *qoph* "signifies nature's submerged stratum. Literally, the APE. Related to the subliminal consciousness. The evolutionary stage which is behind us." Its mystical number is 100. In serial order, Q represents the seventeenth (or sixteenth) place. And, as a further bit of confusion, in some medieval notations, Q (not D) equalled 500, not 90 as it was known to the ancient Greeks. It could also perhaps be noted that although many men have felt this letter to be superfluous, ducks haven't.

Perhaps, if I have tempted readers to discontinue this study by dashing any hopes for the great wealth that Tory has so lavishly promised, I may be pardoned by pointing out that it is a true love of letters that Tory continually mentions. And, as I have previously counted on that "true love" to help my readers persevere, so now I trust that you will continue without the lure of worldly riches. Some wealth you may yet gain, however; it comes in many forms.

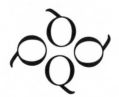

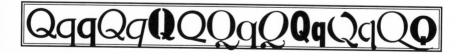

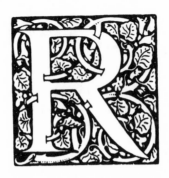

R—THE EIGHTEENTH LETTER of the English alphabet, the seventeenth of the Roman—is descended from the Greek letter *rho* and the letter *resh* of the early Semitic writing systems. Nerdinger believes that it was derived from a P-form, which was an ancient stylized sign for the human head. And, in fact, the Phoenician *resh*—a sort of angular, reversed P— is thought to mean "head" and to depict a human profile. Although the capitals P and R are quite similar in form, they have independent histories and derivations. However, for much of its history, R closely resembled the modern form of P. Although the early Greek forms of the letter generally followed the Phoenician, the letter was gradually made vertical and its bowl rounded to make a more exact mirror image of the modern P. Its boustrophedon counterpart, which the Etruscans adopted, completed the resemblance.

It is the development of the letter in its Roman forms that brought us our accustomed modern sign. This was achieved in various stages. First, the letter was established in its left-to-right (P) written form. Then, to distinguish it from the sign for P, which was also evolving into its classic modern form, the R began to grow a tail—at first a very small stubby appendage similar to some earlier western Greek alphabet variants of *rho* (though never commonly used, they probably influenced the Roman form). By the time of the classic Roman inscriptions, the tail of the R had lengthened in a graceful curve to meet the base line of the alphabet.

Let us return briefly to the Greek letter and its sound. In Plato's *Cratylus*, Socrates says that *rho* appears as the letter expressing motion, perhaps because the "imposer of names...had observed that the tongue was most agitated and least at rest in the pronunciation of this letter." The sound symbolized by the letter R has generated a great amount of commentary. R is one of the four liquid letters, those letters of "easy virtue" according to Tory that have a profound and variable effect on vowels preceding them in words. This is very much true of the letter in English, where R is technically termed an "open-voiced" consonant. Because of its sound, R came to have a special name. Tory explains: "When dogs are angry, before they begin to bite each other, contracting their throats and grinding their teeth, they seem to be saying R, for which reason the poet Persius, the most pleasant of caustic satirists, calls it *Litera canina*, the canine letter." Ben Jonson expressed the same idea in English by calling R "the dog's letter" in his *Grammar*. Others have concurred, Brewer also calling it the "snarling letter" or "dog letter" in his *Dictionary of Phrase and Fable*.

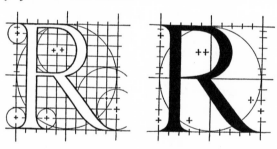

Tory's letter R

Tory, as was his custom, made an attempt to draw the "ideal" form of the Roman capital R—and a very attractive and graceful form it was indeed, even if not considered ideal by other designers who have continued to devise their own versions of the letter. It is this basic classic form that Donald Jackson commented upon in *The Story of Writing*, where he fancied that "even in the best regulated inscriptions the letter R often strides defiantly outside its invisible half-square." And it is this vitality of good letters (whether typographic or calligraphic), their defiance of rigid mechanical constructions, that Graily Hewitt wrote of

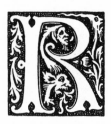 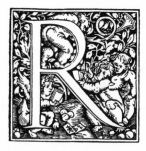 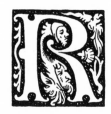

in his important book, *Lettering*: "Letters have something more than the substance necessary for their stability; they should have vitality. Their stems spring from the ground; they have, when well drawn, a vigour as of growing things, not the strength of posts and rails. They can never, therefore, be satisfactorily drawn with compass and set-square, but need the free hand to give them this expression."

Hewitt felt that what we consider a letter's legibility is established by custom and convention, not by any supposed ideal design. Frederic Goudy agreed while getting in a few extra punches: "Tory's simple assumption that there is a relation between the shapes of letters and the contours of the human body is no more erroneous, however, than the hypothesis that there is one ideally correct form for each letter of the alphabet; erroneous, because the shapes of letters have been in constant process of modification from their very beginnings. Indeed, the shapes of the letters in daily use are due entirely to a convention." Although Goudy conceded that the basic forms of the letters have become fixed or classic, "nevertheless we may give to one face of type a quality of distinction, or of novelty in mass, which differs from the quality presented by another face of the same general character similarly employed." This is design.

  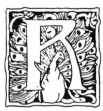

RrRrRRRrrRRRrRrRrRRrRR

Alphabet design cannot alter too radically because the signs must remain recognizable to the human eye. But within that range (which is surprisingly large), letter shapes can vary greatly—especially since letters grouped into words and sentences are even more legible than they are by themselves. The eye does not readily grasp a word whose meaning is unknown. Some complaints of illegibility are based on the vocabulary of the reader, not on the form of the letters. Robert Bridges felt that true legibility consists in "the *certainty of deciphering*; and that depends not on what any one reader may be accustomed to, nor even on the use of customary forms, but rather on the consistent accurate formation of the letters."

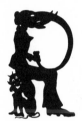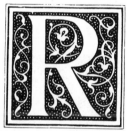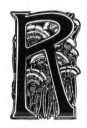

As we have seen in tracing the history of various letters, the great range and variety of letter forms is certainly not a recent development. The contemporary type designer Hermann Zapf maintains that few who read consider how the letters came to be, and yet each letter has been shaped by "the constant effort to render its image suitable in purpose and beautiful in form." Well, maybe that effort hasn't been exactly constant, but the general evolution of the Roman letters has been towards regularity and symmetry. And certain letterforms did tend to be influenced by others, such as F by E, Q by O, and G by C. When P assumed a similar shape, R received its distinguishing stroke. According to B.L. Ullman: "Numerous variants of the letters, some of them very strange and unusual, may be found in the records which have been preserved to us. But they have disappeared as a result of the operation of the law of the survival of the fittest." Whether or not this sort of literal Darwinism actually applies, many letter forms have certainly fallen into oblivion over the course of the centuries. (Galway Kinnell has called

RrrRRRrrRrRrRRrRRrR

death a traveling the "path of vanished alphabets.") Legibility, simplicity, beauty, and adaptability to pen and ink or metal typecasting have all affected the development and survival of letters.

Donald Anderson claims that the predominance of right-handed people also has had a determining effect on our letter forms and upon the direction of our writing. When letters were inscribed in stone or impressed in clay the direction of writing mattered little, and thus boustrophedon as well as right-to-left forms could flourish. With pen and ink, however, a right-handed scribe writing from right to left would drag his hand over the still wet ink; consequently, the left-to-right direction gained greater favor and finally became universal in Western writing. The position and shape of some of the letter strokes were also directly influenced by right-handed writing.

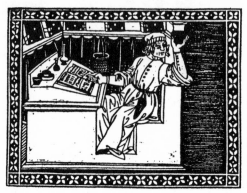

Illustration of a scribe from an Italian book of 1493; while pointing to the ms. with his right hand, he appears to be requesting more ink (or beverage?) for the container in his left.

The form of R began to change noticeably with the semi-uncial script—the bottom of the bowl of the R became detached from the stem, and the tail was shortened to a small curve coming off the bowl. This change became more pronounced in later forms, culminating in our lower-case form of the letter—r. (Martin Luther made unusual use of the R forms in his 1545 translation of the Bible. To distinguish the old

R ɼ RRR⌐RRℜ ɼɼ

Uncial, semi-uncial, various Insular, and three black letter forms of R

RrRrRrrRRRrRrRrRRRr

D£nn ſo ſpricht der H£rr H£RR / Jr habts
Fürſten Jſrael / Laſſet abe vom Freuel vnd Gewalt / vn
gut iſt / vnd thut ab von meinem Volck ewer austreib

Section from Luther's Bible showing distinctive use of HErr and HERR

Hebrew names of God, Adonai and Elohim, he employed the visual distinction of the upper- and lower-case letters—HErr and HERR.) Although many different forms of this letter (and the others) were current during the medieval period, since the development of printing there have not been distinct national scripts; we have had instead a universal roman alphabet which has adopted countless variants of its classic typographic form. These contemporary typographic variations are generally not as extreme or diversified as were the early medieval letterform varieties, letters now being recognizable in virtually all of their forms by any basically literate person. As Laurence Scarfe says: "The practice of typography has saved mankind from riotous alphabets: the machine has put at the disposal of men who are not all scribes, a wide collection of previously well-designed letter forms."

Typesetting based on classic letter forms may have saved us from riotous alphabets (at least in book faces if not in advertising fonts), but a tremendous variety still exists. Walter Tracy states that R is a key letter in identifying a typeface, and he finds it "remarkable that so much individuality can be contrived from just three elements: a vertical stem, a bowl, and a leg stroke." The noted artist Ben Shahn said that "the uses and the understanding of type are a life's work." He went on to point out that "all kinds of letters that exist—and that includes type letters and amateur letters—have their own intrinsic moods and meanings. Lettering is, for all its perfectionism, an expressionistic art." Artists, designers, and printers are probably most sensitive to the moods, personalities, and tones of different typefaces; but most readers can easily perceive the

THE SHAPE OF
CONTENT

Highly distinctive lettering by Ben Shahn for one of his books

RrrRRRRrRrRrRRRrRrRRR

altered effect of the same word set in two very different typefaces—for example, **modern** and *moḃern*. Type can be static, dynamic, solid, fanciful, and much more. As Beatrice Warde said: "The best part of typographic wisdom lies in this study of connotation, the suitability of form to content. People who love ideas must have a love of words, and that means, given a chance, they will take a vivid interest in the clothes which words wear." Members of the art (or anti-art) movement known as Dadaism were interested in these ideas, and Apollinaire (among others) created works that played with the idea that letters set in different typefaces can detract from or augment the meaning of the words they construct.

  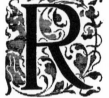

Not only the forms of the letters but also their rhythm or flow in combination influences the way we perceive them. Warren Chappell maintains that "the *soul* or *spirit* of the alphabet is in its rhythm, and there must be very few who have been deeply involved with letters who have failed to sense it. This is not so much a matter of theory as of feeling." A successful book type must balance two opposing characteristics: each letter must be distinct and easily recognizable; yet if a letter is too distinctive it disturbs the flow of reading. Most readers have probably encountered a typeface in which one or more of the letters irritates or disturbs them as they read, sometimes even making it difficult to concentrate on the meaning of the words. Even if the particular offending form is attractive in itself, it stamps the whole face with the mark of failure. Such was the case of the otherwise anonymous "R-printer" in the early years of printing. His design for the capital R stood out boldly on the printed page, distinguishing his work from that of his contemporaries. As Harry Carter points out: "The reading eye learns to rely on the excrescences from letters as much as on their essentials, especially when the impression is imperfect."

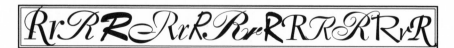

R R R

Early versions, including three Insular, of the letter R

In calligraphic lettering, the letters are allowed much more extensive decoration, embellishment, and elaboration than they are in typography; but the goal of rhythm and harmony is still paramount. In this regard, it is interesting to read a passage by William Gass in *Fiction and Figures of Life*: "The elaboration that can be accorded the letter *r*, for example, far outruns its meaning, yet it would receive no elaboration at all if it were not a letter. One is tempted, therefore, to see in the elaboration some explication of the meaning of the letter, some search for mystical essence even, while at the same time the elaborations reduce it to a pure design whose interest lies wholly in the movement and harmony of lines in space." Donald Anderson adds that "if the graphic identity of the letter is not totally lost, the calligrapher can do whatever he likes with it.... The struggle between the calligrapher and the alphabet is one of honor: he must preserve the identity of the individual letter and get his own way at the same time." Sometimes the victories are equivocal, as Beverly Boyd notes: "One of the most troublesome signs in fifteenth-century English vernacular manuscripts is a reflex curve on r at the end of a word, which traditionally indicated a final *e*, but which often became confused with flourishes in the scribal handwriting. Sometimes the rhymes are the only evidence of the correct reading."

Geofroy Tory seems to treat the dog's letter most sympathetically in his analogical system. He relates the letter to the Liberal Art Geometria, and in his man of letters R represents the heart. Perhaps the misanthropic (and surely the cynical) would wish to consider Tory among their number, seeing his "perfect" man with a dog's heart; but just as surely many caninophiles would consider that to be a more true and fitting mark of perfection.

In the runic alphabet, R was named *rad*, meaning "riding"; and usually a horse was mentioned in describing this name. According to

RrRrRrRRRrRrRrRrRrRR

Zolar, the Hebrew letter *resh* "signifies individual movement, determination, and progress. Literally, means head....Indicates independence, self-help, self-initiated endeavor. Also, direction, a center of generating motion starting of its own accord." Its mystical number is 200. The letter R had darker connotations in the ancient Irish tree-alphabet. According to Graves, R—*ruis*—was associated with November 25, the last month of the year and the symbolic end of many festivals and reigns. Its tree was the elder or myrtle, which was often associated with witchcraft and calamity. In medieval numerical notation R equalled 80; and in serial order the letter represents the eighteenth (or seventeenth) place.

R R r R r

This letter has gained some notoriety and use in modern phrases. Many gourmets are aware that the "R months" (September through April—each month's name containing an R) are the period when oysters are in season. The most famous R-phrase is probably the "Three R's" of education—"reading, riting, and rithmetic"—unfortunately, seemingly not a quality education. Other variants include the Three R's of Theological Controversy: "Romanism, Ritualism, and Rationalism." And there is also one variant that I hope not too many are presently aware of—the Three R's of the inexperienced writer of books: "Rhetoric, Reflex, and Repetition."

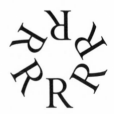

Rrr*Rr***R**R*Rr*R R_pR R_r**Rr**R_RR

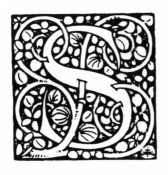

S IS THE NINETEENTH LETTER of the English alphabet and the eighteenth
letter of the Roman. It is descended from the Greek letter *sigma* (Σ),
which in turn came from the Phoenician letter *shin*, which is practically
the same form turned 90°, resembling our modern letter W. Nerdinger
believes that the symbol originated from an early sign that depicted the
displacement of split halves of the sun sign—perhaps somewhat similar
to the Chinese yin-yang symbol—and that it stood for the summer
solstice. Donald Anderson, however, believes that it descended from a
pictogram depicting mountain peaks. The Phoenician *shin* is thought
by scholars to have meant "teeth," which the multiangular letter does
seem to illustrate. The Phoenicians actually had three letters signifying
various [s] sounds: *samech*, with a sharp [s] sound, was used by the
Greeks for [x]; *tsade* or *sadhe*, a [ts] sound, was used briefly in some early
Greek alphabet variants but was later dropped; and *shin*, which technically had an [sh] sound but was used by the Greeks for their softer, basic
[s] sound. The Book of Judges records a terrible story in which thousands of Ephraimites were killed by their foes from Gilead as they came
to cross the Jordan River. A test word—"shibboleth"—was given, which
the unfortunate travelers pronounced "sibboleth," resulting in their
immediate execution. This is a most brutal illustration of the potential
weight of even such a seemingly small thing as a letter's sound and
pronunciation, while it also illustrates how different peoples use differing language sounds, even when the spelling of the words is identical.

Once established by the Greeks, the sound represented by the forms of the letter has remained virtually unchanged through the millenia and has had a great influence on the lore and interpretation surrounding the letter. Technically, in modern English, S is called a "voiceless sibilant." In Plato's *Cratylus*, the Greek *sigma* was called a letter expressive of shaking, shock, and shivering—all that is windy—because its pronunciation is accompanied by "great expenditure of breath." An old story relates that during the wars of the Greeks and Persians, at the retreat of the ten thousand, Xenophon, the great general and historian, needed a pot-hook and made it out of a *sigma*. Perhaps the story appealed to an ancient Greek sense of humor, or maybe it was intended to illustrate the importance of letters and writing in Xenophon's military campaigns.

 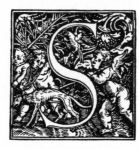 

The Romans must be given credit for rounding the letter form into its familiar sinuous shape, so complementary to its represented sound. Geofroy Tory claimed that in order "to show the changeable nature of the said letter S, the Ancients represented it as twisted in shape." The "changeable nature" he referred to was due to the various effects S has on other letters adjacent to it in different words. Although not quite as disreputable and unpredictable as the whorish liquid letters, S was still somewhat suspect and was certainly not a letter of pure and unimpeachable character. In Tory's words: "As there are men who have few good parts, and are of little use, except in their number, like the numeral 0, which by itself makes no number, but with others multiplies their value, so it is with the letter S, which is sometimes a quasi-liquid, making the vowel that precedes it long, and sometimes not, and very often vanishes and is lost to sight in respect to metrical quality."

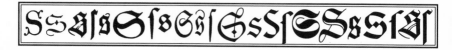

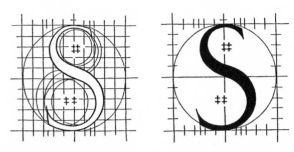

Tory's letter S

The Greek writer Lucian, in his tale "The Consonants at Law," referred to this mutable characteristic of S, as well as to the spelling changes and developments that all languages undergo through time. In this witty little work, S, which calls itself "a much-enduring letter," feels that it has endured enough and appeals to the Court of Vowels for justice and protection, complaining that other consonants (particularly T) are stealing away words formerly spelled with S. S maintains that if T is not stopped in its assault and robbery, S will have nothing left, be ejected as a letter, "and shall be no better than a hiss." Unfortunately, the court is unable to do much about the problem; however, S did retain some of its words and remain in the alphabet, although T's pilfering is still evident in modern English spelling and pronunciation—for example, the suffix "-tion," which is often pronounced as though it were spelled "shun."

This characteristic of S, becoming inarticulate in the pronunciation of certain words and thus often being dropped in later spellings of the words, is especially characteristic of Latin and the Romance languages. Some ancient writers considered S to be an ignoble letter that was without force. It therefore came to signify "silence," and Tory claims that for this reason "the ancients often wrote it alone above the door of the place where they ate and drank with their good friends; in order to put it before their eyes that such words as they should speak at table must be spoken soberly and listened to in silence." The Romans also used ST as a symbol for silence; and Tory records the fact that the great nobles who built mansions and palaces would "cause an S or ST to be written, painted, engraved or carved over the doors of their halls and kitchens, in order covertly yet plainly to impose silence on a parcel of roisterers who

SsSsSsSSsSSsSsSSsSsSSsS

make more uproar after drinking than a hundred starlings in harvest-time."

The ancients played upon both the sound of the letter S and its connotation of silence by calling its sound a hissing like that of a red-hot poker being dipped in water just before falling silent. It is this hissing sound coupled with its shape that brings S its most characteristic and appropriate name—the serpent letter.

S "is a most easie, and gentle Letter, and softly hisseth against the teeth in the prolation. It is called the *Serpents* Letter, and the chiefe of the consonants. It varieth the powers much in our pronunciation." Thus wrote Ben Jonson in his *English Grammar* of 1640. The name well suits the letter. And it is interesting to note that some of the qualities that led Tory and ancient writers to consider S weak and ignoble, Jonson finds to be strengths—its many applications in the language influence him to call it the chief of consonants. It is the case, however, that S has a stronger sound in English than it has in Latin and many Romance languages. In modern English more words begin with S than with any other letter; it

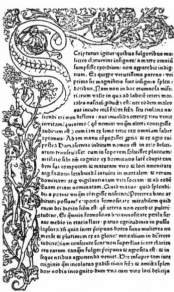
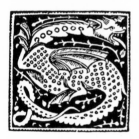
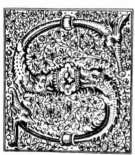

Medieval forms of S as a dragon or serpent, including S as the Serpent with Adam and Eve

$$Ss\,Ss\,Ss\,SS\,Sss\,Sss\,SSs\,Ss\,SS$$

is also one of the most frequently occurring letters within the bodies of English words, and its sound is seldom lost.

Like many things quite common and overused, the letter S can be something writers would often wish to avoid, although still remaining a temptation and challenge to be used in striking and novel ways. Virginia Woolf may have had some such idea as this in mind when she wrote that S "is the serpent in the poet's Eden." Happily, the form of the letter itself would make sense of the image even if there were no other reflections behind it.

Although the Romans established the modern S form in their monumental capital alphabet, another form of the letter developed in late Roman–early medieval times with the semi-uncial book script of the seventh century. Essentially it was a flattened, elongated ascending letter—somewhat similar to our lower-case f without the cross-bar—that was extensively used in various scripts of the Middle Ages. By the gothic period (eleventh century) there were two common S forms—the flattened or long S, which was used throughout words (quite often at the beginning and in the middle), and the modern or short S, which was used for word endings. Following the example of the earlier manuscript books, the early printers generally adopted this practice. The short S, which became our modern lower-case form of the letter, was just a smaller version of the classic capital letter.

Uncial, semi-uncial, many Insular, and two black letter versions of long S and short S forms

The Italian language helped put an end to the use of the long S form. Italian words generally lack S endings, and gradually the convention became confused as medieval Italian scribes began to use the short and long S indiscriminately in initial and medial positions in words. During the Renaissance, when Italian scholars and scribes were the dominant influence in learning and book production, they also used the short S extensively in their transcriptions of Latin texts, and soon scribes in other countries began to copy and adopt the Italian practice. The practice was continued and expanded with the early Italian typefaces of the age of printing. The long S form gradually fell out of favor and was discontinued. It effectively dropped out of English usage in the eighteenth century, although it survives in German where medieval black letter types have remained in favor. Medieval English also had a sign for the double S (ß) which has become obsolete, although again a similar sign continues to be used in German.

Most readers would be immediately aware of a long S or double S sign inserted in their reading matter; yet, unfortunately, they do not usually notice type characteristics of a lesser scale. Most ordinary readers are "type blind"—that is, they either don't notice the differences in typefaces or else consider them to be of little or no account. Seán Jennett points out, however, that "type faces are, like human faces, the same in essentials, but vastly different in detail; and the difference in detail is an expression of that indefinable quality called character."

One difference in detail between typefaces—as well as a convenient S-word—involves serifs, the small finishing strokes at the ends of many of the component lines of letters. They are thought by some to have originally developed as an aid to stonecutters to help control and define the carving of the letter lines, and thus became an integral design element of the monumental inscriptional Roman capitals. They soon became a basic feature of letters written with pen and ink. A few scholars and calligraphers claim that this was through simple imitation of the inscriptional letter forms, but others maintain that pen and ink serifs are starting and finishing strokes that come naturally to flat-nib pen lettering. Serifs assume subtly different forms in both historical manuscripts and modern printing typefaces. Some critics maintain that they now serve merely a traditional, ornamental function, being unnecessary in

SsSsSSSSSsSSsSsSSsSsS

the mechanical formation of metal, photographic, and computer-generated type. Beatrice Warde had other thoughts on the subject, however: "Serifs are by no means inessential ornaments: they enable us to distinguish cap. I from lower-case l and arabic numeral 1, they strengthen the descending mainstrokes by forming a buttress against the halation of light from the white paper, they unobtrusively mark the line on which lower-case characters are ranged, and they are essential in preventing such a word as 'illicit' from looking silly."

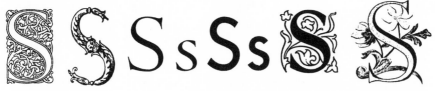

Sans serif type designs were developed in the nineteenth century and have become very popular in the twentieth, advocates claiming that they are very modern in appearance and reflect our streamlined technological age. They not only were considered by many to be purely functional with no unnecessary decoration, but also had the additional advantage of being free from all historical associations. Some sans serif typefaces are quite attractive and have been widely used; but they still are not employed in books to anywhere near the extent of serif typefaces, since most readers prefer traditional typefaces for their general reading matter.

In fact, a basic problem with sans serif typefaces is that many people find them illegible in smaller sizes. Whether this is due to actual design characteristics or only attributable to readers being more familiar with serif letterforms, the perceived illegibility remains. Even if the idea is specious, it seems that if thought to be illegible, typefaces are illegible.

Relative illegibility of different type sizes is not unique to sans serif types, however. Even in a regular roman typeface, to achieve maximum legibility the letters should be redesigned for various type point sizes. A "point" is a typographic unit of measurement—72 points being approximately equal to one inch. In small sizes (6 to 12 point), the letters must be proportionally wider and their stems, hairlines, and serifs thicker than in their larger counterparts. Also, ascenders and descenders must be

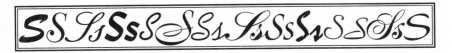

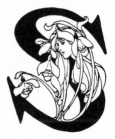   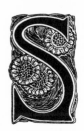

proportionally smaller, and spaces between the letters greater. The printing authority Victor Strauss maintains that "practically speaking, legibility is a consideration of type design, whereas readability refers to the arrangement of types." And a typographer, John Biggs, says that "technical considerations hold the field in the smaller sizes but give way to artistic considerations when dealing with large letters. A small type must be judged on its appearance in the mass, while larger sizes must be considered … as individual letters having an abstract beauty of their own." Frederic Goudy summarized the essential elements: "Legibility depends on three things: first, simplicity, that is, a form having no unnecessary parts (not the bastard simplicity of form which is mere crudity of outline); second, contrast, as shown by marked differences in the weight of the lines composing the individual letters (stems and hairlines), and also as shown in the varying widths of different letters; and third, proportion, each part of a letter having its proper value and relation to the other parts and to other letters—these three things in connection with the aspects of purpose and use."

According to Robert Graves, S—*saille*—was one of the seven most important letters of the *Beth-luis-nion* alphabet and was associated with

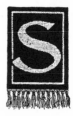 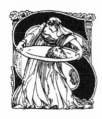  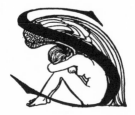

the moon and Monday. It relates to the lunar month beginning April 15 as well as to the willow—a tree important to witches and witchcraft, as was also, of course, the moon similarly important. In chemistry, S is the symbol for sulphur, which, if not popular with witches, is commonly associated with their leader and inspiration, Satan. In the runic alphabet, however, the S sign—*sigel*—meant "sun." The Hebrew letter *shin* has been considered one of that alphabet's three "mother" letters. Because of its hissing sound, it corresponded to fire and represented the season of summer. Zolar says that *shin* "signifies light movement and sweet sounds. Esoterically it symbolizes that part of a bow from which the arrow darts hiss. It is the sign of relative duration." Its mystical number is 300.

It seems fitting that S should begin the word "superstition." As Gary Jennings reports: "It is a minor wonder that the letter S is still with us; it and its sibilant siblings in other alphabets have long been abhorred by people who perceived in them the shape or sound of the dread serpent or the monogram of the even more dreaded Satan. The Yezedi Arabs won't pronounce the letter. The Hebrew scribes took care not to use it in the opening pages of the Scriptures."

In a series, S represents the nineteenth (or eighteenth) place. As an abbreviation of *salutem* ("wishing health") it was used by Romans to end their missives. And I have not forgotten Geofroy Tory. He associates the letter with the Liberal Art Rhetoric, and it forms the spleen of his man of letters. Much probably could be said about this, but I prefer to recall Tory's mention of the ancient use of the letter and write it down here to discourage ill-bred chattering and to wish you health. S.

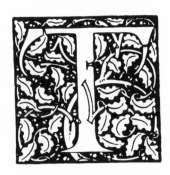

T, THE TWENTIETH LETTER of the English alphabet, was the nineteenth letter of the Roman. It is descended from the Greek *tau* and the ancient Semitic *tav* (*taw* or *tahv*). In the oldest Semitic scripts, *tav* had an X shape, which became more generally turned to a cross shape (+) with the Phoenician script. The early Greek alphabets copied this form but gradually raised the horizontal bar; the familiar T shape was in common use by the time of the classical Greek alphabet. *Tav* was the last letter of the Semitic alphabets. In the Phoenician, *tav* is thought to have meant a mark or cross. Nerdinger believes that it was derived from an early sign for the crossed spokes of a wheel. Moran, however, identifies *tav* with the bull (Taurus)—just as the first Semitic letter, *aleph*, was associated with the ox or bull. Thus, both the first and last letters of the alphabet were associated with the Taurian Age (c. 4000–2000 B.C.), and the cross (sign of *tav*) became the symbol of God. In early Greek alphabets *tau* was also the last letter until the creation of *omega*, which assumed the terminal place and with it many religious associations.

Throughout the centuries, a great deal of commentary regarding the letter T has involved religious matters—much of it relating to Christianity with its special symbolic use of the cross. A tale from what has been called a "collection of pious frauds," the alleged second century pseudo-*Gospel of Thomas,* tells of a dispute between the young Jesus and his schoolmaster. The schoolmaster grew increasingly frustrated by Jesus's superior knowledge of the alphabet and its significance. When they came to the letter T, the pedagogue, overcome by rage, struck the child and prophesied his crucifixion, then fell senseless to the ground. Other variants of the tale assert that the teacher was struck dead for his audacity. Robert Graves retells the story in a fascinating but believable way in his excellent novel *King Jesus*. In both Christian orthodoxy and mysticism, exegetical interpretations and analyses have been quite common and varied regarding the use of T in various biblical words and passages. Rudolf Koch says that the T form is known as Saint Anthony's cross, the Egyptian cross, and the Tau cross. Saint Francis of Assisi used it as his signature mark.

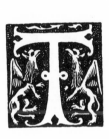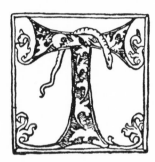

Even when not directly associated with Christianity, much commentary about the letter has had theological connotations. According to tradition, T was the form of the cross that Moses used to lift up the serpent in the wilderness, foreshadowing the crucifixion of Christ. The annual ritual Sacred King of many ancient cultures was crucified on a T-shaped cross of sacred wood. In *King Jesus*, Graves reports that among the ancient Israelites a T-shaped cross "was tattooed as a royal caste-mark on the brows of the clansmen from whose ranks the Sacred King was chosen." *Tav* was also said to be the sign that will be marked in blood on the brows of the Jewish faithful to protect them from the slaughter of the "Great Day of the Lord." However, in his book, *The Olive Leafe*, Alexander Top speculated that for his crime Cain was marked on his forehead with the letter T because it not only signified a mark but was also the last—and, hence, somewhat disreputable—letter of the Hebrew alphabet.

It is T's disreputable connotation that Lucian wrote about in "The Consonants at Law." We have seen that S brought suit against T for thievery, and in so doing issued the following lament: "Men weep, and bewail their lot, and curse Cadmus with many curses for introducing *Tau* into the family of letters; they say it was his body that tyrants took for a model, his shape that they imitated, when they set up the erections on which men are crucified. *Stauros* the vile engine is called, and it derives its vile name from him."

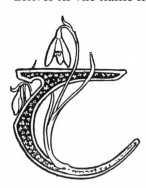 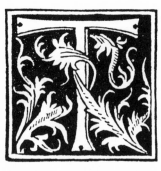 

Not all writers have had bad things to say about T. In the dialogue *Cratylus*, Plato says simply that *tau* is expressive of "binding or rest at a place" because of the closing and pressure of the tongue against the roof of the mouth in pronouncing it. And Chaucer in his translation of Boethius's *The Consolation of Philosophy* found a pleasant connotation for T: he said that it signified the contemplative life. In his man of letters, Tory associated T with the "virile member"—certainly a most interesting part of the body, and one with all kinds and degrees of pleasant or unpleasant connotations, depending upon one's particular state of mind (or body). Tory also related the letter to the Muse Thalia, who is generally regarded as the Muse of comedy—which, again, many may consider to be rightly associated with the virile member.

Robert Graves mentions that T was one of the seven most important letters of the *Beth-luis-nion* alphabet. It was connected with the planet Mars and with Tuesday. It corresponded with the lunar month beginning July 8 and was also associated with the holly or prickly oak. In *The*

TtTtTt*t*TtT*Tt*TtTtTTTtT

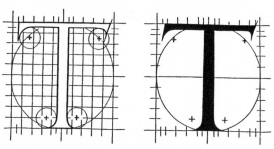

Tory's letter T

White Goddess, Graves mentions that the goddess Carmenta invented the letter T, which introduced half of her calendar year, and that T was also associated with Christianity at an early date in the British Isles. In Graves's account (here simplified greatly), T, associated with Jesus and Christianity, was involved in a struggle for dominance with the letter D (considered its twin), which was associated with the oak tree, the Druids, and John the Baptist. The letter T—*tinne*—the prickly oak or holly oak (also known as the kerm or evergreen oak), rules the waning part of the year and originally was D's executioner: the oak king crucified on a T-shaped cross. The account appears to have become a bit confused in imposing Christian figures on what may be more easily understood as a pagan calendrical myth regarding the waxing and waning of the solar year. But I will leave it to others to challenge the myth or Graves's interpretation if they so desire; I am content to allow that myths have more depth and levels of meaning than the surface or literal meaning.

The White Goddess develops the important idea that a new alphabet and a new religion are often closely related and can develop hand-in-hand. I have mentioned earlier the Coptic Christians; the Mormons of the mid-nineteenth century also tried to establish a new script with their "Deseret Alphabet" after they had made their way with Brigham Young

†6 †1 80 ? †1 †6 ‌‌‌‌4‌‌‌‌1 80.

Шᴈ ᴑᴑ †‌‌‌‌4. ‌‌‌‌‌Ꝑᴈ †6 †‌‌‌‌4. (Is it so? It is not so.

We go in. He is in.

Ꝋᴑ Ⴟ ᴑᴑ †‌‌‌‌4 ? ‌‌‌‌ᴊ ᴊᴑ †‌‌‌‌4 †1. Do ye go in? I am in it.)

Sample of the Mormons' Deseret Alphabet (with translation)

TtᴛTtTᴛTTtᴛᴛTttTtTᴛᴛTt

to the isolated American West. Their alphabet was short-lived, however, as the Mormons soon became assimilated into the more general American lifestyle and abandoned their dreams for a separate nation.

Even when a religion does not create a new language, it often helps to establish and codify languages. It has been said that our alphabet followed the sword with Rome, then the cross with Christianity—becoming established where those forces triumphed. Alphabets and languages both can often change rapidly until the language receives a canonical expression in a religious text, which then serves to restrain and stabilize the language. As Oswald Spengler pointed out, once a script has been canonically sanctified it retains its power even if other elements of the language continue to develop around it. "The conviction that the letters contain secret meanings, penetrated with the Spirit of God, finds imaginative expression in the fact that all religions of the Arabian world formed scripts of their own, in which the holy books had to be written and which maintained themselves with astounding tenacity as badges of the respective 'Nations' even after changes of language."

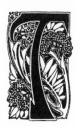 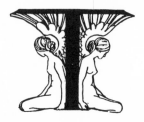 

In the ancient Semitic and Greek alphabets there was another T-related letter: *theta* in the Greek and *teth* in the Phoenician. Both represented variant [th] sounds. The Romans did not adopt *theta*, using instead the digraph TH to express the basic sound. (Some scholars believe that the Romans did use the sign for *theta* (Θ) to express the number 100, and in time it became simplified to the classic C-form Roman numeral.) Old English used two signs—the *thorn* and the *thok* or *eth*—to express [th] sounds. It is interesting to note in regard to Graves's comments about the letters D and T that the *eth* sign (ð) was created by Insular scribes crossing their d form. The *thorn* (þ) was

TtTTtTtTtTtTtTtTtTtTtT

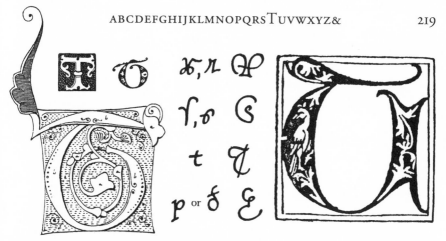

Decorative medieval Ts, with Old English handwritten R, S, T, thorn, and eth signs (center)

originally a runic sign—one of the two most influential on the English alphabet—whose merit was early appreciated. By the ninth century both [th] signs were used indiscriminately, the *thorn* becoming especially popular. With the advent of printing, there was no *thorn* sign in the fonts (which were usually cast on the Continent), so it was represented by the lower-case y, which it somewhat resembled. A misusage and contrived archaism is still found in phrases like "ye olde English pub," where what actually is being written is "the"—ye being not a synonym but instead a variant form of "the." In any event, the invention of printing hastened the dropping of these signs from the English alphabet, which, like the Roman, now uses the letters T and H in combination to represent all variants of the sound—although linguists complain that true pronunciation differences are not accurately reflected.

This last complaint is one common to all alphabetic writing systems. Good as the letters are, they are too few in number to accurately express

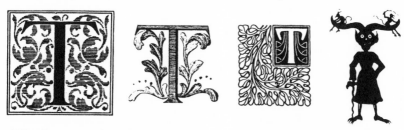

all of a language's sounds. Also, as languages and their pronunciation have changed, the orthography has not kept pace, remaining fixed in traditional or canonic forms. This condition is especially bewildering to foreign and beginning students of a language. English is especially notorious in this regard, and T has to assume a share of the blame. It has a variety of sounds between different languages and within the English language itself, including an unusual [sh] sound in some words. George Bernard Shaw provided a witty illustration of this in his variant spelling of the word "fish," which he maintained could as well be spelled "ghoti" by taking the gh from "enough," the o from "women," and the ti from "nation." Shaw was a great advocate of spelling reform and offered a substantial amount of money in his will to anyone who could devise a new and consistent English alphabet following certain basic principles. The prize remained unclaimed for a number of years, although finally a script that had 48 characters won the award and was used in a special edition of *Androcles and the Lion*. Thus far, however, it does not seem to have gained popular acceptance, and we remain with our familiar 26 letters. Therefore, for want of a better, let us continue our study of what we have.

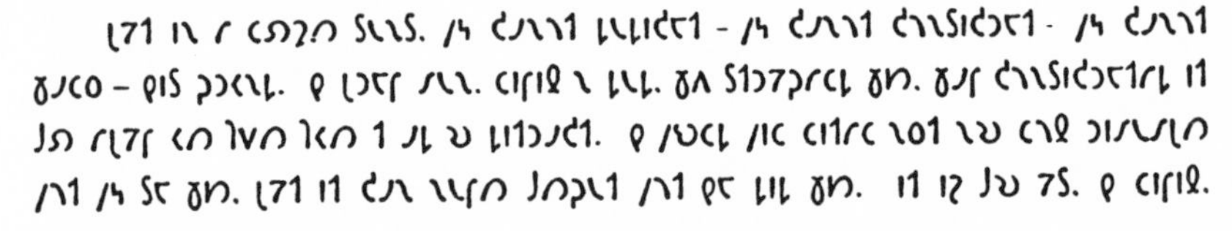

ᒐᒄ ᓇ ᒉ ᑕᘚᓄ Sᐧᓚᔕ. ᔭ ᘔᐱᓇᒐ ᒦᒥᐧᒉᒐ - ᔭ ᘔᐱᓇᒐ ᘔᐱᔕᒉᑐᒉᒐ - ᔭ ᘔᐱᓇᒐ
ᓍᒍᑕᐤ - �ᓚᔕ ᓴᑕᐢᒪ. � ᒪᘔᒉᒐ ᒥᐧᐧ. ᑕᒥᒉᘔ ᘁ ᒦᒪ. ᓍᐱ Sᒪᘔᒐᓴᒉᒪ ᓍᓄ. ᓍᒥᒐ ᘔᐱᔕᒉᑐᒉᒐᒪ ᒦ
ᒍᓄ ᒉᒪᒐᒐ ᑕᓄ ᒥᐧᓄ ᒈᑕᓄ ᒉ ᒍᒪ ᐢ ᒦᒐᒍᒉᒐ. � ᒍᘔᘔ ᒦᑕ ᑕᒦᒐᒐ ᑕᐧᒐ ᑕᐧ ᑕᒦᘒ ᒍᒥᒍᘒᒦᓄ
ᒦᒐ ᔭ Sᒐ ᓍᓄ. ᒐᒄ ᒦ ᘔᐱ ᒐᐧᒍᓄ ᒍᓄᘒᒐ ᒦᒐ �ᒐ ᒦᒦ ᓍᓄ. ᒦ ᒦ� ᒍᐧ 7S. � ᑕᒥᒉᘔ.

An example of text in the 48-character Bernard Shaw ("Shavian") alphabet

According to Tory, the first century writer Pedianus recorded that in ancient Greek criminal trials the letter *tau* was written by jurors on a slip of papyrus to signify acquittal, and *theta* for conviction. I am not certain that Lucian was aware of this usage of the letter T, which would definitely seem to work in its favor in a court of law; but, since T has remained in the alphabet despite the many attacks against it, it seems to have been assured legal success.

Zolar claims that *teth* "signifies an asylum, a refuge, which man provides for himself for his protection." Its number is 9. *Tav* "signifies

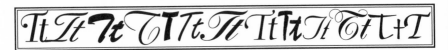

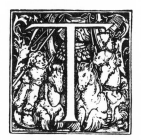

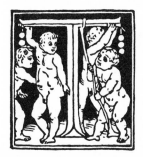

reciprocity. The ancient Egyptians regarded this letter as a symbol of the universal soul. It stands for sympathy and for perfection, of which it is the emblem." Its mystical number is 400. Besides the *thorn* sign, the runic alphabet had a sign for T called *tir* which is thought to have been the name of a guiding planet, star, or constellation. In Scandinavia, T is known as the letter of Thor because it has the shape of his "world-defending" hammer. Joseph Campbell, in his important multivolume work *The Masks of God*, mentions that for centuries Scandinavians have hung around their necks the T-shaped bone from the tongue of a sheep as a protective amulet. Others wore tiny gold or silver hammers or other T-shaped relics invoking the protection of Thor. Many Christians, of course, have worn a †-shaped cross for similar reasons. The wearing of protective charms, phylacteries, and amulets greatly antedates Christianity and has been practiced by many cultures. Special scriptures or charms are often inscribed on the amulets, but single letters and other signs of special power and significance also have been used.

T is one of the few Roman capital letters whose breadth can vary greatly in its pleasing use in calligraphy and typography, a fact that helps to explain even as it calls into question the common phrase, "it fits to a T" (which, it should be added, others say refers to precision mechanical drawing with a T-square). Like B and F, T also developed a somewhat elongated form in the Roman Rustic script, which helped influence its

Uncial, semi-uncial, various Insular, and two black letter forms of T

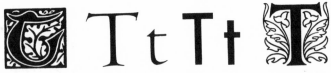

subsequent lower-case form. However, it was with the humanistic script of the early Renaissance that a true minuscule form of the letter developed, with an ascender rising above the cross bar and thus forming a more true cross. Earlier forms such as the uncial and semi-uncial had rounded the letter by curving the stem and base and lowering the cross bar. Still, it is surprising to most people studying the forms of t to see that the ascender is usually very low, almost always shorter than the ascenders of b, d, f, h, k, and l. Another distinctive design feature is that t is often made thicker at the base to avoid the appearance of falling backward. The cross bar has always remained essential to define the letter in all forms of T, and the phrase to "cross your t's" means to be precise, thorough and meticulous.

T is one of the most commonly used letters of the English language. In a serial order it signifies the twentieth (or nineteenth) place. In medieval times it was occasionally used as a symbol for 160. It is called the point-breath-stop consonant of Bell's Visible Speech scale. And, having made that point about our much used, oft abused letter T, let us take a breath … and stop.

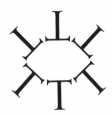

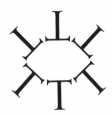

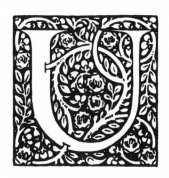

U IS THE TWENTY-FIRST LETTER of the English alphabet, and I shall consider it the twentieth letter of the Roman according to its representative sound—although the Romans did not commonly employ the present-day rounded shape for the letter, using instead the angular V. In other words, in Roman times the V sign had both a vowel and a consonantal sound, and not until Renaissance times were separate signs used to distinguish the two. Following the English order, I will first discuss the use of the Roman letter as a vowel and later focus on its consonantal variant.

U is one of many letters that can be said to have descended from the Greek letter *upsilon* (or *ypsilon*), which in that alphabet also designated both vowel and consonant sounds. Since the early Semitic writing systems did not signify vowels, there is really no Phoenician equivalent for the U. Also, those systems ended with T; both the Greeks and the Romans added other letters to meet their language needs. Many scholars believe that *upsilon* came to be adapted from the Semitic consonant *vau* (or *waw*). We have seen that *vau* briefly was also associated with the Roman letter F but was dropped from that part of our history at an early date, long before the classical Greek alphabet was formalized. In any event, the Romans derived their letter U (V) from the Greek *upsilon*, and it was used to signify the sounds [u], [v], and [w]. Its incised classic capital form was almost always the V shape; but in later written scripts U and V were considered interchangeable—either or both forms might be used, even in the same word and to express the same sense and sound. Not until the tenth century did the custom arise of writing V before a vowel and using U elsewhere.

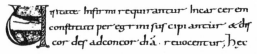

French writing from 9th century with rounded forms of U (left); Florentine incised letters from 12th century showing both U and V forms (right)

The U form did not truly develop until the advent of late classical–early medieval uncial and semi-uncial scripts in which many letter forms—including V—were rounded. These early forms closely resembled our modern letter U, yet the classic capital V was still considered the true form of the letter by the Renaissance theorists and designers, including Geofroy Tory. He illustrated only the V form of the letter in *Champ Fleury*, but discussed the fact that it represented both vowel and consonantal sounds. Tory related the letter to one of the three Graces, Pasithea—also called Aglaia (or Brilliance personified)—and it formed the right shoulder of his literate man. He mentioned that the Romans used the V to indicate the number five, as it is the fifth vowel of the alphabet. Other scholars have different derivations for this particular Roman numeral, as we shall see in the next section.

According to the *Chronology of Books and Printing*, "one of the earliest known attempts to distinguish between the lower-case letters u and v according to modern usage appears in *Dyalogus between Salomon and Marcolphus*, printed by Leeu, Antwerp," about 1492. Generally speaking, the U and V forms were considered interchangeable until about 1530, when they began to assume separate forms on the Continent. This development reached England by the year 1600; and by 1630 the lower-case forms (which were simply smaller versions of the capital letters) were commonly distinguished. However, V served as the capital

U u 𝖀𝖀 U 𝖀 𝖀 U 𝖀 u u

Uncial, semi-uncial, eight Insular, and two black letter versions of the letter U

form for both lower-case letters until about 1700, although Ronald McKerrow points out that rhymes and puns reveal that "the Elizabethans called V by the name we give to U." And as recently as the mid-nineteenth century the two letters were often combined under one heading in English dictionaries.

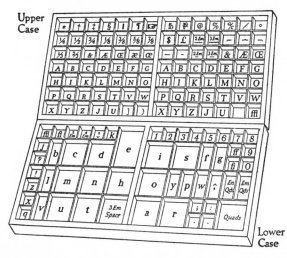

Upper Case

Lower Case

A pair of printer's cases from D.B. Updike's *Printing Types*

In the cases which hold the metal type letters or "stamps" that type compositors use in hand setting type (and which are the basis for upper- and lower-case terminology for the capital and minuscule letters), the compartments for the lower-case letters are of different sizes and are arranged according to how frequently the various letters are used. The capital letter compartments are in a case placed above the minuscules— hence the names upper and lower—and these compartments are in alphabetical order. However, exceptions to this are J and U, which are placed at the end of the order, indicating their late acceptance as full-fledged letters. A type compositor reads metal type as it is set—that is, reversed and upside down when it is set by hand. This ability may seem almost marvellous to the layman, but it is basically just a matter of practice and habit. And, as Seán Jennett points out, it helps illustrate that we could read in different ways and different forms, that our letter forms and writing tradition are a convention, not a necessity.

UuUuUUUUu*u*UuUuU*u*U

Although our writing tradition is only a convention, it is one that is so strongly ingrained as to remain virtually unthreatened by all attempts over the centuries to contravene or supplant it. Randall Jarrell called the conventions of grammar and capital letters "the last twigs on the tree of life." Changes almost always have been of a most subtle nature, occurring gradually over a great many years. Only very rarely are major alphabet changes sudden; however, the conversion of German printing from black letter to roman type was one that was. As S.H. Steinberg reports, this change was imposed by the German government. Originally, the Nazis had extolled black letter type as the natural expression of the Aryan soul. However—either because as their plans for world domination evolved they wanted a more universal type for propaganda purposes or because Hitler actually believed the notion—on January 3, 1941 it was decreed that "the so-called gothic type" had been invented by the Jews and, thus, roman type would henceforth be the "normal script" of the Germans. According to Steinberg, it was, "despite its nonsensical argumentation, the one good thing Hitler did for German civilization."

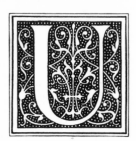 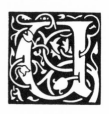 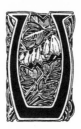

The new alphabets proposed by linguistic or artistic reformers have become mere footnotes and curious period pieces in the general history of writing. Some alphabets were never intended for general acceptance or even any actual use, however, being merely literary appendages or embellishments. These include what Geofroy Tory called Utopian or Voluntary letters—named after the alphabet devised by Thomas More in his *Utopia*. These letterforms are a literary conceit or exercise in ingenuity meant to give a flavor of authenticity to fictional accounts of the civilization of imaginary societies. Another example readers might

UuUuUUuuUuUUuuUuU

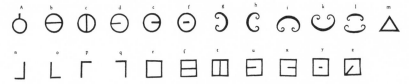

"Utopian" letters from *Champ Fleury*

have encountered is the novel alphabet in the Venusian stories of Edgar Rice Burroughs.

In the *Beth-luis-nion* alphabet, U was called *ur* or *ura* and corresponded to heather as well as to the time of the summer solstice. Among its connotations was "passion"—being sympathetic to summer's heat. In the runic alphabet, U was also called *ur*, but the meaning of the word in this script was an auroch or wild ox.

The vowel U has at least six sounds in modern English, plus others in various letter combinations and dipthongs. To call A, E, I, O, U the five vowels of English is to talk merely about the letters, not about sounds. English employs one of the greatest number of vowel sounds among world languages. The *Oxford English Dictionary* lists almost fifty vowel sounds that the five letters represent, as well as other sounds that result from vowel combinations. Although some of these sounds are duplicates—both A and E can represent the same sound, for example— it is little wonder that English spellings and pronunciations can vary so greatly. This situation of different letters sharing sounds can prompt intricate linguistic and philosophic speculation. Jacques Derrida wrote of "Differance"—the substitution of an "a" for the normal "e" can be "written or read, but it is not heard. It cannot be heard....It is put forward by a silent mark, by a tacit monument." It is a purely graphic distinction—the written sign clothing the sound, as it were. So what then is the difference between "differance" and "difference"?

UuUuUUuuUuUUuUUuU

Vowels were generally much more extensively used in letter mysticism than were consonants, vowels supposedly having a correspondence with the deeper mysteries, realities, and "soul" of the cosmos, whereas consonants were more mundane and this-worldly. Also, the fact that vowels were not written in Hebrew added to their mystical aura. According to an old hornbook rhyme, "A E I O U God's Great Name doth spell. Here it is known, but is not known in hell." Mystics of many persuasions found special significance in the seven Greek vowels, relating them to the major heavenly bodies: the sun, the moon, and the five known planets. One Gnostic version of the "real" name of God was composed of the seven Greek vowels: "Iaōouēe." The Gnostics also related them to the "seven heavens," and they inscribed them on magic triangles (one *alpha* at the top, then two *eta*s on the next line, and so on to seven *omega*s at the bottom) to be worn as amulets. According to Budge, amulets originally "were believed to give the wearer of them health, strength, virility and prosperity, and had a much closer relation to magic and medicine than to religion. It was the Gnostics who by adopting them gave them their religious significance."

Religious mysticism also made great use of the most distinctive attribute of vowels—their ability to be vocalized as "pure" sounds. There were some magical formulas involving consonants, but they could not be chanted without vowels and so were considered less powerful. Vocalization of sound often seemed more important than the writing of the letter signs, although there are examples of both types of practice. Such uses could be either sacred or profane. One famous example is the syllable AUM. As Joseph Campbell reports, the letter U is identified with the state of "dream consciousness (heaven and hell, that is to say)"; the

letter A relates to waking consciousness, while M is identified with "deep sleep…. The mystical union of the knower and the known, God and his world." Others have related AUM to the One Supreme Spirit manifested in the three personifications of Brahma, Vishnu, and Siva.

Chants and mantras were used in many cultures and periods to invoke or honor the gods. The vowels (especially the Greek seven) were frequently linked with Apollo and his seven-stringed lyre, thought to bring harmony to creation. Less harmoniously, the droll laugh-chant of Hell's devils in Goethe's *Faust* is "Aa! Ee! Ii! O! U!" (their "hornbook" obviously different from the one mentioned above). Most likely somewhere in between is a fifteenth century motto of Austria—A E I O U: *Austriae Est Imperare Orbi Universo,* which, in a like manner, freely translates into "Austria's Empire Is Over all Universal."

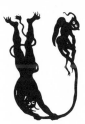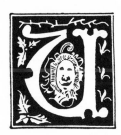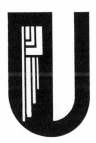

According to Rousseau, the vowels express passions, the consonants express needs. In his magnificent novel *The Recognitions,* William Gaddis wrote of a strange passion linked with the vowels in his character Friar Eulalio, "a thriving lunatic of eighty-six who was castigating himself for unchristian pride at having all the vowels in his name." Wellek and Warren write that E and I express thin, clear and bright things, O and U clumsy, slow and dull things. And Edmond Jabés likened words to bodies, the body parts being letters and the sex of the word-body always expressed by a vowel. Those more perceptive than I may be able to determine which sex and which vowels are linked.

U was linked with the color green by Rimbaud, who wrote of the "divine vibrations of green seas" in connection with the letter. In his essay "In Praise of the Vowels," Ernst Jünger makes a number of

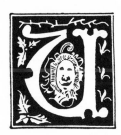

interesting comments about our fifth vowel. He says that U is the most difficult vowel to characterize. It expresses a more elemental deepness than does I. It evokes the dark source of being—the secrets of procreation and death. It is the ur-sound. It has deeper roots than does logic, and can involve the demonic, the ghostly, and the saturnine. As it relates to Life it involves the deep mysteries of the Mother and fruitfulness. It is the letter of Mother Earth (at least the German part). Through one of my unparalleled maneuvers, I have been able to relate Jünger's observation linking U and earth with a line from Thomas Pynchon's novel *Gravity's Rainbow*: "… sans-serif Us at the entrances to underground stations pointing in smooth magnetism at the sky to bring down steel angels of exaltation." However, I will leave it to Mr. Pynchon to explain exactly what he meant by this image. I just felt strangely drawn to it.

U Uu Uu U

When used in a serial ordering, U signifies the twenty-first (or twentieth) place. In chemistry and physics, U is one of the more well-known symbols of the nuclear age: it signifies the element Uranium. I do not feel anywhere near as drawn to this; however, the unstable quality of the uranium atom, and the energy and new combinations released through its ability to split apart or fission, can be seen to be appropriate for the letter that designates it—for our modern letter U is but a remnant, a split half, of an earlier whole. Our next section concerns the other part of this unit. To slightly alter the words and sense of a rather recent popular song: "I'm going to sit right down and write myself a letter; and make believe it came from U…"

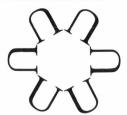

UuUUUuUUUuUUuuUu

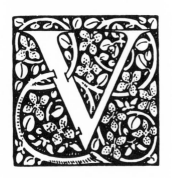

V IS THE MODERN LETTER that is the twenty-second of the English alphabet and what I will consider to be (along with U) a variant form of the twentieth letter of the Roman alphabet. Much of its history has been discussed already in our study of the letter U, since the two forms were not considered independent letters until the Renaissance and in some cases even well into the nineteenth century. Prior to this, from Roman times the letter U (V) had served as both a vowel and a consonant. I have chosen to consider U the basic ancient letter and V the variant form and later independent offshoot. Since their first representation by the Greeks, the vowels have generally assumed a dominance in discussions of the letters and their relative importance, representing as they do basic vocal sounds necessary for the articulation of any word, while the consonants serve to modify those basic sounds. To make things a bit complicated and confusing, however, it is the V form that the Romans most commonly used to designate both the vowel and the consonant sounds. Appropriately enough, the ancestry of the letters is also mixed: U and V are descended from the Greek vowel-consonant *upsilon* and from the ancient Semitic consonant *vau*.

In *Voyages and Excursions*, Victor Hugo conceived associations for the letters based on their shapes and was able to account for the confusion of U and V: "U is the urn, V is the vase (that is why U and V are often confused)." Though it might not convince scholars, it should charm them.

ΥͶΥVᐯVᐯᐱᵿᵿᵿᵿᵿᵿᵿᵾ

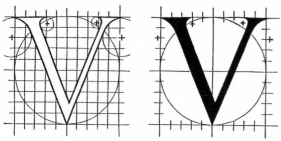

Tory's letter V

Although the vowels have generally been preeminent among the letters, there is an interesting exception. It is well known that the ancient Semitic writing systems did not contain vowel signs and that among the ancient Hebrews it was forbidden to write or even accurately pronounce the sacred name of God with vowels—signs or sounds. This resulted in the Tetragrammaton—JHVH—the common written name for what today we write "Jehovah," the God of the Judeo-Christian religious tradition. What is not as commonly realized is that the Roman name of their chief deity, Jove (Jupiter), could have been legitimately written in ancient times with all vowel signs—IOUE. For well over 1500 years the Judeo-Christian god has eclipsed the Roman deity, providing one example in which consonants have certainly attained a dominance over vowels—at least in some written representations of the metaphysical world.

As mentioned, the Romans and those who adopted their alphabet generally used the V form for both consonant and vowel sounds. The Romans and the English Elizabethans pronounced the vowel sound [u]; and, although a rounded U form had developed before the eighth century, there was no consistent usage and separation of the two forms until about the sixteenth century. McKerrow claims that in early English printing "v and u were differentiated according to position, not according to pronunciation; v being always used at the beginning of a word and u always medially." Trissino, the Italian Renaissance scholar, was one of the first to consistently use and require the V form for the consonantal U (that is, [v] or [w]) sound in his writings, as he also discriminated and distinguished between I and J. This division was well-established by the

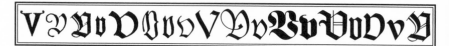

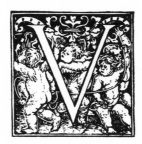
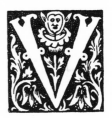

middle of the seventeenth century and was legitimized in dictionaries by the nineteenth century.

Long before Trissino, the first century Roman emperor Claudius proposed adding a new letter to the alphabet to signify the consonantal [v] or [w] sounds. The sign he proposed for the new letter resembled an upside down and reversed F (Ⅎ). In Robert Graves's novel *Claudius The God*—one of his two very accomplished fictionalized accounts of that most unusual Roman emperor—Claudius is portrayed discussing his linguistic reforms: "I pointed out that though one was brought up to regard the alphabet as a series no less sacred and unalterable than the year of months, or the order of the numerals, or the signs of the Zodiac, this was not really so: everything in the world was subject to change and improvement. Julius Caesar had reformed the Calendar; the convention for writing numerals had been altered....So with the Latin alphabet.... The Latins borrowed and altered these alterations of alterations....And still in my opinion the alphabet was not perfect." Yet, although the linguistic reform of Claudius was very reasonable and was officially adopted during his lifetime, the new letter did not catch on with the public and was soon abandoned.

Coin from Roman Britain portraying the emperor Claudius

Alphabets change, but not often radically or suddenly. Societal conventions or apathy can usually triumph over imperial decrees that seem to threaten or alter established writing traditions. Claudius should

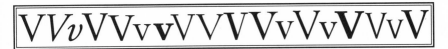

not really have expected a much better reception for his reforms. As our history of the letters U and V reveals, centuries of erratic usage generally elapse before alphabet changes become commonly used; additional centuries often pass before this use becomes formal and official practice. Even the possibility of major change seems to shrink as literacy becomes more universal and conventions more widely established. In modern times, great resistance to even relatively minor type design changes is common—at least for book typefaces meant for lengthy texts (we allow advertising and display types considerably more design latitude). As Warren Chappell points out: "As far as type is concerned it is helpful to realize that the letters of the alphabet, being symbols and abstract in themselves, are most successful when their forms come closest to being free from idiosyncrasy."

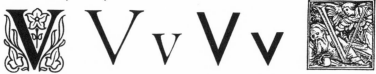

In her collection of essays, *The Crystal Goblet*, Beatrice Warde was concerned with the idea of typographic unobtrusiveness. In her mind, good typography was similar to a crystal goblet used for drinking wine, which should only elegantly contain the beverage while allowing its qualities to show through unimpeded. So, too, type should not call attention to itself, for it can thus become a "typographic impertinence" rather than being the unobtrusive vehicle of an author's thoughts. "Type well used is invisible as type, just as the perfect talking voice is the unnoticed vehicle for the transmission of words, ideas." Others have seemed to disagree, however—at least in practice, if not in theory. Ben Shahn wrote about his early impressions on immigrating to America: "It seemed to me there were thousands of letters in the American alphabet, all shapes and styles and sizes. They were intimidating, but also quite wonderful." Typefaces abound, many of which I'm certain could be found typographically impertinent by some people. Of course, as mentioned, with display or advertising type much more distortion of the basic letter shapes is allowed, since their first and foremost purpose is to

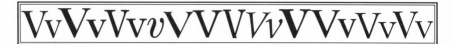

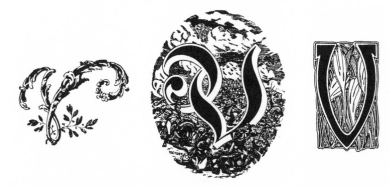

attract attention while, if need be, retaining only a bare legibility. However, the basic (strictly unanswerable) question remains even here: when does a shape cease to be a letter? Nicolete Gray probably has given as good an answer as any: "In my opinion the criterion as to whether a letter is an 'A' is whether the writer thought of it as such. This does not mean that all such 'A's are good, but that neither identity nor goodness are derived solely from conformity to the Roman letter. A letter must have identity to be recognizable, but this identity refers to a composite, flexible idea in the mind."

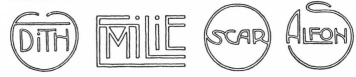

Distorted letter shapes in names by H. Nowack

Even if we do not consider advertising and display letters, the experienced reader is aware that different text typefaces—all seeking to be strictly legible and non-gimmicky—have different moods, tones, character, or feeling; and many designers feel that their true challenge is matching an appropriate typeface with a particular text so as to actually complement or even augment an author's work. According to them, the reason typefaces have proliferated is to serve different communicative functions. As Hermann Zapf wrote: "The projected purpose of a type determines its form in design. A type contrived for newspaper text will hardly be suited to a volume of lyric verses, any more than an evident advertising face would be for the rendering of a lengthy text."

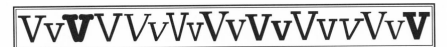

Perhaps the gap between these two design philosophies is not as great as it might seem, for many who value Warde's ideas could maintain that they also seek type that is harmonious with the ideas expressed in the writing, and that as long as the type doesn't distract from the text it is not an impertinence, even if it is not so unobtrusive as to seem transparent. But there is yet another challenge to the idea of invisible type, and that is type that consciously seeks to express the "spirit of the age," no matter what text it embodies—this despite the fact that very often writing naturally reflects its era. People familiar with the history of the alphabet and writing can often identify the time when a letter was written by its distinctive style—Rustic, uncial, Insular, Merovingian, etc. The same often holds true for printing types—Old Style, Transitional, and Modern types are characteristic of certain historical periods—and many claim that they reflect the spirit of their particular time. As Adrian Frutiger expressed it: "The human spirit of each century resounds from its type forms."

 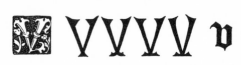

Three medieval decorative Vs surrounding four Insular and one black letter U-V form

In the twentieth century, although typefaces from many periods are commonly used, at least two major attempts have been made to construct letter forms reflective of the "modern" age. The first style, especially noteworthy from 1920 to 1940, was championed by the Bauhaus school and made use of sans serif type to echo the clean, spare functionalism of those modern times. It was successful to the point that sans serif types have become more commonly employed and accepted; but still no typographic revolution followed. In fact, with the passing of the years, the more blatantly "modern" book productions of those years became dated by their very distinctiveness. So, in that regard, they succeeded— but only in reflecting the spirit of that brief era, not that of the modern age or even of the twentieth century.

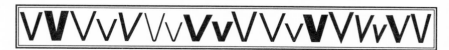

Attempts to make new alphabet signs distinctive and representative of our time generally fail when they stray too far from the basic letter forms, as they then appear artificial, contrived, or idiosyncratic. The later twentieth century technological revolution—computer type—has definitely affected typography, expanding its range but at the same time presenting new problems and challenges. At first, the aim was to create letter forms that could be easily read and generated by computers; unfortunately, however, they were not so easily discerned by humans. The challenge of designing characters for world-wide application, which would transcend language barriers, may yet serve to modify our basic letter forms in the years to come, although computer and software manufacturers soon were stressing that their products could produce regular roman type forms, and they no longer emphasize the more unusual computer letter versions of only a few years ago. Outline font design technologies as well as sophisticated design models and printing devices have now enabled computer generated type to achieve a high level of quality which technology should only further improve.

However, new challenges also have arisen. Alexander Lawson cautions about the wide gap that "currently exists between the technology's almost astonishing potential for excellence and the supply of traditionally oriented practitioners who are skilled in the construction of letter forms. Indeed, it is ironic that a machine with sophisticated abilities may be subjected to the caprice of an operator who lacks any understanding of traditional typographic practices." In addition, computer magazine articles and software manufacturers have encouraged individuals to

ABCDEFGHI
JKLMNOPQR
STUVWXYZ

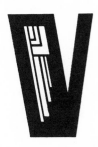

An early version of computer type (center) flanked by medieval and 20th century Vs

create "a font of one's own" by modifying existing typefaces or even by starting from scratch. The results should pose no serious threat to the existing letter forms, although, like an illegible handwritten scrawl, they may wreak havoc on a more personal level. But the experiment at least promises to "increase one's appreciation of typography."

As long as people must continue to personally deal with the cultural artifacts of our civilization—including books and manuscripts—it seems safe to assert that, despite the computer revolution, our letters will not change too radically in the foreseeable future. And human beings can still do things that computers can not. According to some authorities, a major problem with computer alphabets is that they have to be extensively programmed manually. Optical character recognition, that is, the ability of computers to "read" manuscripts, is generally quite limited because there is such great variation in how individual characters are written—for example, the computer might read one person's "l" as an "e" because it is shaped more like a traditional "e." Here, the human ability to discern and discriminate is much more rapid and accurate than is the computer's. And, though computers can be programmed to quite accurately "read" a particular individual's writing, they could then be even less able to recognize characters in another hand.

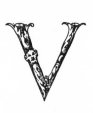 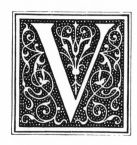

The letter V is one that is distorted in almost all of its parts by a dot-matrix system of computer printing—diagonals and curves having to be constructed by step-like blocks which, when enlarged, reveal extremely rough and jagged line edges in contrast with the clean knife edge of traditional forms. The lower-case v is but a smaller version of the classic capital. V was used by the Romans to express the number five. Many

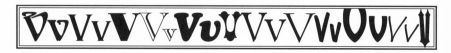

scholars believe that this derived from an early use of the fingers to designate numbers. One through four are easily understood as represented by the extended fingers of the hand. For the number five, the four fingers and opposing thumb are thought to have been extended in a V form, which became represented graphically as V. In modern times, Sir Winston Churchill extended the index and middle fingers in a V to represent "victory." Other politicians have adopted the practice, some with less reason or grace. With the protests of the 1960s, this form also came to signify "peace"—although the graphic symbol for that concept is a different form. Thomas Pynchon used the letter V as the title for one of his richly allusive novels; and Haydn's Symphony 88 is known as "the letter V symphony."

In chemistry, V represents the element Vanadium. In English, V's sound is technically termed the labio-dental voiced spirant. It is not generally used in serial orders—nor in cereal orders ("vheat" being about as close as you can get in English; and even then you will most likely get stares rather than wheat if you so venture to order). *Caveat lector!*

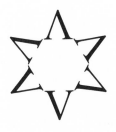

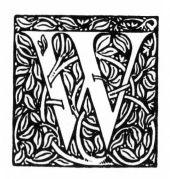

With W we wend our wondering, wandering (wary, weary?) way to the twenty-third letter of the English alphabet and the last of our alphabet additions unknown to the Romans. Like V, its near relative, it has a somewhat confusing history. It was originally descended from the Semitic letter *vau*, that most prolific of the early signs, being the progenitor of five letters of our modern alphabet—F, U, V, W, and Y. However, the W form was unknown in antiquity. In the ancient Greek alphabet the letter form F (*digamma*) represented a [w] sound. The Romans had no real use for this and used the Greek *digamma* in combination with an Etruscan sign to represent the [f] sound. Eventually F standing alone came to represent its modern sound, and the [w] sound was left without a sign of its own in the Roman alphabet. When it was used in Latin it was considered a modified consonantal U and was subsumed under and represented by the V sign.

Over time certain Romans realized that there was some use for the [w] sound, a need that the alphabet reforms of the emperor Claudius would have helped fill; but after his death they were soon discontinued, probably having been adopted, as Robert Graves says, only to gratify the emperor's fancy and not from any understanding of their utility and merit. According to some accounts, certain Roman writers adapted the Greek letter *omega* to represent the [w] sound—especially for transcribing Greek words. (In some Greek scripts of the Christian era *omega* was occasionally written like a W—particularly in its minuscule forms.) It

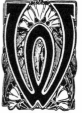

ewly

lefewy

Greek writing from c. 100 B.C. showing minuscule *omega* as w form (left; copied by Alexander Nesbitt); decorative *omega*-like W (right)

was due to this usage that some medieval and Renaissance writers referred to W as both a vowel and a consonant and considered the digraphs AW, EW, and OW to be independently articulated vowel combinations.

Despite these early forms and associations, we can fairly claim that the W as we know it came into existence in the Anglo-Saxon writing of the seventh century. Although the Roman Empire had extended into the British Isles, use of the Roman alphabet seems to have generally disappeared with the retreat of the Roman legions as the Empire declined. With the Anglo-Saxon invasion of about A.D. 500, the runic alphabet became the dominant script in Britain. Although different runic variant alphabets developed, they were basically used by Germanic and Scandinavian peoples. Runic writing is thought to have been based on an alphabet of Etruscan origin used by sub-Alpine tribes of northern Italy from the fifth century B.C. to the first century of the Christian era. It is thought to have then migrated northward, while being gradually modified in the process, and to have eventually settled in northern Europe, where it flourished between the third and twelfth centuries and assumed an aura of power and mystery.

First six (futharc) characters of runic script (left), with 14th century runic writing

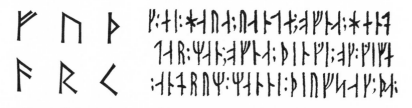

The name "rune" connotes a secret or mystery, and the alphabet was likely used by an elite priestly and ruling class. It was used more for talismans, marks, and brief inscriptions than for long texts; and it was almost always carved or incised on wood and bone rather than being written in pen and ink on hide or parchment. In the eddic *Havamal*, the god Odin (Woden) describes the runes as powerful enough to raise the dead; and in the *Prose Edda* it is recorded that Odin hung wounded from a tree for nine days as a sacrifice to himself in order to gain knowledge of the runes, which healed him and gave him wisdom. This respect for the basic power of letters was shared by other peoples. Budge reports that "letters to the early Hebrews were the essence of things and…the Romans described all human knowledge as 'letters,' using the word as the peoples of the North used 'runes.'"

The basic runic alphabet consisted of twenty-four signs arranged in three groups of eight, probably according to a magical principle or formula later forgotten. The alphabet was called "futharc" after the sounds of its first six signs. The Anglo-Saxon runic alphabet had thirty-three signs, but it fell into increasing disuse with the introduction of Christianity to Britain about A.D. 700—two hundred years after the Anglo-Saxon invasion. Only in Celtic Wales and Ireland did earlier Christianity persist under the onslaught of the Saxon invaders; but there was little intercourse between the two groups, the Celts seeming to hate the invaders too much to try to save their souls. However, by the beginning of the eighth century the missionary impulse prevailed and Irish monks began to reintroduce Christianity to England, accompanied by the Roman alphabet and their beautiful semi-uncial script. This spurred an awakening of education and literature. Some English monastic scribes tried to incorporate futharc into the Roman alphabet and Latin language, or at least find Latin equivalents for the runic script rather than suppressing it as pagan. As a result of their efforts, two runic signs—the *thorn* (þ) and the *wen* (ƿ)—came to be added to the Roman alphabet in Britain and continued to be used for centuries. These two signs (both somewhat resembling an angular lower-case p) are among the most distinctive and unusual found in Old English writing.

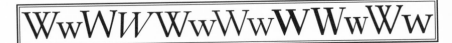

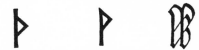

Thorn and wen signs with English courthand W (c. 14th century)

The runic letter *wen*, according to some authorities, is an English dialectical variant of the true name, *wyn*, which meant "joy." Its sound was close to the [w] sound used in the English language, which gradually supplanted the Celtic. Withstanding the Norman invasion of the eleventh century, English incorporated French words rather than being supplanted by French. The Norman Conquest did consolidate and expand the use of the Roman alphabet, and soon a practice began of using two U's or V's in combination to designate the [w] sound. At first, the most commonly used form was the rounded U, due to the influence of semi-uncial and gothic scripts, and the two U's were often connected in the process of writing them. Later, as the classic Roman forms came into renewed favor, the angular double V became the accepted form of the letter. The English name for the letter came from the vowel, however; and it seems fitting that both U and V thus contributed to the

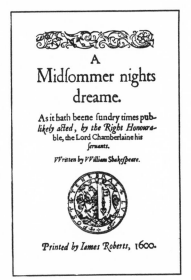

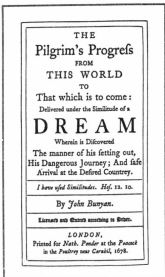

Title pages of two well-known English books, revealing changing W form in 17th century

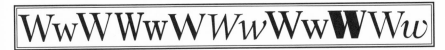

form and name of the new letter. Yet, if some people still feel that the appropriate name for the letter is "doublevee," most would probably concede that "doubleyu" is preferable to the letter's technical phonetic name—the "gutturally-modified bilabial voiced spirant."

By the time of the Renaissance, the new letter W had acquired enough power and popularity to eliminate the competing runic *wen* sign, which soon thereafter generally was dropped from English writing. In France and most of Europe the letter W was unknown at the time— Tory makes no mention of it in *Champ Fleury*. In time it became an accepted letter in the German and other northern European alphabets; but it has never been a full-fledged member of the Romance languages' alphabets, having only a very limited use in words of foreign derivation. So we can say of W that it might be joyous, but it's not romantic!

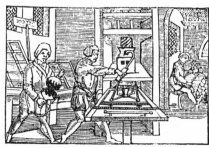

Initial W, and a woodcut of a printing shop— both from 16th century English printed books

Generally speaking, in the first years after the invention of print-ing—as in the period before—authors and printers employed the Latin language with its Roman alphabet. Soon, however, the alphabet was used in the service of the various European languages, and this tended to help define and consolidate them. More than most other countries, England kept its language alive during the early days of printing. This was due especially to the work of the great fifteenth century scholar and printer William Caxton, who printed eighty percent of his work— including Chaucer's *Canterbury Tales* and Malory's *Morte d'Arthur*—in English, thus helping establish the victory of English over Latin. His successor, the industrious printer (and mouthful of W's), Wynkyn de Worde, further consolidated the victory by also printing many books, including English language grammars, in the vernacular.

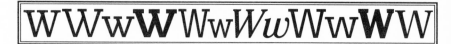

Ber kis/take compaynie With Wyse men and studie in their bookis/fle kfingers/for the lyers speth not but for Vnknowing of reason and of her saukes/the left farme that can fall to after/is that no man biketh him of nothing that he

Type from one of William Caxton's 15th century printed books

At an early date, the English language assimilated elements from many others—including, as we have seen, Celtic, Saxon, and Norman French—expanding upon its Germanic roots; and it continues to do so, adding words to the language from virtually all linguistic families. This keeps English a living, growing language; but spelling has lagged behind pronunciation changes, making English one of the most difficult languages to master. Not only that, but Philip Gaskell points out that until the late seventeenth century, printers setting type with justified (that is, even) columns employed many contractions and even intentionally varied the spelling of words to make them fit in the lines. Thus, for example, we find "do" and "doe," and "here" as well as "heere" intermixed in Shakespeare's plays and many other works of the period.

Interestingly enough, Noah Webster and other eighteenth and nineteenth century lexicographers and pedagogues who are honored for helping bring order to the tangle of words and their different spellings are partly to blame for the well known problem of English's idiosyncratic spellings and pronunciation. Ambrose Bierce defined lexicographer in his *Devil's Dictionary* as "a pestilent fellow who, under the pretense of recording some particular stage in the development of language, does what he can to arrest its growth, stiffen its flexibility and mechanize its methods." Before Webster's time spelling was variable—an art—able to keep pace with pronunciation changes. He and others who tried to make it an exact discipline unwittingly helped destroy one benefit of a phonetic alphabet—the correspondence between spelling and pronunciation. As a result, the spoken and written forms of the language began to drift apart—and the rift grows wider with the years. This has led to the half-humorous claim that to be able to spell correctly

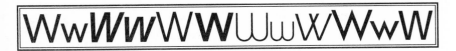

is a gift of God. It should be mentioned, however, that many "great" ones are perversely proud of their poor spelling and illegible writing, feeling that it shows them to be above those more clerical tasks. Preoccupied with "important" things, they cannot be distracted by such niceties. Hamlet mentions that once he "did hold it, as our statists do, a baseness to write fair." The implication, however, is that he changed his mind.

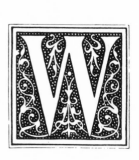 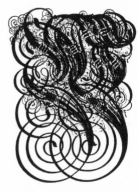 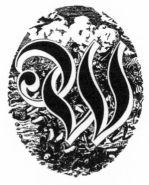

Mario Pei points out that "when a written form is achieved, the result is generally greater stability in the spoken tongue"; but English written forms were often standardized incorporating many unusual and often mutually inconsistent spelling–pronunciation correspondences. Consider what a nineteenth century doctor claimed was an accurate spelling according to the basic and accepted rules of English pronunciation: Ghoughphtheightteeau. What does it spell? Potato. "Gh stands for p, as in the last letters of hiccough; ough for o, as in dough; phth for t, as in phthisis; eigh stands for a, as in neighbor; tte stands for t, as in gazette; and eau stands for o, as in beau." (These potatoes seem to go quite well with Shaw's fish.) Though it is true that spoken forms of a word may not alter as rapidly once a written form is standardized, what changes do occur cannot be accommodated by easily changing the spelling. And languages are always changing.

The capital W is commonly the widest of all the letterforms in typefaces, even though many fonts use a contracted version which crosses the two interior arms of the letter. The poet Robert Southey commented on the fat and hungry look of certain letters in a printed sentence when he wrote: "And sprawling W's, and V's, and Y's, / Gaped prodigiously." In typical tests of the recognizability of type characters W is commonly found to be the most legible, probably in great part because of its width. Optically, the strokes of the W must be slightly curved at the bottom in order to appear straight. The lower-case form of the letter is a smaller version of the capital.

British writers have often poked fun at the poor taste or education of some Englishmen who mistakenly use the sound of the letter W in pronouncing certain words. Some of Charles Dickens's characters interchange the sounds of V and W, as, for example, in "winegar" and "vicked." Another common mispronunciation involves the substitution of W for R, as in "wubbish"—used in *The Pickwick Papers* and also, more recently, by Bugs Bunny's poor foil, Elmer Fudd, who further extended W's range by also incorporating L, as in "that wascawy wabbit!" and the wonderful "west and wewaxation at wast!"

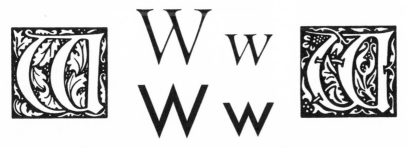

W is very seldom used in serial orderings. In chemistry, it represents the element Tungsten—which may seem a bit odd but is actually based on the original name of the element: Wulfram. Zolar, the twentieth century mystic, also uses W as the English equivalent of the Hebrew letter *vau*, which he writes *waw*. We have seen that it is the parent form of five of our modern letters, and he finds it to be correspondingly rich in mystic significance. Its mystic number value is six, and it "signifies the eye of man and becomes the symbol of light; it also represents the ear and becomes the symbol of the sound of the air; the wind....It is the emblem of water and represents the taste and the appetite. As a gram-

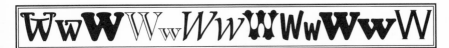

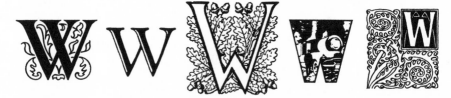

matical sign it is considered to be the image of mystery most profound and most incomprehensible, the symbol of the knot that unites, and of the point which separates Being and Non-being." After all that, maybe it should be called *wow!* instead of *waw.* What more can I say except to add that it is the first letter of many of the most common interrogatory English words, including what?, when?, where?, and why? Why, I don't know; nor what to make of it.

Why not continue our survey? When? Now. As Elmer Fudd might say: "No west for the vicked!" We can take that as a humbling reminder that we have not yet reached the point where we can claim all the bounties that Tory has been so lavishly promising us.

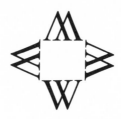

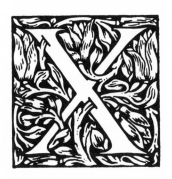

WITH THE LETTER X WE MARK THE SPOT where we finally return to a proper letter of ancient times. X is the twenty-fourth letter of the English alphabet and was the twenty-first of the Roman. It is descended from the Phoenician letter *samech*, one of their three [s] sound letters, but a letter of obscure origin and unknown meaning thought by various scholars to have meant a prop, a support, a post, or even a fish. Zolar, speaking of *samech*, relates it to S and claims that its mystical number is 60 and that it signifies hissing: "It is considered to be the type of a bow and esoterically represents the great cosmic bow, the string of which hisses in the hands of mankind." The Greek letter of related form and sound that was descended from the Phoenician *samech* was *xei* (also known as *xi* or *ksi*). The form of both the Greek and Semitic letters differed from the common X shape, which both scripts used to signify other letters. Nerdinger believes that the X was first used as an early landmark sign. In Plato's *Cratylus*, *xei* is mentioned as one of the letters expressive of "shaking, shivering, and windy" notions due to the great expenditure of breath used in pronouncing it. Its basic sound was—and remains—[ks].

The Romans adopted the basic [ks] sound from the Greek letter *xei* but assigned it to the X form of another Greek letter, *chi*, for which they, like the Etruscans, had no use. (Similarly, the Phoenicians had used the X form for their letter *tav*—ancestor of the modern letter T.) It is from the association with *chi* that many modern X forms, abbreviations, and symbols have been derived, particularly those associated with Christ—

for example, Xmas for Christmas. The use of X as a signature mark of the illiterate has been thought to represent the sign of the cross and to attest to the good faith of the individual. It is also possible that the phrase to "cross out" a mistake or error (as well as its graphic representation) could be associated with Christ crossing out a person's sins through His redemption and sacrifice, though the simple graphic explanation also makes sense. Further, the use of X at the end of notes and missives to represent a kiss may derive from an association with Christ and love, although it could just as well be derived from the [ks] sound of the letter.

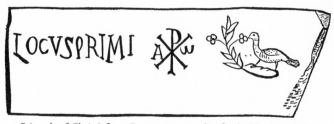

A "chrismon" (mark of Christ) from Roman catacombs, flanked by inscription and picture

Although a number of Greek words began with X, no Latin word did; and the Latin name of the letter—*ex* or *eks*—is a reversal of the Greek name, perhaps for that reason. Until about A.D. 50, X was the last official letter of the Roman alphabet. According to Geofroy Tory, X is one of the two double letters (*duplices*) of the alphabet, and therefore is not really necessary, for it represents the letters KS (and, for Tory, CS and GS) in combination. In late Latin, X became more commonly used, replacing earlier letter combinations—for example, "Rex" supplanted the earlier spelling "Regs" (from whence regicide, regent, regina, reign).

Tory related the letter X to the Liberal Art Dialectica—which, in English, is dialectic, or philosophical and intellectual dialogue, discussion, and argumentation. I have little argument, however, with his association of the letter X with the navel of his man of letters. It, being the center of the body, seems quite appropriate for this quintessential place-marking letter. Argument did continue to center on X, however, as to whether or not it was a legitimate letter of the alphabet. Although Tory, following Roman tradition, considered X to be a real if somewhat

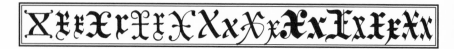

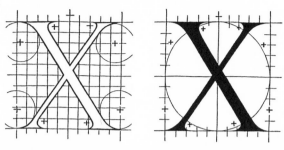

Tory's letter X

unnecessary letter, the English poet Ben Jonson was a bit more strict. In his *Grammar* he said that X "is rather an abbreviation, or way of short writing with us, than a Letter. For it hath the sound of *k* and *s*." Yet majority opinion has pragmatically sided with the party of Tory, and X has long been accepted as a full-fledged part of the English alphabet—although Bierce's acceptance was rather grudging: "X in our alphabet being a needless letter has an added invincibility to the attacks of the spelling reformers, and like them, will doubtless last as long as the language. X is the sacred symbol of ten dollars...." X has three phonetic values in English: [ks] (most common), [egz], and [z], which is used in all cases for initial X (symbols and abbreviations such as X-ray and Xmas being, of course, excepted).

A member in good standing of the alphabet it may be; yet, as it is in Latin, X is somewhat underemployed as a beginning letter of words, being the rarest initial letter in the English language. Most of the words it does begin are of Greek origin. X does get slightly more use in the bodies of words; but still not much, being twenty-fifth among the letters in relative frequency of use in the English language. Poe's story "X-ing a Paragrab" makes use of the common nineteenth century printing practice of substituting x for any letter of type that the compositors had run out of in typesetting copy for printing. I mentioned earlier that one of the characters in that tale—a newspaper editor named Bullet-head—had a great love for the letter O. In order to confound a rival editor who attacked him for his overfondness of that letter, Bullet-head responds by composing a paragraph in which the letter O was used in superabundance. Unbeknownst to him, however, his rival has sabotaged his type-

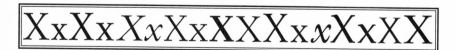

cases, absconding with all the O's. His apprentice, discovering the fact but facing a deadline to get the copy printed, follows traditional practice and substitutes x's for all the o's in the text. The printed result causes an uproar in the town. The townsfolk, seeing the mysterious paragraph, believe at first "that some diabolical treason lay concealed in the hiero-glyphics," and want to ride Bullet-head out of town on a rail. But he has already left, "and not even the ghost of him has ever been seen since."

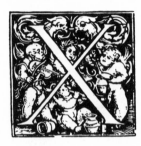

Trouble (and great humor) can also result from typographic errors in which the wrong letters or words are substituted, drastically changing the meaning. Familiar to many readers and most copy editors, such mistakes can happen regardless of the technology, but they seem to have been more common in those days when manuscripts were truly hand-written and type was set by hand. Many are spurious errors—as when George Moore wrote of "dew-drops from freshly blown noses" having been substituted for his intended "dew-drops from freshly blown roses." Some errors could occur when a type compositor accidently picked up the wrong characters or misread the original manuscript—such as with one of my favorites. The printer, misreading the writing, "His manners would adorn a drawing room," set the copy to read: "His manners would alarm a drowning man." To the printer, it must have been pretty bad handwriting; to me, those are awfully bad manners!

A discussion of the letter so commonly used as an abbreviation and also considered a kind of short writing by Ben Jonson seems an appro-priate place to briefly discuss more true systems of shorthand writing. The aim of such systems is to write quickly and succinctly, using easy-to-write symbols, which are often abbreviations of phrases, words, or

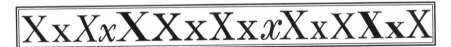

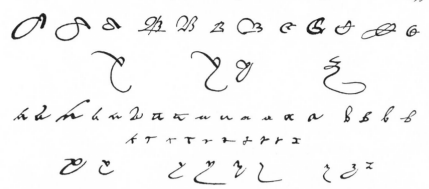

Elizabethan writing: various capitals ABCXYZ (above), and minuscules abcxyz (below)

syllables. They are not intended to be secret, as it is necessary for others to be able to transcribe the notes. It is known that as early as the fourth century B.C. the Greeks had developed a system of shorthand. The most famous shorthand system of antiquity is the Tironian Notes, invented, according to tradition, by Tiro, a slave of Cicero, who used them to transcribe his master's orations. As a reward he is supposed to have gained his freedom. Although some scholars doubt the story, the Notes proved to be very popular and influential, continuing to be used up to the thirteenth century. During the Elizabethan period when Jonson was writing, there was a great deal of interest in developing shorthand systems, mainly because of their utility to the rapidly growing mercantile and commercial class. Others used shorthand systems in their private diaries and notes—Samuel Pepys being perhaps the most famous of those diarists—but their motives no doubt also included the desire for privacy from prying eyes. Since the sixteenth century, well over 300 shorthand writing systems have been used in England and America, and more continue to be developed.

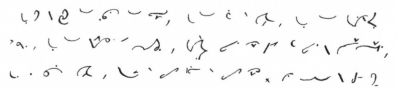

Sample of a popular shorthand system (Pitman)

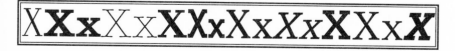

Uncial, semi-uncial, two Insular, two black letter and two medieval capital Xs

The lower-case x, following the pattern of the final letters of the alphabet, is merely a smaller version of the capital. In the semi-uncial script, however, one bar of the X descended. This form, which is occasionally found in medieval manuscripts, was rejected by Italian Humanistic and Renaissance writers, and other scribes quickly followed their lead. With the development of printed type this form was permanently dropped. Lower-case x has achieved some notoriety in printers' terminology. The classic Roman capitals are written as if they were bounded by two imaginary lines establishing their height. A minuscule or lower-case alphabet is written between four imaginary height lines to accomodate ascenders, descenders, and the smaller body size of the letters. This body size of lower-case type is called the x-height of the letters of the particular font of type since that letter clearly sets both measures.

$$AbCgHIj\ x$$

Letters illustrating use of four imaginary lines, the middle two establishing the x-height

It has been established that it is the top line of the x-height that the eye follows in reading. Experiments that split letters in the middle of the x-height with a horizontal line, first masking the top half of the letters, and later the bottom half, reveal that the top part generally conveys the letters' meaning while the lower part establishes a rhythmic coherence. That is, people can usually identify a letter when the bottom half is covered (especially when written in words), but not vice-versa. The better the alphabet or typeface distinguishes these two halves, the more legible it is generally found to be. As Donald Anderson says: "In effect, meaningful features hang on the top line of any string of lowercase letters." Anderson also makes an interesting observation about x and its fellow angular lower-case letters—k, v, w, y, and z: "Curiously, these late

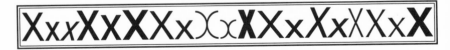

additions and refinements of the original Latin alphabet retain an echo of geometric Greek inscription letters, and they are difficult to compose within the group and with other letters. They lend the necessary variety in visual content that makes our lowercase alphabet interesting, but they do not appear often enough." However, Alfred Fairbanks felt that "some letters of our alphabet are much more likeable as shapes than others." He preferred A, B, C, D, and E to V, W, X, Y, and Z.

X is used as the Roman numeral ten. Some scholars believe that it derived from two V (that is, five) forms—one placed over the inverted other—supposedly stemming from such a use of the two hands and their fingers in primitive counting systems. Certain medieval mystics related the Roman numeral X to the concept of Justice. X is also used to denote a member of a serial order; but in the twentieth century it has achieved much more prominence and notoriety in rating systems, particularly of motion pictures, where it represents something suitable for adults only, usually due to sexually explicit or, less often, extremely violent material. To many, X-rated means obscene, immoral and pornographic, synonymous with "smut." To others, such a rating could hint at Art—unfettered as is proper. To most of either opinion it piques curiosity about the work in question to find out why it received such a brand.

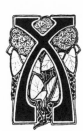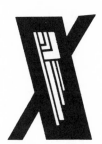

In chemistry, X stands for the element Xenon. In mathematics, x is used as a symbol for an unknown or variable quantity. This algebraic use relates to perhaps the most common and enduring use of the sign—that of X to mark a location, usually of something hidden and unknown. This very ancient usage has come down through the millenia and makes use of X more as a simple geometric figure than as a letter of the alphabet;

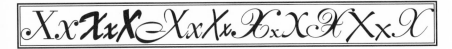

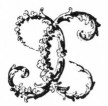
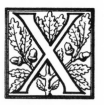

but perhaps it is because X is also a letter that phrases using it have become common in the language. The phrase "X marks the spot" comes neatly to the pen, the tongue, and the imagination.

Victor Hugo wrote that "x signifies crossed swords, combat—who will be victor? Nobody knows—that is why philosophers used x to signify fate, and the mathematicians took it for the unknown." It is merely a coincidence, but a rather appropriate one, that scholars do not know the meaning of the runic name—*eolhx*—of that script's X letter, although some believe that it may mean "elk."

Not all unknowns are considered alluring or promising, and X can also be a letter or sign of mystery, danger, or warning. X-ray, of course, is a radioactive ray, symbolizing a threat as well as revealing what would otherwise be hidden and unknown. Because of its resemblance to the crossed bones symbol of pirates and poison, X has often been used to represent the dangerous. Wallace Stevens perhaps had this in mind when he wrote of "the vital, arrogant, fatal, dominant X." Stevens, who often mentioned alphabets and various letters in his poems, seemed to find X one of the most noteworthy. In another poem, Stevens referred to "the big X of the returning primitive"—possibly alluding to the associations of X with illiteracy as well as to its pre-literate importance as a basic sign. Again, possibly not; yet if I am in error, his use of the letter then fits well for me with its connotation of the unknown.

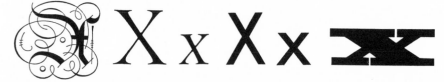

Various forms of X, including a decorative script typeface and a distorted x-shape Fat-face

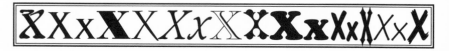

Much can be made of the meaning of the mysterious letter X in literary analyses as elsewhere, and often the search can reveal a treasure. Frequently, however, the mystery is to be found in the mind that conceives it, the reality being perhaps as simple as the substitution of one letter for another in a printer's paragraph because the correct letter could not be found—as in Poe's tale. After the darkest imaginings and fears subsided, opinions on that affair varied. As Poe relates it: "One gentleman thought the whole an X-cellent joke. Another said that, indeed, Bullet-head had shown much X-uberance of fancy. A third admitted him X-entric, but no more....The more common conclusion, however, was that the affair was, simply, X-traordinary and in-X-plicable." And with that, we have an X-ellent place to end our X-cursion.

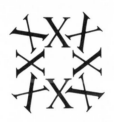

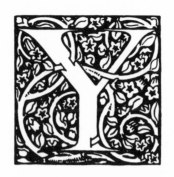

We have marked the spot of X, the letter of mystery, and now come to a letter of even deeper and richer significance—Y, which for more than 2000 years has been seen as the philosophical letter, the letter of destiny. It is the twenty-fifth letter of the English alphabet and was the twenty-second letter of the Roman. It is also one of the five modern letters descended from the Semitic letter *vau*. The Greeks used *vau* as the basis for both the vowel *upsilon* (or *ypsilon*) and the consonant *digamma*. From Roman and medieval developments of the alphabet it has become the ancestor of F, U, V, W, and Y. Nerdinger believes that the Y sign (like X and V) was originally an ancient landmark symbol.

The letter Y itself was actually a late Roman addition to the alphabet. Although both the Semitic *vau* and the Greek *upsilon* had variant Y-shaped forms, that form was originally neglected by the Romans, who used the V-shaped variant for their letter U (V). At first, the Romans did not include Y among their letters, but in time, with the influx of Greek words into their language, they revived the form and used it with the [y] sound for the Greek vocabulary additions. Some believe that the letter was created as early as 80 B.C. during the time of Sulla, although other scholars (perhaps referring to the widespread use and acceptance of the letter) date it from late in the first century A.D. The new letter was added to the end of the alphabet along with the letter Z. It was regarded by many Romans as somewhat of an intruder, hardly belonging to a proper alphabet. Before the Y was adopted, the early Romans had occasionally

ΥꟿΥΥꞒΥΥꞒꝴꟲꝴꞄ𝒴𝒴ꝴ𝓎𝓎

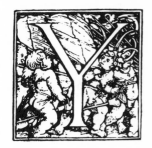
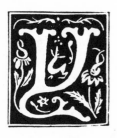

Medieval versions of Y, two of which feature stems turned to the right

used a V in the spelling of Greek words, and also used I as a consonant to express a [y] sound.

It is not from its history, however, but because of its shape, that Y has been called the philosophical letter. Since at least the time of Hesiod (eighth century B.C.), Y has been seen as the symbol of moral decision—the choice between two paths—and has been important in Greek, Roman, Gnostic, and Christian mystical thought. Xenophon, Cicero, and Virgil are among the important writers who have discussed the letter; but Geofroy Tory summarizes the essential thought as well as anyone. He calls Y the letter of Pythagoras, the Greek philosopher who, according to tradition, invented it. Others have also called it the Pythagorean letter and the Samian letter, after the island of Samos, the home of Pythagoras. According to Tory, Pythagoras invented the Y, "in which letter he represented the age of adolescence, when youth is drawn toward pleasure or toward virtue; the allegory being that Hercules, that is to say, man inclined toward virtue, when he was…walking one day through the fields alone, and lost in thought, came to a broad road which forked and divided into two roads, one of which was very broad and the other very narrow; and on the broad road was a dame named Pleasure, who held out her hand to him to bid him come; and on the narrow road was another named Virtue, who likewise wished to make him enter upon her road."

Tory made a special drawing of "this divine Pythagorean letter Ypsilon" to help point out the allegory and the moral choice to be made by all of us Herculean souls. The upright stem of the letter represents adolescence, the broad arm is the road of pleasure, the narrow arm the path of virtue. He drew this picture in order "that you may make of it a guerdon of your good memory and virtuous contemplation, to hang in your study and closet. On the slope of the road of Pleasure I have drawn and attached a sword, a scourge, rods, a gibbet, and a flame, to show that at the end of Pleasure wait and follow all lamentable ills and grievous torments. On the side of the road of virtue...I have placed and attached the figures of a laurel wreath, palm leaves, a sceptre, and a crown, to give it to be known and understood that from Virtue proceed all pure glory, all reward, all honor, and all royal preeminence."

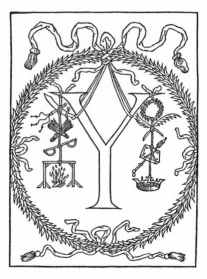

Tory's first drawing of the "divine Pythagorean letter" Y

Among those who have called Y the Pythagorean letter was Felice Feliciano, the first Renaissance letter theorist and designer. An example of its related representation in classical times is found in the poem *"De Y littera"* by the Latin poet Maximinus, which begins: "The letter of Pythagoras, divided by its fork into two horns, seems to proclaim the meaning of human life." In the twelve stanzas of the poem, Y is described as the symbol of existence which, starting from the straight path of its beginning, divides into the narrow and difficult way of virtue and the broad and comfortable road of vice—an interpretation which was held

YyYYyYYyyYYYyYYyYyyYyY

to be propounded by Pythagoras. The connection between Y and that philosopher has continued and been carried into English literature. A couplet from Alexander Pope's *Dunciad* re-echoes the tradition:
"When reason doubtful, like the Samian letter,
Points him two ways, the narrower is the better."

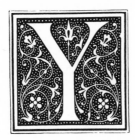

Various forms of Y, including a three-forked decorative version (left)

As the reader has had many occasions to note, an alphabet is a conventional system of graphic signs representing spoken sounds. We find instances where certain letters appear to be unnecessary, the sounds they represent already covered by other letters; and, conversely, we often find a seeming shortage of letters, one letter having to do many tasks, representing sounds with seemingly arbitrary impunity. Any alphabet is an imperfect tool—the very paucity of signs which makes it truly functional works against the fully accurate representation of language sounds. The problem is further complicated when an alphabet created for one language is adopted by people speaking another language with different sound components and requirements. Such is the case with our own alphabet, coming from the Phoenician through the Greek to the Roman and then to the various European languages—all with different needs and elements. Compounding this is the evolution of pronunciation within a language while the orthography generally remains much more static and conservative—leaving us with archaic spellings where the pronunciation of some words has often changed radically. Difficulties always exist, even though they may not be as terrible as those encountered by the Ephraimites in the Old Testament. (That slaughter is, unfortunately, only one example of the mispronunciation of a test

YyYYYyyYyYYyYyYyYYYYyYyY

word leading to the mistreatment of those whose language or dialect did not employ the sound. History records Saxons killing Danes, Sicilians Frenchmen, and Englishmen the Dutch using similar methods.) Even "sacred" letter constructions are not immune from variations. The Tetragrammaton—the Hebrew four-letter designation of God—which I have written JHVH from "Jehovah," is also known as JHWH and YHWH from the variant spellings "Jahweh" and "Yahweh." It is a bewildering state of affairs for students of all languages—and English is one of the most notorious problem cases. All of which is perhaps just to say that the alphabet is not "as easy as ABC"...or XYZ, for that matter.

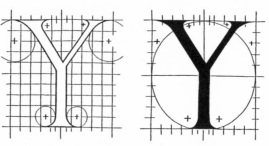

Tory's letter Y

Which brings us back to the letter Y. Being a Roman adaptation, related to U as both vowel and consonant, Y had both a modified vowel and consonant value. In English, the letter has also represented both types of sound. In fact, although it is commonly regarded as a consonant, according to the O.E.D. Y has five vowel sounds and only one consonantal sound. Also, though Y has a historical connection with U, its common English vowel sounds relate more to I. (If one tries to pronounce Y followed with a [u] sound, as, for example, in *ypsilon*, the result is a type of [i] sound.) This goes back to medieval traditions. In Old English, the letter Y represented an [i] sound which scholars consider to be a mutation of [u]. It was used commonly and alternately with I. According to some scholars, after the twelfth century y was used to represent ii. I discussed earlier how the i came to be dotted and how the j form was used to distinguish two adjacent i's. The idea is that this ij form became joined by the calligrapher's pen into a ÿ, which soon became a Y form proper. By the middle of the thirteenth century, with

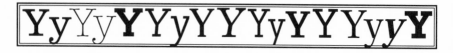

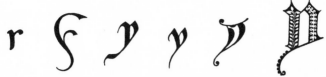

Uncial, Insular, three black letter, and one medieval decorative version of Y

the dominance of the angular and quite illegible black letter scripts, y was occasionally used to break up a line of lower-case letters—being used especially for i with m's, n's, and u's in order to promote legibility and ease of reading. With the invention of printing and the coming of standardized type forms for each letter, the i was generally restored to its common use, and y was used at the ends of words, before i, and to represent the letter V in Greek words.

Y became a popular letter in English—much more often employed than it was in Latin. Curiously, it is the frequency of its use that leads some critics to maintain that the English language is not as well suited to the basic Roman alphabet as was Latin. Frederic Goudy expressed it: "Lower-case y is difficult to make so that it will not appear to 'rain' tails through a page if the tail of the letter is not just right in length and shape." Latin uses relatively few descenders, and many calligraphers and printers feel that this makes for a more attractive written page than does English with its frequent descenders, a great many being y.

The runic sign for Y was a relatively new sign, found only in the English runic alphabet. Its name was *yr*, but its meaning is uncertain—perhaps "bow." Rudolf Koch, speaking of Y more as a geometric sign than as a letter, says it was called the *furca*, or fork, and was a medieval symbol for the Trinity as well as having its Pythagorean moral connotations. As mentioned, y was used as a substitute for the runic *thorn* sign in some pseudo-archaic constructions.

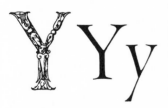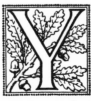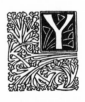

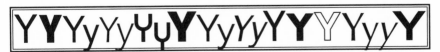

Y is known phonetically as the voiced palatial spirant. It is used in serial representations and is often seen designating the penultimate unit. In chemistry, Y stands for the element Yttrium. In mathematics and in Logic it is the second in a set of unknown or variable quantities, which Pynchon probably alludes to in *Gravity's Rainbow* where he writes: "Most of his calculating these days is with marks and pfennigs, not functions of idealistic r and ø, naive x and y."

And, even if naive, Y's meanings or allusions are certainly varied, as Victor Hugo appreciated: "Have you noticed how picturesque the letter Y is and how innumerable its meanings are? The tree is a Y, the junction of two roads forms a Y, two converging rivers, a donkey's head and that of an ox, the glass with its stem, the lily on its stalk and the beggar lifting his arms are a Y. This observation can be extended to everything that constitutes the elements of the various letters devised by man."

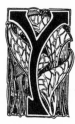 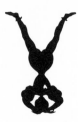 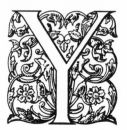 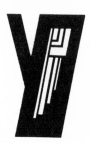

Oh, yes! After bringing him along this far, I would hate to leave Tory's man of letters at an unknown fork in the road. Y forms his left shoulder, and is related to Aglaia (Brilliance), one of the three Graces. The attentive reader will note that Tory related the letter U to the Grace Pasithea—commonly also known as Aglaia—whereas the third Grace is generally known as Thalia. But, as Thalia is also the name of one of the nine Muses, Tory obviously tried to take a simple path by omitting Thalia from the Graces and using both names of one to distinguish two separate Graces. Thus, the seemingly easy path becomes difficult.

Although Tory may have taken the wrong path in this matter, his standards regarding the alphabet were high. In this he anticipated by a few hundred years Eugen Nerdinger, who wrote: "The alphabet is to be

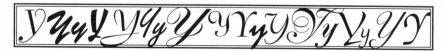

sure a servant, but not a prostitute; it is to be used but not bought." However, Nerdinger felt that often it was bought and misused for advertising and commercial purposes. It also has been a victim on the altar of Progress—for example, in the nineteenth century when type design and quality suffered in the interests of printing speed, and more recently with the ungainly early computer alphabets.

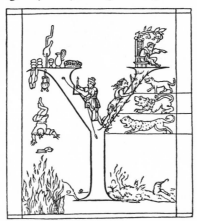

Tory's second didactic drawing of the letter Y

Our age has achieved magnificent technological capability but little true concern for letterforms. So, let us take leave of our moral letter with advice from Geofroy Tory: "Look well to it, therefore, o ye young children, and leave not behind you the knowledge of well-made letters —the true buckler against adversity and all ills, and the means to attain to the supreme felicity of this mortal life, which is perfect virtue; which at the last bestows upon us the prize of honour, the wreath and the palm, leaving the slothful and the vicious behind, to perish wickedly in their ordure and their execrable life." To reinforce the point, he also added another drawing of the letter Y, that "you may make such profit of it as you can, taking in good part my humble diligence in giving you pleasure and honest service."

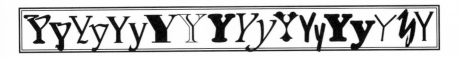

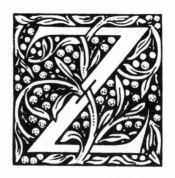

WE CONCLUDE OUR STUDY of the individual letters with what I can call a happy ending—the tale of a letter cast out from its place, reviled, and then forgotten until recalled from seeming oblivion to answer the need of its fellows and once again join the honored ranks in battle against the inarticulate, illiterate unknown. Let the reader be informed!—we have here a comedy, not the tragedy (s)he may have thought.

Z is the twenty-sixth and final letter of the English alphabet; it was also the last (albeit twenty-third) letter of the classical Roman alphabet. Originally, however, it was the seventh letter of the Roman alphabet and was descended from the Greek letter *zeta* and the Phoenician letter *zayin*, both of which were also among the first letters of their respective alphabets. Each of these letters represented a basic [z] sound, and both had a similar form—akin to a modern capital I, but with extended bars or serifs at the top and bottom of the stem. The Phoenician *zayin* is thought by some scholars to mean a dagger (although, frankly, it would seem to be a rather blunt one); however, Nerdinger believes that the sign was an inversion of an early N sign, relating to lightning. In the mystic realm, Zolar informs us that the Hebrew letter *zayin* (or *zain*) "signifies whistling and applies to all piercing noises which penetrate the air and reflect themselves in it. As a symbol it is represented by a stroke, a dash, or an arrow. Everything that tends to a given point. As a grammatical sign it is the abstract image of a tie which connects things with one another." Its number is seven.

The early Roman alphabet borrowed the sign with its [z] sound from the Greeks; but the Romans had little use for the sound, which for their purposes was adequately covered by the letter S. The early I-form Z thus fell into disuse and, according to tradition, was finally abolished from the alphabet about 312 B.C. by the censor, Appius Claudius Caecus. Its place in the order was taken by the new letter G, leaving the developed alphabet of the Roman Republic with twenty-one letters.

During the last centuries of the Republic, increased contact with Greece led to Greek words becoming more common in Roman usage. To meet the greater need for the [z] sound, the Romans at first used an S and then a double S to represent it. Finally, in the first century B.C., the more recent Attic and Etruscan Z form began to be used, and by the middle of the first century A.D. Z was again a fully accepted letter of the alphabet. However, all was not as it had been before—besides having a new form, Z also joined the new letter Y at the end of the alphabet instead of assuming its former place.

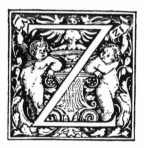

Although restored to the ranks of the letters, Z, like Y, was still considered by many Romans to be an interloper; they were not fully legitimate letters because they were only used in the spelling of Greek words. The Romans called the two letters by their Greek names—in the case of Z, *zeta*—an exception to their general rule of phonetic names for the letters based on the simple sounds of the particular signs. The English name for the letter—zed—derives from the Greek and Roman name, while the American name—zee—follows the general Roman and English letter-naming practice. This letter is therefore also exceptional in having two different names within the same language group. This is unusual, but not too surprising considering the many names that the letter has had throughout English history. One early English name for Z was "izzard," which probably derived from the French *et zede* ("and z"), from the custom of putting in an "and" before the last letter in oral recitations of the alphabet. Other recorded English variants of the letter name include zad, zard, ezod, and uzzard.

Z was seldom used in Latin documents of either Roman or medieval times, yet at least two minuscule forms still developed. One was a smaller version of the classic Roman capital, which we are familiar with today as the lower-case type form of the letter. The second version featured a descending hook shape, somewhat approximating and probably influencing certain modern cursive handwritten forms of the letter.

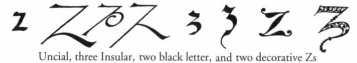

Uncial, three Insular, two black letter, and two decorative Zs

Even though Z has had an unusually turbulent history in and out of the alphabet in its various forms and with its different names, it must again take a back seat to the alphabet itself. According to many scholars, it is "a rather incredible fact" that we still use any of the letters of the Roman alphabet, let alone use as models for our letters forms that were created more than 2000 years ago. The advance of the alphabet is even more remarkable when it is recalled that it was essentially devised more than 3000 years ago for a Semitic language. Although different modern languages employ variant spellings, auxillary marks, and a few different characters to help make the basic Roman alphabet suitable for their purposes, that alphabet remains easily recognizable across widely divergent language boundaries. So, if the triumph of Z is great, that of the alphabet is even more noteworthy.

ABCDEEFGCGLHIKLMMNNOPQRST VX Z

ABCDEFGHILMNOPQRSTVXKUWYZ

Carved letters from the 8th to the 10th century (top); imitative version of early Roman letters drawn in the 20th century by Edward Johnston (bottom)

ZzZzzZzzZZzZZzzZZZZzZ

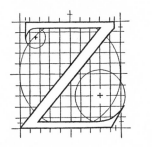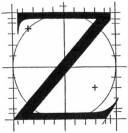

Tory's letter Z

Doubts continued to be expressed about the right of Z to a place in the alphabet even long after Roman times, however. Many Englishmen also considered it to be unnecessary. In *King Lear*, Kent exclaims to Oswald: "Thou whoreson zed, thou unnecessary letter!" thus rather effectively making known his opinion of the latter (and the letter). In Shakespeare's time, Z generally was omitted from contemporary dictionaries. In the ancient Irish *Beth-luis-nion* alphabet, according to Robert Graves, the equivalent of Z was a double S, which was considered a subdivision of S and, like it, related to the lunar month beginning April 15 and to the blackthorn tree. Geofroy Tory considered Z to be one of the two *duplices* or unnecessary letters of the alphabet. To him it represented a double S or also an SD in combination. He quoted the Latin writer Martius, who said that Z was not a true letter but rather a double hissing sound. Appius Claudius, who was said to have abolished the letter, detested it "because, when it is pronounced, it resembles the teeth of a dead man, who usually has his teeth all awry."

Geofroy Tory, however, was not a man to let the last official letter of the alphabet go by without finding something more positive to say about it, something appropriate to his analogical method. Therefore, he also quoted Celius Rhodiginus, who wrote that "Zeta is not only the name of a letter, but signifies the seat of the judges and masters of the Chamber of Accounts in the old days in Athens…before whom those persons were summoned and compelled to come who were in arrears and did not pay in full." I would have to agree that Z is an extraordinarily powerful letter if it could command the attention and dread it now takes three letters to fill—I.R.S.!

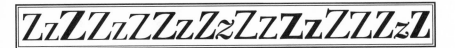

Tory went on to find even higher levels of significance for the final letter. "I can say that the worthy ancient fathers covertly and purposely placed this as the last letter in alphabetical order, to indicate that those who are perfectly accomplished and learned in well-made letters are inspectors and sovereign judges of the revenue and of the knowledge of the seven Liberal Arts and of the nine Muses, without knowledge of whom man can be neither learned or perfect." The reader who feels sufficiently accomplished may wish to try this argument in answering a tax audit or in applying for the position of Tax Commissioner. Tory himself, content to tax his readers' patience, related Z to the Liberal Art Grammatica (Grammar) and to the groin of his man of letters—which I will leave to the individual reader to fit into the rest of the analogy as he or she so desires.

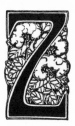 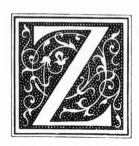 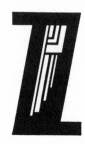

The paean continues. "This noble letter Zeta contains within itself every token of perfection. I have so drawn it below that the seven Liberal Arts and the nine Muses with their Apollo are placed therein in such marvellous proportion and disposition." Tory's drawing includes steps cut in the angled cross-member of Z. "These steps signify in allegory the upward path to beatitude, which they can follow easily enough who have perfect knowledge of well-made letters, and of arts and sciences. In connection with which I have drawn above the letter a small divine spirit, standing upon his feet ready to award the crown, the sceptre, the palm, or the laurel wreath to all those who shall well and diligently labor to acquire learning, rising from step to step, even to the state of perfection." So, if Y can be said to reveal the path, Z can be seen as the final ascent to our goal…even if we have to carve toeholds into the form to reach it.

ZzZzZzZzZzZZZzZzzZZ

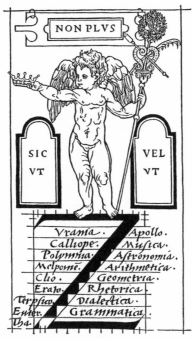

Tory's drawing of the letter Z with a "small divine spirit"

We thus find that, far from being disgraced at the end of the column, Z is the most honored rear-guard of our conquering alphabet army; or, to vary the image somewhat, Z is the caboose of our freight train of thought, where one can find more comfort and honor than in the boxcars ahead. That is probably more than sufficient as far as varying of images goes, and we could perhaps well attend to one writer's words: "He was headed straight as a Z for immortality." In a more truly poetic vein, William Blake, a man deeply concerned with "the upward path of beatitude" that Tory associates with the letters, wrote that "Poetry admits not a Letter that is Insignificant." Stretching his intended meaning somewhat, we can apply it to the alphabet itself, in which a disgraced and rejected letter like Z not only can be returned to the order but credited with great significance and importance as well. In fact, in relating Z to lightning, Victor Hugo also related it to God, the heavenly source of that power—represented in Greek mythology by the chief god and lightning bearer, Zeus.

ZzZZzZZzZZzZZz1ZZzZZz11

Z is commonly the last of any alphabetic serial order and has come to be used allusively for the "end" of something, as in the phrase, "from A to Z." In representing the finish, Z has also come to have connotations of accomplishment, learning, or mastery. As to know the ABCs about something is to be well-prepared to begin, so to know the XYZs is to have mastered the subject. Wallace Stevens referred to this when he called Z the "polymath"—one who is outstanding in his or her learnedness, having great understanding in many areas of knowledge. In the poem "An Ordinary Evening in New Haven," Stevens writes of "twisted, stooping, polymathic Z, / He that kneels always on the edge of space." The last line not only imaginatively relates to Z's shape, which can be seen as a kneeling attitude, but also places Z at the end of the order, adjacent to the as yet inarticulate void.

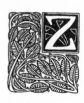  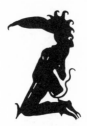

To have escaped the void is in itself a small triumph; it is much better to be the last of anything than not to be at all—as is pointed out in the story within John Irving's fine novel *The World According to Garp*. The characters are assigning a letter rating to an establishment especially displeasing to them: "'They have fallen past Z,' said old Johanna. 'They have disappeared from the human alphabet.'" Z did not.

Z is known phonetically as the "blade-open-voice-consonant." In mathematics it is a symbol for the third of a set of unknown or variable quantities; and it is used abstractly in Logic (if not always logically in Tory's—or this—abstract).

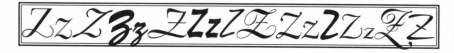

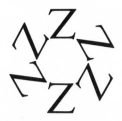

I shall leave it to a "small divine spirit" to award sceptres, laurels, or palms to those readers who feel they have earned them—such a spirit should know the reader's heart, sincerity, attentiveness, and comprehension better than I. In keeping with our themes of ascension to beatitude and perfection, and the comedic resolution typified by the letter Z, I just wish to remind the reader that in his *Divine Comedy*, Dante, as he ascended in his vision toward the unspeakable majesty of God, beheld that angelic beings of light formed letters in order to honor and praise the Divinity. Which letters they were is not recorded; but I would not be surprised, and would feel it to be quite appropriate, if *each* letter was represented in the blazing heavenly display.

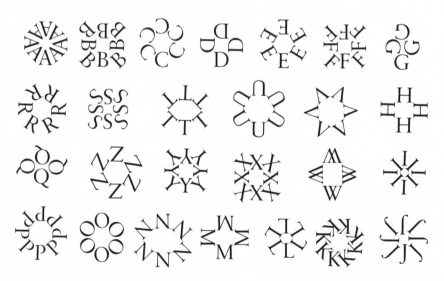

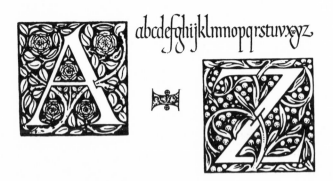

abcdefghijklmnopqrstuvwxyz

THOSE WHO HAVE READ *The Divine Comedy* no doubt realize that Dante did not conclude it with Canto 18 of the *Paradiso* in which the poet saw the heavenly letters of light near the throne of God; he had a bit more of which to stand in awe and report. Similarly, I feel that if the individual stories of the letters are so noteworthy, a chapter devoted to the entire order together is eminently fitting. And, throughout history, much interest has centered upon the alphabet as a whole.

The basic order of the alphabet has remained remarkably consistent since it was first established as we know it with the Phoenician script. Although letters were added or dropped by successive groups who employed the system, and though the letter forms were often altered or refined, the basic alphabet has remained recognizable. In some ways, of course, it is not too surprising that people becoming literate would retain their basic model, even if they did not fully understand it—as was the case of the Greeks with the Phoenician letter names and their meanings. It is more surprising that after being adopted the alphabet was so infrequently altered, the signs being retained and stretched, as it were, to fit different languages' requirements. Exactly why the ancient Semitic alphabet originally was put into its particular order is not known, although a few theories on the subject have been mentioned. Whatever the reason, the order is of great antiquity and has been confirmed in ancient writings as well as by many archaeological relics, including student writing tablets and instructional devices. For example, scholars

ABCDEFGHIJKLM

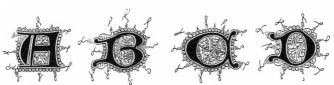

maintain that Psalms 9 and 10 (among other biblical examples) appear to have been an acrostic corresponding to the traditional letter order.

There is a long-standing belief in the alphabet as a power-laden microcosm of the universe. During medieval times, the letters often were written on the floor of a church or cathedral at its dedication to represent all of God's creation being sanctified. According to Peter Metz: "When a church is consecrated, two lines of ashes are drawn along the floor, each crossing the other, to opposite ends. This cross has the shape of an X, the initial of Christ. Into this form the bishop writes the Greek and Latin alphabets, the alphabets of the Church which has become the spiritual home of the nations of the earth." Somewhat related is the mystical idea that the alphabet is the expansion or articulation of the all-encompassing ecclesiastical signs Alpha and Omega. In almost all known periods and cultures the entire alphabet has been used in chants, recitations, and lists to help release the latent power of the letters. A more mundane power or wisdom still practiced today is found in the advice given to Augustus Caesar by Athenodorus of Tarsos: recite the alphabet silently before taking any action when angry.

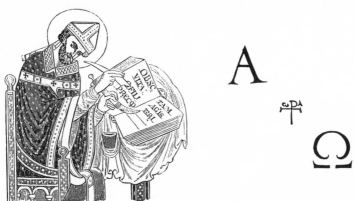

St. Dunstan writing, from old manuscript (left), with Alpha, Omega and chrismon signs

A custom of Strassburg was recorded in 1665 in which a pious man on first waking recited the entire alphabet because it would contain all possible prayers—leaving it to God to order and arrange the letters into the words He wished, for He knew best what should be asked for and done. The phrases, "Alpha to Omega" and "A to Z," referring respectively to the complete Greek and Roman alphabets, generally have come to imply a complete system or the whole knowledge of something. Such a phrase usually implies an accomplishment reflecting knowledge or honor. William Styron used it effectively in *Sophie's Choice*: "To tell what a great human being Max Tannenbaum is I must use the entire English alphabet! From A to Z I will tell you about this beautiful man." Occasionally, however, the concept can reveal depths of anguish or frustration well expressed in Don Gibson's song lyric: "I've thought of everything from A to Z; Oh, lonesome me!"

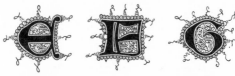

Most of us feel that it is easier to learn the alphabet "A to Z" than to accomplish the equivalent in other areas of learning and life. Young children (and poets) might certainly (and rightly) disagree. The thrill of accomplishment many of us felt upon first reciting the alphabet without error has generally faded in our memories and been further dimmed by the fact that being able to recognize and use the individual letters in reading and writing is a longer, more gradual process without an equivalent moment of triumphant achievement. The accomplishments are worthy of celebration, however, and are not always easily come by. History records that in the second century A.D., a young son of Herodes Atticus was having difficulty learning the alphabet. His father, a wealthy Athenian, devised a pedagogical aid beyond the means of most concerned parents. He took twenty-four of his slaves, equipped each with a sign depicting a letter, and had them parade in front of and attend his son until the youth learned the alphabet. (It is not recorded, but I think it safe to assume that another method was used to teach the boy to read

𝔄𝔅ℭ𝔇𝔈𝔉𝔊ℌ𝔍𝔍𝔎𝔏𝔐

and write.) And, in Dickens's *Pickwick Papers*, the elder Sam Weller voices the opinion: "Vether it's worth-while goin' through so much to learn so little, as the charity-boy said ven he got to the end of the alphabet, is a matter o' taste,"—possibly articulating the sentiments of certain readers of this book.

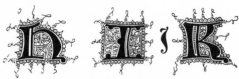

Through our regular association of the letter signs with the sounds that they represent, we generally fully equate the two—only A and a are the signs for the sound [a] and are nothing else;...and so on down the line with B, C, D, etc. Yet the letterforms are only a conventional representation. Throughout history those forms have been used for decorative purposes with no alphabetic association. On the other hand, many systems have been experimented with that substitute other figures for our conventional letterforms. Any graphic device will serve the purpose—all that is required is consistent usage and a societal convention; that is, one that can be taught to prospective readers of the new script. It is likely that thousands of such scripts have been devised—many frivolous or for the sake of amusement only, such as the Utopian alphabet of Sir Thomas More, others seriously intended "improvements" on the alphabet. None, however, has successfully challenged the

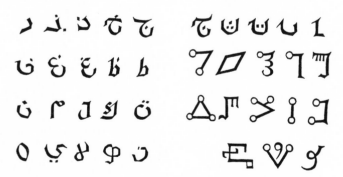

Tory's drawings of certain unusual letters from various scripts

accepted system; all have lacked the popular support necessary to effect any major change. Still others were formed for more esoteric purposes: to be used by the knowledgeable few and kept hidden from the many. These range from playful schoolboy ciphers to extremely serious Kabbalistic variant scripts using unfamiliar symbols.

In a somewhat related vein, many alphabetic substitutions have been created for special purposes. One such is the "Flower Alphabet," in which certain flowers are designated to represent the letters. Using such a system, lovers can send messages through the bouquets they present to the objects of their affection. Unfortunately, there is no universal standard system—although there are a few claimants to such—so one should be certain his beloved is using the same system in deciphering the meaning of the bouquet, or he may have an unanticipated response! Other substitution systems are more widely known and conventionally accepted—including naval flag and light codes, Morse code, and Braille. All of these have proven extremely valuable in answering the special requirements they were designed to fill.

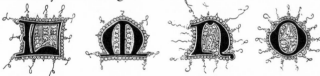

The English names of the letters, with so many ending in the same vowel sound, are very poor when used for verbal identification; therefore, operational names have been devised. One of the most common systems is: Alfa, Bravo, Charlie, Delta, Echo, Foxtrot, Golf, Hotel, India, Juliet, Kilo, Lima, Mike, Nectar, Oscar, Papa, Quebec, Romeo, Sierra, Tango, Uniform, Victor, Whiskey, X-ray, Yankee, Zulu. Of course, other names can be (and have been) used.

A rather different case of special letter substitutions is ciphers, which are meant to be undecipherable to anyone without the key. Ciphers have been used since ancient times, but are generally found only where writing is a common practice; writing itself is an esoteric mystery to most people in less literate periods and cultures. Julius Caesar employed ciphers in his military campaigns, and scientists including Galileo and

A B C D E F G H I J K L M

Huygens used anagrams and ciphers to establish that they had made certain discoveries yet keep that knowledge concealed from others. To be a true cipher, whether simple or complex, a pattern must be followed, however well disguised it is. This pattern is what cryptologists seek to disguise and what cryptanalysts look for. Without such a pattern there is only a random grouping of signs, meaningful only to the individual who created it. The idea of a cipher is to communicate with others, though the intent of the cryptologist is to restrict that communication to a select few. In order to enlarge that reading audience, cryptanalysts employ methods based on the frequency of letter use in the language. Tables of frequency have been made for the individual letters and also for bigram and trigram combinations of letters. There is rather remarkable consistency in the frequency of letter use in languages—even in relatively brief passages of text. In normal, unspecialized English texts the most widely used nine letters account for approximately 70 percent of the signs.

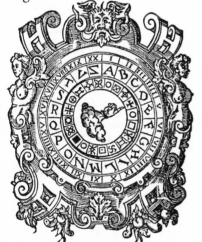

ฮธ21 ฮฟ๋ฮป I ๋ฮ ฤ2ฮง
This   table   servith

8ฤ๋ ฮ6 ๋3ฮ๋๋ 23 ฮ6
for   to   enter   in   to

ฮงฮ ฮฟ๋ฮป 68 ๋ฮฤฮ
the   table   of   equa-

ฮ263 68 ฮงฮ ฤ630
cion   of   the   moñe

63 ๋2ฮงฮ๋ I2Rฮ
on   either   side

Drawing of 16th century cipher disk of Giovanni Porta (left); and a cipher by Chaucer from *The Equatorie of the Planetis* (c. 1390)

Cryptanalysts categorize three basic frequency groupings of letters: 1) high (E,T,A,O,N,I,S,R,H); 2) medium (L,D,C,U,P,F,M,W,Y); and 3) low (B,G,V,K,Q,X,J,Z). According to Frank Higenbottam: "The re-

N O P Q R S T U V W X Y Z

markable characteristic is that the high-frequency group will invariably consist of the same letters in the same order, whatever the text, provided that it is reasonably long. The letters in the medium-frequency group are also remarkably consistent, although their position in the group may vary from text to text. The low-frequency group is also very consistent, with the rare letters always turning up as Q, X, J, and Z." *Brewer's Dictionary of Phrase and Fable* alters the order slightly while confirming it in essentials. It set up a table where the most commonly used letter was used 1000 times. The corresponding use of the other letters was as follows: E-1000, T-770, A-728, I-704, S-680, O-672, N-670, H-540, R-528, D-392, L-360, U-296, C-280, M-272, F-236, W-190, Y-184, P-168, G-168, B-158, V-120, K-88, J-55, Q-50, X-46, Z-22. Used as initial letters of English words, the order of frequency is: S,C,P,A,T,D,B,M,F,I,E, H,L,R,W,G,U,O,V,N,J,Q,K,Y,Z,X. In English, French, and German, E is the most common letter. In Italian, E, I, and A are all about equal; in Russian, O is used most frequently. Vowels make up about 40 percent of an English or German text, 45 percent of French, 47 percent of Spanish, and 48 percent of Italian and Portuguese. Using such information, no matter what signs have been substituted for the letters (whether other letters or strange marks), cryptanalysts can eventually work out the original pattern of correspondences, given a sufficient amount of text. In theory, no monoalphabetic substitution cipher is unbreakable, although in this era of complex machine-generated, one-time use ciphers, many are in practice. Poe's story "The Gold Bug" is perhaps the most famous of the many examples of the use of ciphers in literature.

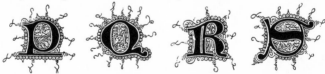

I have mentioned that studies of the legibility of typefaces have also been done. Much, of course, depends on the faces chosen to be tested as well as the different readers testing them; but from the various tests some general results emerge. One test involving twenty-six different typefaces resulted in the following ranking of Roman capital letter legibility (from

abcdefghijklmnopqrstuvwxyz

most to least legible): W,M,L,J,I,A,T,C,V,Q,P,D,O,Y,U,F,H,X,G,N, Z,K,E,R,B,S. According to the researcher, Miles Tinker: "Legibility was attributed to letter form (least important), letter size, heaviness of typeface, width of white margin surrounding letter, position of letter in letter group, and shape and size of adjacent letters." It has been found that distinctive, characteristic parts of letters (such as the stroke of the T, the curve of the J, etc.) should be clearly defined for maximum legibility. A typical test for lower-case letter legibility revealed the following order (most to least legible): k,d,q,b,p,m,w,f,h,j,y,r,t,x,v,z,c,o,a,u,g,e,i,n,s,l. Individual capital letters are generally found to be more legible than lower-case forms; but words in lower-case are more legible than words constructed with capital letters—revealing that familiarity plays a great part in legibility.

It may be surprising to many to learn that some of our most frequently used letters are also considered to be among the least legible. But we have had ample opportunity to see that much relating to the alphabet is quite surprising and not always strictly rational (or at least expected). A further example is provided by the typewriter: its standard keyboard is known to be inefficient and slow and, in fact, was designed to be so. The father of the typewriter, Christopher Sholes, laid out the familiar keyboard in the 1870s after it was discovered that his first machines kept jamming when typists went too fast. To slow them down, he spread the most common letters all over the board and made it so that common combinations (such as "ed") had to be struck by the same finger—the slowest motion. Although the mechanics of the machine gradually improved, once the keyboard was well established there was great resistance to change. Recently, however, a new keyboard pattern has been gaining popularity and is said to be able to increase the output of the average typist by about fifty percent. In contrast to printed type, which establishes different widths for each letter, the typewriter letterforms are distorted through their less variable widths since each letter is set within a uniform space, resulting in the distinctive look of typewritten material as contrasted with printed typography.

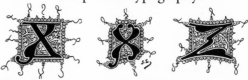

A through Z—the series as we know it is complete. There are other alphabets and other letters, but the English alphabet has retained the preceding twenty-six for more than 300 years, and they have generally proved adequate to its purposes—and perhaps even excessive to some who have completed this survey. To paraphrase William Blake, every letter has been studied and "put into its fit place." And, while I'm at it, another phrase from the Talmud will add an appropriate note of importance to the enterprise: "The omission or addition of one letter might mean the destruction of the whole world." Pretty important stuff, no doubt.

And it is, in fact. When Alphonse de Lamartine said that "letters are symbols which turn matter into spirit" he was referring, of course, to the grouping of letters into words to accomplish this miracle. That is the primary function of the letters; and it is more than a lifetime task—so that one can never truly claim to know the letters "A to Z." It is this on-going miraculous power of the letters in combination that underlies

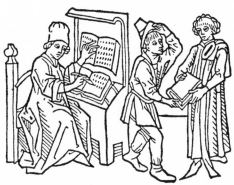

Woodcut of scribe and bookseller from a book printed in Germany in 1491

many of the grandest pronouncements regarding the alphabet. As Emanuel Geibel said, the alphabet is the greatest human achievement, "for in it lies the deepest wisdom; yet only he can fathom it, who truly knows how to put it together." And thus, patient reader, we have examined this greatest of accomplishments from A to Z, and completed a book…but not a task, hope, challenge, and promise. That lies beyond the "sniffing drainpipes" that Bob Dylan linked with merely reciting the alphabet. We have examined the keys on the ring; the challenge now is to unlock the doors.

In *One Hundred Years of Solitude*, Gabríel García Marquez wrote of a mysterious condition—a loss of memory—afflicting the inhabitants of Macondo: "Thus they went on living in a reality that was slipping away, momentarily captured by words, but which would escape irremediably when they forgot the values of the written letters." It would be wise to realize that we all inhabit such a Macondo, facing such a plight. John Irving expressed a similar idea on a personal and perhaps more poignant level in his most famous novel: "'Ar,' he moaned. He had lost the *P*. Once a Garp, then an Arp, now only an Ar; she knew he was dying. He had just one vowel and one consonant left."

Perhaps I should let Geofroy Tory have the last words on the subject—the words with which he concluded his own discussion of the Roman letters. "From letters one makes syllables, from syllables words, and from words discourse. Do your duty by them."

NOPQRSTUVWXYZ

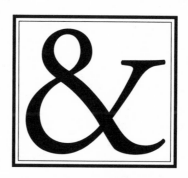

AFTER MUCH THOUGHT AND DELIBERATION on the matter, I have
concluded that since Tory had the last word in his book on the alphabet,
I did not need to let him have it again in mine. For those who are
beginning to wonder if this book will ever end, I will first note that the
true study of letters is more than a lifetime's task which I am hereby more
fully assisting; but I will also promise that this is the concluding section
of the present book—the appendix, if you so desire, after having deemed
the preceding chapter the epilogue. This is a healthy appendix, I hasten
to add—its removal would leave an unsightly scar and unfortunate gap
in our ideal man of letters.

This section is concerned with some of the auxiliary marks and signs
of our language: signs that are not proper letters but are important in our
use of the alphabet. Let us begin with the & (ampersand) sign itself—
one of the most widespread international abbreviations. It is said to have
been devised in 63 B.C. by Marcus Tiro as part of his 500 Tironian Notes
or shorthand system. According to William Mason, it is actually a
ligature combining the letters of the Latin word *et* ("and"). The old-
style form, &, distinctly shows the two letters. The English name of the
sign is actually an abbreviated form of its meaning: "and per se and ..."
(that is, "and by itself, which is and"). In his *Handy-book of Literary
Curiosities,* William Walsh recorded an amateur etymologist's amusing
derivation of the name: "The sign & is said to be properly called
Emperor's hand, from having been first invented by some imperial

"'&!@#–$%-^*( )—...æ≤

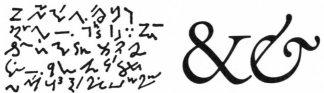

Example of Tironian Notes (left); with two forms of the ampersand (right)

personage." Donald Anderson writes: "The early printers were devoted to manuscript styles, and in attempting to reproduce them in type they were caught in a trap. They felt the necessity of making characters of every ligature, accent mark, abbreviation, and mark of punctuation occurring in Greek or other manuscripts. Gutenberg had to design almost three hundred different letters, ligatures, and abbreviations. Today we use about forty characters in the lowercase, with seven or less ligatures. The ampersand is the only abbreviation."

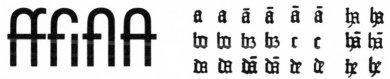

Various f-ligatures (left); and a few ligatures and alternate letters used in Gutenberg's Bible

Other signs have also been commonly associated with writing, most notably those found on the typewriter keyboard. Many of these are actually ideographs—that is, they directly represent an idea or concept—and as such are a remnant of an early stage in the development of writing. These signs include quotation marks, punctuation marks, apostrophes, parentheses, and diacritical marks. Interesting explanations and comments are associated with many of them. For example, according to Mason, the dollar sign ($) is probably a modified figure eight denoting a "piece of eight"—eight reales—a Spanish coin at one time of about equal value to a dollar. The section mark (§) was probably derived from the initial letters of the Latin *signum sectionis*—"the sign of the section." The interrogation mark (?) is described by Bilderdijk as a combination of the first and last letters of the Latin word *quaestio*—"question"—placed one over the other as was a quite common early

+=[]{};:,./<>?¡£¢¥∞§¶•—≠'""

practice in writing abbreviations: Q̊. This was later simplified by cursive scripts and printing types to the modern form. The same authority says that the exclamation mark (!) is formed from the Latin word *io*, meaning "joy," written vertically: ᴵₒ. It also was later simplified to our modern form. This explanation, I'm certain, would have pleased Geofroy Tory. Many would be pleased by reading *ABC Et Cetera* by the brothers Humez, in one chapter of which punctuation is charmingly examined. Also, the recent *Elements of Typographic Style* by Robert Bringhurst is an incredibly valuable resource, including information on punctuation.

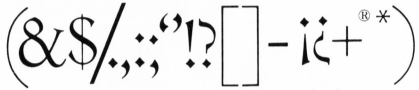

A few of the commonly used alternate characters and marks

Not all punctuation marks have been used consistently. In the sixteenth and seventeenth centuries parentheses and square brackets were used for emphasis the way we now use italics, boldface type, or quotation marks. In fact, use of the two apostrophe marks before and after quotations was not common until late in the eighteenth century. Even today many authors do not use them, instead often employing long em dashes (—) or guillemets (« »), and thereby reminding us that our language signs are a convention, not a necessity.

In their earliest stages, Greek and Roman writing did not use any form of punctuation. Later, in some classical inscriptions we find the beginnings of word divisions either with a space or a dot centered between the words. Gradually the space between words became more popular and was quite common by A.D. 600. The dot was used somewhat irregularly to designate phrases or full sentence stops. In some early manuscripts the punctuation mark for a stop was the same as our colon—two vertical dots (:). Later, one of the dots was dropped. The remaining dot served as a period, colon, or comma depending on whether it was placed even with the top, middle, or bottom of the minuscule letters. The Carolingian minuscule script is the model for our modern practice,

SICEQVIDEMDVCEBAM.NIMOREBARQVEFVTVRVM
FEMPORADINVMERANSNECMEMEACVRAFEFELIT
QVASEGOTETERRASETQVANTAPERAEQVORAVECTVM

A EDEM·ISIDISTERRAE·MOTV·CON
AFVNDAMENTO·P·S·RESTITVIT· HVN C·DECVRIONESOB
CVM·ESSET·ANNORVM·SEXS·OR DIN I·SVO·GRATIS·AD

Roman inscriptions without divided words (top), and with word divisions (bottom)

although it was somewhat influenced by earlier Insular writing. Texts were divided into paragraphs, paragraphs into sentences, sentences into words, and capitals were often used to begin sentences. Punctuation marks were used irregularly to indicate various breathing stops. According to Mason, "it was Alcuin who first systematized the punctuation of manuscripts. He insisted that copyists should pay attention to the pauses—'per cola et commata.' Later, commas, colons, periods and hyphens were used; but the full system of punctuation as followed today was not completely developed until after the invention of printing."

Geofroy Tory was one of the people most responsible for helping to establish modern punctuation marks and practices; and some people find this to be the most useful part of his book *Champ Fleury*. He mentioned eleven different marks but only drew the three he considered most important—the period, comma, and dash. Tory claimed to have found most of his punctuation ideas in the writings of the ancients— ideas "divinely inspired" but virtually forgotten: "I can truly say and conclude, without boasting, that I have drawn forth this ancient secret from the darkness, and first of all modern authors have brought it into

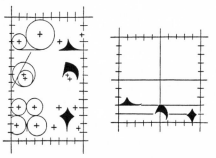

Tory's drawings of punctuation marks (the dash, comma, and period)

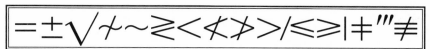

plain sight and set it down in writing, thereby to do devoted & heartfelt service to the public weal, to which I have always dedicated myself." Our dedicated author did not identify all of the modern punctuation marks; but within a short time the system we now use was virtually completed.

Elizabeth Eisenstein credits this conventionalized system with helping to reorder the thoughts of readers as they began to consistently use it. She also points out that after the advent of printing "visual aids multiplied, signs and symbols were codified; different kinds of iconographic and non-phonetic communication were rapidly developed." That is, now that there was a means of regularly reproducing signs, they became standardized; and a glance at any medical, chemistry, physics, mathematics, or astronomy book will reveal that a great many such signs are in common use supplementing our alphabet signs.

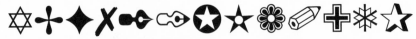

A few of the hundreds of dingbats and other marks readily available today

A long-standing problem we still face today involves the relation of the alphabet signs to the language sounds they endeavor to represent. Although no alphabet perfectly accomplishes this task, some are more accurate than others; and the same basic alphabet is more suited to certain languages than it is to others. The theoretical ideal goal of an alphabet is to reproduce every shade of sound with the greatest possible exactitude. Unfortunately, this seems to be impossible to achieve in practice—the more thorough an alphabet is, the more complex and, hence, unusable it is in daily commerce. Alphabets designed for practical use satisfy more general requirements, such as reproducing the phonemes of a language. Phonemes are basic, general linguistic sounds that are essential to the meanings of words (as contrasted with dialects, accents, and individual idiosyncratic pronunciations). There is generally a close correspondence between the letters and phonemes of a given language, but it is hardly exact in any language. If there are more phonemes than letters, letter combinations are generally used to express the sound, or individual letters can express more than one phoneme. If

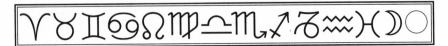

there are fewer phonemes than letters, the same phoneme can be expressed by different letters or combinations.

The English language uses 44 or 45 phonemes served by the 26 letters; and, in contrast to other European languages, it commonly uses no accent or diacritical marks to help expand the range. English actually experiences both phoneme–letter correspondence problems, the second one because of its developmental history—the pronunciation of many words changed over the years, but spelling often persisted at an earlier stage, resulting in different spellings of the same sound. Because writing is more conservative than speech, in almost all languages modern spelling represents the speech of an earlier period. There is at least one advantage to the multiplicity of languages and their constant change, however; this situation helps counteract the human tendency to confuse words with their objects.

∧ \ / ~ o ı ı

Diacritical marks used in various languages in conjunction with the Roman letters

For centuries, the freedom and lack of uniformity in English spelling helped keep spelling–pronunciation differences to a minimum. But spelling became more fixed and the gap widened with the invention of printing. Noah Jacobs wrote that "English spelling is a monumental witness to the misguided erudition of pedants and printers...and could be abolished entirely in favor of shorthand without impairing communication. We are in reality spelling imaginary sounds. The appearance of a word is irrelevant: different meanings can be attached to the same word (*sound, mean, bill*); a word can be given a different meaning when differently pronounced (*sewer, wound, lead*); and the same significance may adhere to words which do not look alike" (such as transliterations of foreign words).

In 1768, Benjamin Franklin proposed a new phonetic alphabet to fit English writing to its sound. Many others have also advocated such a reform, and an English poet laureate, Robert Bridges, actually printed some of his work in a phonetic alphabet. Such an alphabet endeavors to represent actual speech in written form. To accomplish this requires

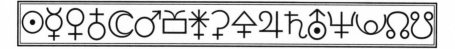

They wer amid the shadows bj njht in lonlines obsclir Wavkiŋ forth i' the voyd and vasty dominyon of ADES; As bj an vnçertan moonŗey sacretly illumind

Sample of phonetic alphabet used by Robert Bridges

more letters, as well as a disregard for traditional orthography. Many phonetic alphabets have been developed through the years, but they are commonly used only by linguists and other scholars. A simplified system of 44 signs called the Initial Teaching Alphabet has been used in teaching English to young children and other students; it supposedly helps prepare them for some of the orthographical inconsistencies they will later encounter by teaching them how a word should be pronounced properly. The most widely used phonetic alphabet is that of the International Phonetic Association; it has a great many signs—including nineteen for vowel sounds—but even this is insufficient for some languages.

hamlet: tʊ bee, or not tʊ bee: jhat is jhe kwestion:
   Whejher 'tis nœbler in jhe miend tʊ suffer
   Jhe sliŋs and arrœs ov outræjus fortuen,
   Or tʊ tæk arms agænst a see ov trubls,
   And bie oppœsiŋ end jhem. Tʊ die: tʊ sleep;

Nœ mor; and bie a sleep tʊ sæ wee end
   Jhe hart-æc, and jhe jhousand natueral ſhocks
   Jhat fleſh is ær tʊ, 'tis a consummæſhon
   devoutly tʊ bee wiſht. Tʊ die, tʊ sleep;
   Tʊ sleep: perçhans tʊ dreem; ie, jhær's jhe rub;

Lines from *Hamlet* set in Initial Teaching Alphabet

Throughout history there have been attempts to solve the problem by adding letters to the common alphabet. In the second century B.C. there were experiments with double consonants and double vowels in Latin; and we have seen that the emperor Claudius unsuccessfully attempted to reform the Roman alphabet by adding three new signs: Ⅎ for the [w] sound; Ⱶ for a vowel between [i] and [u]; and Ↄ for the [ps] and [bs] sounds. Only one gained acceptance—some 1500 years later, using a different sign. There have been many other attempts—most more serious but hardly more important than Dr. Seuss's introduction of newly invented letters in his book *On Beyond Zebra*—all of which have been private crusades that failed when they were unable to elicit popular support. There also have been scribes' variant forms of the letters lost

ᴰɓčɗəyųɣꭓλᵐŋɔʄɖrᵛš₁ᵛɷ₎ᵞž

when others did not imitate them. The historical battlefield of the alphabet is strewn with dead letters; that graveyard, like our own, perhaps vivified only by what Galway Kinnell calls the "languished alphabet of worms."

Early medieval forms of letters that did not survive in popular use

Periodically, attempts have also been made to reverse the curse of Babel by creating a universal language and alphabet. The movement reached its peak in the seventeenth century when it was thought that it would facilitate the search for "universal truths." Thus, Francis Bacon, in the *Advancement of Learning* (1605), called for "real characters" able to give precise expression to basic things and ideas. In 1668, John Wilkins, in his *Essay Towards a Real Character and a Philosophical Language*, devised one of many such systems. In our own time, universal languages such as Esperanto have had their zealous proponents, while others have seriously suggested that the world adopt an ideographic system such as Chinese to bring down the language barriers between us. Still others place their faith in an improved version of the Roman alphabet, which is still dominant in the world and continues to gain new subscribers.

Punctuation is a rather fluid field where auxiliary marks can expand the reach of language. So also can unusual combinations such as the mixture of signs to indicate profanity, or the combination ?! to indicate exasperation, among other things. Duplication of signs indicates augmentation—??, !!, ...—and can say a great deal in a small space; but one can soon bog down in ambiguity with such a method.

The Faustian human spirit is never satisfied, and writers continually strain the resources of language in their assault on the Unknown, the Unexpressed, even the Inexpressible. As an integral part of language, the letters come under continued stress and scrutiny; and some people feel that to increase their number would be to extend the range of writing. Those of a mystic bent seem especially sympathetic to such an idea. A small book on numerology for popular consumption by Juno Jordan directly expresses such thoughts. After claiming that the letters (through their numerical values) represent our essential cultural human reality or accomplishment, she continues: "In the early times the Hebrew alphabet contained twenty-two letters or symbols. Our present day alphabet moving forward through the past ages of civilization contains twenty-six letters. It will eventually contain twenty-seven letters, as mankind moves forward into a better understanding of the Brotherhood of Man." What that letter will be or symbolize is not revealed, so I suppose mankind still lacks understanding. It would be fun but perhaps not fair to mention that the Russians and other users of the 32-character Cyrillic alphabet may have long ago moved beyond Jordan's "understanding" (and they might possibly be quick to agree), but I will assume that she believes the spiritual world to be transcribed with the Roman/English alphabet.

More seriously, some Kabbalists have mentioned a missing Hebrew letter. In his book *Kabbalah and Criticism*, Harold Bloom writes of the mystic Kabbalah as "a collective, psychic defense of the most imaginative medieval Jews against exile and persecution pressing on them *inwardly*. So, some Kabbalists spoke of a missing twenty-third letter of the Hebrew alphabet, hidden in the white spaces between the letters. From these openings the larger Torah was still to emerge." Poets, too—perhaps especially—have felt the need to go beyond the powers of the letters in rendering their visions. Dante, Milton, and Blake come readily to mind, but the idea is superbly expressed by the German poet Heinz Piontek in lines from his book *Prewartime*: "How do I say it / without fear? / Through / sign language. / Through my language signs, / which include / the white between the letters, / which remain unspeakable."

Writing in 1920, William Mason claimed that "the evidence is quite too overwhelming to be doubted that our present alphabetic signs are but the corruptions of primitive pictures, each having lost through the attrition of ages its peculiar pictorial character, having passed through the transforming hands of many different nationalities and races, each contributing its share of alteration or modification, until they have become conventionalized and simplified into their present, latest arbitrary form. We cannot say their last form, for future generations may yet mold and modify these alphabetic signs as past generations of men have

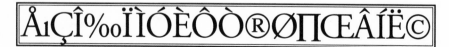

done; but we may confidently assert that no further radical change ever will or can be effected....It may safely be claimed that the final chapter is practically completed, and that the long historic development of our written characters forever is a closed book."

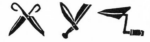

Since Mason wrote the above, both single-character alphabets of the mid-twentieth century as well as computer alphabets of more recent years have tried to challenge his conclusion. However, the public rejected the first; and with the development of laser printers and more sophisticated dot-matrix, vector-curve drawing, and object-oriented systems, most computer alphabets now closely resemble classic roman letterforms, as this book bears witness. It is also true that our almost universal literate print culture has helped "freeze" the classic forms, even though advertising and display types constantly test the limits of letter character recognition. So, there is perhaps a great deal of validity to Mason's words. But, if we have learned anything in this study, it should be that it would be foolish to ever imagine a "closed book" in regard to the alphabet. As Nicolete Gray writes (and a million typographic advertisements remind us): "A letter has no fixed shape, it does not even have a skeleton shape, it has *identity*, and this exists in the mind." As we saw with Plath and Marquez, that identity is as fragile as our minds. A character in John Barth's novel *Letters* restates the case one more time: "I couldn't write, couldn't even read. Our alphabet looked alien as Arabic; the strings of letters were a code I'd lost the key to; I found more sense in the empty spaces, in the margins, between the lines."

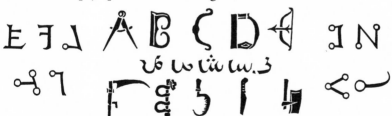

Some fantastic letterforms by Tory, including some "alien as Arabic"; in fact, they are Arabic.

ABCDefghijklmnopqrstuvwXYZ

Bruno Schulz wrote a story about an old man who went back to the first form at school in his effort to continue learning. The headmaster called him a "veteran of the alphabet." You, too, dear veteran, should be ready again to reenlist. If there is one lesson to be learned and relearned and learned again from all this, it is the miracle of it all. I cannot express it any better than did Vladimir Nabokov in *Pale Fire*: "We are absurdly accustomed to the miracle of a few written signs being able to contain immortal imagery, involutions of thought, new worlds with live people, speaking, weeping, laughing. We take it for granted so simply that in a sense, by the very act of brutish routine acceptance, we undo the work of the ages,...I found myself enriched with an indescribable amazement as if informed that fireflies were making decodable signals on behalf of stranded spirits, or that a bat was writing a legible tale of torture in the bruised and branded sky."

Future abecedariums (also known in times past as "battledores") may contain different elements than those we now know, my understanding and most patient reader; however, as long as words are written, the story of the alphabet will continue ... although what form it will take is yet unknown.

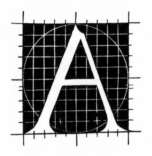

AbcdefghijklmnopqrstuvwxyZ...

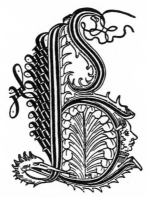

SELECT BIBLIOGRAPHY

Alexander, J.J.G. *The Decorated Letter*. New York, 1978.

Anderson, Charles. *Lettering*. New York, 1982.

Anderson, Donald M. *The Art of Written Forms*. New York, 1969.

Baikie, James. *Egyptian Papyrus and Papyrus-Hunting*. New York, n.d.

Bain, George. *Celtic Art: The Methods of Construction*. New York, 1973.

Barth, John. *Letters*. New York, 1979.

Bayley, Harold. *The Lost Language of Symbolism*. London, 1951.

Beckett, Samuel, et al. *Our Exagmination . . . of Work in Progress*. London, 1972.

Bennett, Paul, ed. *Books and Printing: A Treasury for Typophiles*. Cleveland, 1951.

Benson, John Howard, and Arthur Graham Carey. *The Elements of Lettering*. New York, 1950.

Bierce, Ambrose. *Collected Writings*. New York, 1946.

Bigelow, Charles, and Donald Day. "Digital Typography." *Scientific American*. 1984.

Bigelow, M.S. *Alphabets and Design*. Minneapolis, 1967.

Biggs, John R. *An Approach to Type*. New York, 1962.

Bloom, Harold. *Kabbalah and Criticism*. New York, 1975.

Blumenthal, Joseph. *Art of the Printed Book: 1455–1955*. New York and Boston, 1973.

Bombaugh, C.C. *Oddities and Curiosities of Words and Literature*. New York, 1961.

Borges, Jorge Luis. *The Book of Imaginary Beings*. New York, 1970.

Boyd, Beverly. *Chaucer and the Medieval Book*. Los Angeles, 1973.

Brewer, Ebenezer C. *Dictionary of Phrase and Fable*. New York, 1870.

Bringhurst, Robert. *The Elements of Typographic Style*. Point Roberts, WA, 1992.

Bruns, Gerald L. *Modern Poetry and the Idea of Language*. New Haven, 1974.

Budge, E.A. Wallis. *Amulets and Talismans*. New York, 1961.

Butler, Charles. *The English Grammar*. Oxford, 1634.
Calas, Nicolas. *Art in the Age of Risk*. New York, 1968.
Campbell, Joseph. *The Masks of God: Occidental Mythology*. New York, 1976.
———. *The Flight of the Wild Gander*. South Bend, IN, 1977.
Carter, Harry. *A View of Early Typography*. London, 1969.
Cartier, Francis A., and Martin T. Todaro. *The Phonetic Alphabet*. Dubuque, IA, 1971.
Cavendish, Richard. *The Black Arts*. New York, 1967.
Chao, Yuen Ren. *Language and Symbolic Systems*. Cambridge, 1974.
Chappell, Warren. *A Short History of the Printed Word*. Boston, 1980.
———. *The Living Alphabet*. Charlottesville, 1975.
Clodd, Edward. *The Story of the Alphabet*. New York, 1904.
Connell, Evan. *The White Lantern*. New York, 1980.
Coulmas, Florian. *The Writing Systems of the World*. Oxford, 1989.
Cowper, B. Harris, ed. *The Apocryphal Gospels*. London, 1910.
Dante. *The Divine Comedy*. Translated by John A. Carlyle and Philip H. Wicksteed. New York, 1950.
Day, Lewis. *Alphabets Old and New*. London, 1910.
Degering, Hermann. *Lettering*. New York, 1965.
Denman, Frank. *The Shaping of our Alphabet*. New York, 1955.
Diringer, David. *The Alphabet*. New York, 1968.
———. *The Book Before Printing*. New York, 1982.
———. *Writing*. New York, 1962.
Doblhofer, Ernst. *Voices in Stone*. New York, 1961.
Donoghue, Denis. *Ferocious Alphabets*. Boston, 1981.
Dornseiff, Franz. *Das Alphabet in Mystik und Magie*. Leipzig, 1925.
Driver, Godfrey R. *Semitic Writing: From Pictograph to Alphabet*. London, 1976.
Drogin, Marc. *Medieval Calligraphy: Its History and Technique*. Montclair, NJ, 1980.
Dürer, Albrecht. *On the Just Shaping of Letters*. New York, 1965.
Eisen, William. *The English Caballah*. Marina Del Rey, CA, 1980.
Eisenstein, Elizabeth L. *The Printing Revolution in Early Modern Europe*. Cambridge, 1983.
Etiemble (Robert Delpire and Jacques Monory). *The Orion Book of the Written Word*. New York, 1961.
Fairbank, Alfred. *A Book of Scripts*. London, 1977.
———. *The Story of Handwriting: Origins and Development*. New York, 1970.
Feliciano, Felice. *Alphabetum Romanum*. Verona, 1960.
Ferguson, George. *Signs and Symbols in Christian Art*. New York, 1966.

Fine Print on Type: The Best of Fine Print Magazine on Type and Typography. Edited by Charles Bigelow, Paul Hayden Duensing, and Linnea Gentry. San Francisco, 1989.

Fisher, Leonard Everett. *Alphabet Art.* New York, 1978.

Fleuron Anthology. Edited by Sir Francis Meynell and Herbert Simon. Boston, 1979.

Frazer, Sir James George. *The Golden Bough.* London, 1922.

Frutiger, Adrian. *Signs and Symbols: Their Design and Meaning.* New York, 1989.

———. *Type Sign Symbol.* Zurich, 1980.

Fry, Edmund. *Pantographia.* London, 1799.

Fugger, Wolfgang. *Handwriting Manual.* London, 1960.

Gardner, William. *Alphabet at Work.* New York, 1982.

Gaskell, Philip. *A New Introduction to Bibliography.* New York, 1972.

Gelb, I.J. *A Study of Writing.* Chicago, 1952.

Gentry, Helen, and David Greenhood. *Chronology of Books and Printing.* San Francisco, 1933.

Gerstner, Karl. *Compendium for Literates.* Cambridge, MA, 1974.

Gill, Eric. *An Essay on Typography.* London, 1936.

Goudy, Frederic W. *The Alphabet and Elements of Lettering.* New York, 1963.

———. *Typologia.* Berkeley, 1977.

Grafton, Carol Belanger, ed. *Bizarre & Ornamental Alphabets.* New York, 1981.

———. *Historic Alphabets & Initials, Woodcut & Ornamental.* New York, 1977.

———. *Treasury of Art Nouveau Design and Ornament.* New York, 1980.

Graves, Robert. *Claudius the God.* New York, 1968.

———. *The Greek Myths.* London, 1960.

———. *King Jesus.* New York, 1946.

———. *The White Goddess.* New York, 1948.

Gray, Eden. *A Complete Guide to the Tarot.* New York, 1972.

Gray, Nicolete. *A History of Lettering.* Boston, 1986.

———. *Lettering as Drawing.* New York, 1982.

Gray, William. *The Talking Tree.* New York, 1977.

Gregg, John R., et al. *Gregg Shorthand Manual Simplified.* New York, 1955.

Halsell, Maureen. *The Old English Rune Poem.* Toronto, 1981.

Hewitt, Graily. *Lettering.* New York, 1981.

Higenbottam, Frank. *Codes and Ciphers.* London, 1973.

Hind, Arthur M. *Introduction to a History of Woodcut.* New York, 1963.

Hlavsa, Oldrich. *A Book of Type and Design.* New York, 1960.

Hugo, Victor. *Voyages and Excursions.* Paris, 1910.

Humez, Alexander, and Nicholas Humez. *A B C Et Cetera: The Life and Times of the Roman Alphabet*. Boston, 1985.

———. *Alpha to Omega: The Life and Times of the Greek Alphabet*. Boston, 1981.

Hutchinson, James. *Letters*. New York, 1983.

Huxley, Aldous. *Tomorrow and Tomorrow and Tomorrow*. New York, 1956.

Irving, John. *The World According to Garp*. New York, 1978.

Jackson, Donald. *The Story of Writing*. New York, 1981.

Jacobs, Noah Jonathan. *Naming-Day in Eden*. New York, 1958.

Jennett, Seán. *The Making of Books*. New York, 1951.

Jennings, Gary. *World of Words*. New York, 1984.

Jensen, Hans. *Sign, Symbol and Script*. Translated by George Unwin. New York, 1969.

Johnson, John. *Typographia*. London, 1824.

Johnston, Edward. *Manuscript and Inscription Letters*. London, 1946.

———. *Writing & Illuminating, & Lettering*. New York, 1977.

Jonson, Ben. *The English Grammar*. London, 1640.

Jordan, Juno. *Numerology*. Santa Barbara, 1965.

Joyce, James. *Finnegans Wake*. New York, 1959.

———. *Stephen Hero*. New York, 1963.

Jünger, Ernst. "Lob der Vokale." *Samtliche Werke*, b.12. Klett-Cotta, 1979.

Kim, Scott. *Inversions*. Peterborough, NH, 1981.

Kinnell, Galway. *The Book of Nightmares*. Boston, 1971.

Kip, Rev. Wm. Ingraham. *The Catacombs of Rome*. New York, 1854.

Koch, Rudolf. *The Book of Signs*. New York, 1955.

The Koran. Translated by N.J. Dawood. Baltimore, 1966.

Kuhn, Alvin Boyd. *Esoteric Structure of the Alphabet*. Elizabeth, NJ, n.d.

Kurath, Hans, ed. *Middle English Dictionary*. Ann Arbor, 1959.

Lamb, C.M., ed. *The Calligrapher's Handbook*. New York, 1968.

Langdon, John. *Wordplay: Ambigrams and Reflections....* New York, 1992.

Lawson, Alexander. *Anatomy of a Typeface*. Boston, 1990.

Lehner, Ernst. *Alphabets and Ornaments*. New York, 1968.

———. *Symbols, Signs and Signets*. New York, 1969.

Lewis, John. *Anatomy of Printing*. New York, 1970.

Lucian. "The Consonants at Law." *Works*. Translated by A.M. Harmon. London, 1927.

Marlowe, Christopher. *Doctor Faustus*. New York, 1966.

Marrou, H.I. *A History of Education in Antiquity*. New York, 1964.

Mason, William A. *A History of the Art of Writing*. New York, 1920.

McKerrow, Ronald B. "Typographic Debut," in Paul A. Bennett, ed. *Books and Printing*. Cleveland, 1951.

McLean, Ruari. *Thames and Hudson Manual of Typography*. New York, 1980.

McLuhan, Marshall. *Counterblast*. New York, 1969.

———. *The Gutenberg Galaxy*. New York, 1969.

McLuhan, Marshall, and Quentin Fiore. *War and Peace in the Global Village*. New York, 1968.

Metz, Peter. *The Golden Gospels of Echternach*. New York, 1957.

Meyrink, Gustav. *The Golem*. New York, 1976.

Moorhouse, A.C. *The Triumph of the Alphabet*. New York, 1953.

Moran, Hugh A. and David H. Kelley. *The Alphabet and the Ancient Calendar Signs*. n.p., 1969.

Morison, Stanley. *Fra Luca de Pacioli*. New York, 1933.

Morris, William. *The Ideal Book*. Edited by William S. Peterson. Berkeley, 1982.

Nabokov, Vladimir. *Pale Fire*. New York, 1962.

Nerdinger, Eugen. *Buchstabenbuch*. Munich, 1955.

———. *Signs + Scripts + Ornaments*. Munich, 1960.

Nesbitt, Alexander. *Decorative Alphabets and Initials*. New York, 1959.

———. *The History and Technique of Lettering*. New York, 1957.

Ober, J. Hambleton. *Writing: Man's Great Invention*. Baltimore, 1965.

Ogg, Oscar. *An Alphabet Source Book*. New York, 1940.

———. *The 26 Letters*. New York, 1948.

Orcutt, William Dana. *Master Makers of the Book*. New York, 1928.

Pei, Mario. *The Story of Language*. New York, 1966.

Perfect, Christopher, and Gordon Rookledge. *Rookledge's International Type-finder*. London, 1983.

Petzendorfer, Ludwig, ed. *Treasury of Authentic Art Nouveau Alphabets*. New York, 1984.

Piontek, Heinz. *Prewartime*. Translated by Robert Firmage. Unpublished ms.

Plath, Sylvia. *The Bell Jar*. New York, 1971.

Plato. *The Dialogues*. Translated by Benjamin Jowett. New York, 1937.

Poe, Edgar Allan. *Complete Stories and Poems*. New York, 1966.

Powell, Claire. *The Meaning of Flowers*. Boulder, CO, 1979.

Pratt, Fletcher. *Secret and Urgent: The Story of Codes and Ciphers*. New York, 1939.

Pynchon, Thomas. *Gravity's Rainbow*. New York, 1973.

Rabelais, François. *Gargantua and Pantagruel*. Translated by Jacques Le Clercq. New York, 1936.

Reed, Talbot Baines. *A History of the Old English Letter Foundries*. Revised and enlarged by A.F. Johnson. London, 1952.

Rimbaud, Arthur. *Complete Works, Selected Letters*. Translated by Wallace Fowlie. Chicago, 1966.

Rose, H.J. *A Handbook of Greek Mythology*. New York, 1959.

Rosen, Ben. *Type and Typography*. New York, 1976.

Ryder, John. *The Case for Legibility*. London, 1979.

Sartre, Jean-Paul. *The Reprieve*. Translated by Eric Sutton. New York, 1968.

Scarfe, Laurence. *Alphabets*. London, 1954.

Schlosser, Leonard B. "A History of Paper." In *Paper—Art & Technology*. San Francisco, 1979.

Schulz, Bruno. "The Old Age Pensioner." In *Sanatorium Under the Sign of the Hourglass*. New York, 1979.

Seligman, Kurt. *Magic, Supernaturalism and Religion*. New York, 1971.

Shahn, Ben. *The Alphabet of Creation*. New York, 1954.

———. *Love and Joy About Letters*. New York, 1963.

———. *The Shape of Content*. Cambridge, MA, 1957.

Sheldon, E.S. "The Origin of the English Names of the Letters of the Alphabet." *Harvard Studies in Philology and Literature*. Boston, 1892.

Solo, Dan X. *Classic Roman Alphabets*. New York, 1983.

———. *Special Effects and Topical Alphabets*. New York, 1978.

Steinberg, S.H. *Five Hundred Years of Printing*. Hammondsworth, U.K., 1974.

Steiner, George. *After Babel*. London, 1975.

———. *The Portage to San Cristóbal of A.H.* New York, 1983.

Stevens, Wallace. *Collected Poems*. New York, 1954.

Strauss, Victor. *The Printing Industry*. Washington, 1967.

Thurber, James. *Lanterns and Lances*. New York, 1961.

———. *The Wonderful O*. New York, 1957.

Tinker, Miles A. *Legibility of Print*. Ames, IA, 1963.

Top, Alexander. *The Olive Leafe: or, Universall Abce*. London, 1603.

Tory, Geofroy. *Champ Fleury*. Translated by George B. Ives. New York, 1967.

Tracy, Walter. *Letters of Credit*. Boston, 1986.

Type Specimen Book, The. New York, 1974.

Ullman, B.L. *Ancient Writing and its Influence*. Cambridge, MA, 1969.

Updike, Daniel Berkeley. *Printing Types*. Cambridge, MA, 1966.

Walsh, William S. *Handy-book of Literary Curiosities*. Philadelphia, 1906.

Warde, Beatrice. *The Crystal Goblet*. Cleveland, 1956.

Wellek, René, and Austin Warren. *Theory of Literature*. New York, 1956.

Werner, E.T.C. *A Dictionary of Chinese Mythology*. Shanghai, 1932.

White, T.H. *The Bestiary*. New York, 1960.

Wilkins, John. *An Essay Towards a Real Character and a Philosophical Language*. London, 1668.

Yee, Chiang. *Chinese Calligraphy*. Cambridge, MA, 1973.

Zapf, Hermann. *About Alphabets*. Cambridge, MA, 1970.

———. *Manuale Typographicum*. Cambridge, MA, 1970.

Zolar. *The Encyclopedia of Ancient and Forbidden Knowledge*. Los Angeles, 1970.

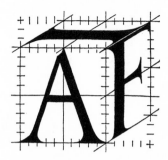

INDEX

A, the letter and its sound, 47–55
A–Z, 276, 282
abbreviations and contractions, 24, 28, 179, 250, 285
abece (abse), 58–59
abecedaries, ix, 13, 45, 76, 139, 294
Abish, Walter, 179
abracadabra, 52, 181
Abraxas, 163
ac, 55
acrophony, 13, 14, 139
acrostics, 75
Addison, Joseph, 180
Agrippa, Cornelius, 160
ailm, 55
aitch, 111
Alcuin of York, 26, 287
alectryomancy, 137–38
aleph, 47–48, 51, 214
Alexander, J.J.G., 190–91
alliteration (tongue-twisters), 181
alpha, 48, 51, 53, 54, 131
Alpha and Omega, 53, 131, 171–72, 275, 276
alphabet, 4, 6–7, 14, 48, 174, 261, 268, 274–77, 282,
    288–89, 292–94; effects of, 151–53; name, 58–59;
    order of letters, 13, 61, 96, 130, 160, 274–75
ambigrams (John Langdon, Scott Kim), 43–44
Amman, Jost (*Book of Trades*), 34, 101, 121, 183
ampersand, 284–285
amulets, 52, 221
anagrams, 180
Anderson, Charles, 102
Anderson, Donald, 18, 37, 67, 81, 107, 113, 121, 127,
    159, 170, 200, 203, 205, 255, 284–285
Anglo-Saxon writing, 23, 24, 27, 130, 178, 184, 241,
    242. *See also* Insular writing.
Apollinaire, Guillaume, 202
Apollo's lyre, 82, 169, 229
Arabic numerals 160, 175. *See also* numbers....
Arabic writing, 8, 15–16
Aristotle, 5
Artemidorus, 138

astrology, linked with letters, 47, 142
astronomy, linked with letters, 47, 95–96, 98, 154
Athenodorus of Tarsos, 275
Auden, W.H., 136
AUM, 228–229
auxiliary marks and signs, 284–291
ayin, 170

B, the letter and its sound, 56–63
Babel, Tower of, 5; curse of, 291
Babylonian writing, 8, 10
Bacon, Francis, 162, 291
Baikie, James, 11
Barth, John, 45, 161, 293
Baskerville, John, 34
battledore, 63, 294
Bauhaus school, 39, 147, 236
Baum, L. Frank, 185
Bayer, Herbert, 147
benefit of clergy, 94, 156, 188
beorc, 62
beta, 56
beth, 14, 56, 57, 58
Beth-luis-nion (Irish tree-alphabet), 54, 60–61, 68,
    79, 84, 92, 106, 109, 122, 148–49, 156, 166, 175, 184,
    195, 204, 212–13, 216, 227, 269
Bible, 9–10, 22, 53, 130, 138, 274–75
Bierce, Ambrose, 101, 116, 245, 251
Biggs, John, 212
black letter (gothic) scripts, 26–29, 120, 225, 262–63
Blake, William, 271, 282, 292
Bloom, Harold, 292
Blumenthal, Joseph, 126
Boethius, 216
Book of Kells, 23, 192
book scripts, 20, 21, 26, 166; book (text) type, 32,
    202, 234–35
boustrophedon writing, 14–15, 18, 177, 196, 200
Boyd, Beverly, 179, 203
Bracciolini, Poggio, 29
branding of letters, 54, 63, 94, 156

Brentano, Clemens, 53
Brewer, E.C. (*Dictionary of Phrase and Fable*), 94, 197, 280
Bridges, Robert, 199, 289
Bringhurst, Robert, 286
Bruns, Gerald, 159
Budge, Sir Wallis, 64, 90, 137, 161, 228, 242
Budgen, Frank, 135
Burroughs, Edgar Rice, 227
Burton, Sir Robert, 182
Butler, Charles, 178–79
Byron, Lord 150

C, the letter and its sound, 64–71, 132, 133; words beginning with, 178
Cadmus myth, 150–51, 216
Caecus, Appius Claudius, 267, 269
Caesar, Julius, 279
calligraphy, 113, 128, 166, 190, 203
Calvus, 186, 189
Campbell, Joseph, 221, 228–29
capital letters (majuscules), 19–21, 22, 67, 121, 127, 146, 224–25, 254, 281. See also upper-case letters.
Carlyle, Thomas, 103
Carolingian minuscule script, 26, 29, 30, 286–87
Carroll, Lewis, ix, 111, 157, 158
Carter, Harry, 126, 202–03
Caslon, William, 189
Caxton, William, 244–45
Celestial Alphabet, 95–96
cen, 68
Champ Fleury, 49, 116, 125–26, 192, 224, 244, 287. See also Tory, Geofroy.
Chancery script, 29, 30
changes in letterforms, 233–34
Chao, Yuen Ren, 174
Chappell, Warren, 38, 44, 128, 202, 234
Charlemagne, 25–26
Chaucer, Geoffrey, 216, 245
chi, 66, 249–50
Chinese invention of paper, 184; writing, 6, 8–9, 291
Christianity and writing, 9, 10, 22, 66, 131, 191, 215, 217, 259
Chrysostom, John, 51
Churchill, Sir Winston, 239
Cicero, 186, 189, 253
ciphers and codes, 278–80
Claudius (Roman emperor), 233–34, 240, 290
Cleland, T.M., 39,
Clodd, Edward, 3, 17, 95
coll, 68
computer type, 40–41, 127, 237–38, 265, 293
Connell, Evan, 16
consonants, 6, 56, 82, 174, 228, 229, 231, 232
Coptic Christians, 89–90, 217
Cotgrave, Randle, 59
cross, 214–15; St. Anthony's, 215; Egyptian, 215; Tau, 215; Greek, 106

crossrow, 59
cummings, e.e., 147–48
cuneiform writing, 10
cursive writing, 21, 30, 165–66, 190
Cyrillic (Slavic) writing, 15, 17, 292

D, the letter and its sound, 72–80, 217
Dadaism, 202
daeg, 79
daleth, 72
Dante, 155–56, 273, 274, 292
De Bry, Theodore and Israel, 45, 156
dead letters, 199–200, 290–91
decorative letters, 23, 24–25, 43, 120–22, 190–94
delta, 72, 77
Denman, Frank, 37
Derrida, Jacques, 227
Deseret Alphabet (Mormons), 217–18
devil traps, 73
diacritical marks, 285, 286, 289
Dickens, Charles (*Pickwick Papers*), 247, 277
dictionary, 130, 245. See also *Oxford English Dictionary*.
differences of letters and typefaces, 201–02
digamma, 89, 240, 258
direction of writing, 13, 14, 15
Diringer, David, 4, 58
disappearance of letterforms and variants, 199–200
display and decorative type, 35–37, 42
dog letter, 197
Dostoevsky, Fyodor (*The Idiot*), 78
dot-matrix printing, 239
dream interpreters, alphabet, 137
Drogin, Marc, 166
Druids, 79
dual-alphabet scripts, 28, 143–44, 146
dualism, 56–57
duir, 79
Dürer, Albrecht, 27, 28, 32, 127, 135
Dylan, Bob, vi, 283

E, the letter and its sound, 81–88
Edda, Prose, 122, 242
Ege, Otto, 47, 56
Egyptian (Fat-face) type, 36
Egyptian writing, 6, 8, 11–12, 183; demotic, 12; hieratic, 12; hieroglyphic, 6, 11, 12, 60
eh, 84
Eisenstein, Elizabeth, 288
English language, 65, 82, 111–12, 130, 133, 179, 208–09, 210, 243, 244–45, 262, 263, 289; Middle English, 99; Old English, 242, 262
eolhx, 256
Ephraimites, biblical story of, 205, 261
epsilon, 81
Erasmus, 76, 135
errors, typographic, 252
Esperanto, 291

eta, 81–82, 83, 107
eternity, letter of, 170
eth, 218–19
Etruscan writing, 15, 17, 18, 61–62, 90–91, 132
etymology, medieval, 184
exclamation mark, 286

F, the letter and its sound, 89–97, 240
Fairbanks, Alfred, 255
"fantastic" alphabets, 192
Faustus, Dr., 92–93
fearn, 92
Feliciano, Felice, 32, 127, 260
feoh, 92
Fleuron, The, 104
flower "language," 75–76
France, Anatole, 75
France, Marie de, 70–71
Francis of Assisi, St., 215
Franklin, Benjamin, 34–35, 289
frequency of letter use, 81, 178, 209, 222, 251, 263, 279–80
Frutiger, Adrian, 44, 236
Fudd, Elmer, 247, 248
Fugger, Wolfgang, 103, 193, 194
futharc. *See* runic writing.

G, the letter and its sound, 98–106, 267
Gaddis, William (*The Recognitions*), 229
games, alphabet, 179–80, 181
gamma, 64, 65, 98, 106, 144, 177
gammadion (swastika), 106
Gardner, Martin, 85
Gardner, William, 193
Gaskell, Philip, 245
Gass, William, 203
Geibel, Emanuel, 282
Gellius, Aulus, 108
Gematria, 161–63
ger, 105–06
Gerstner, Karl, 45, 118
Gibson, Don, 276
Gill, Eric, 40, 43, 189
gimel, 64, 98, 177
Gnosticism, 163, 174, 228, 259
God, name of, 48, 89, 90, 110, 137, 232, 262. *See also* Tetragrammaton.
gods, related to the letters, 1, 8–9, 48, 61, 73–74, 84; Apollo, 115–16; Carmenta, 61, 84, 217; Demeter, 74; Dionysus, 106; Hermes, 8; Hecate, 122
Goethe, J.W. (*Faust*), 229
Goldsmith, Oliver, 76
golems, 90
gort, 106
gothic. *See* black letter scripts. *See also* sans serif typefaces.
Goudy, Frederic, 7, 68, 106, 120, 125, 126, 127, 128–29, 198, 212, 263

Graces, related to the letters, 50, 114, 224, 264
Gradl, M.J., 7
graphology, 104–05
Graves, Robert, 54, 60–61, 68, 78, 84, 89, 109–10, 131, 149, 171–72, 184, 195, 204, 212, 215, 216–17, 233, 240, 269
Gray, Nicolete, 21, 23–24, 24–25, 29, 37, 41, 118–19, 127–28, 157, 235, 293
Greek alphabet: eastern (Ionian), 15, 171, 186; western (Chalcidian or Pelasgian), 15, 17, 18, 171, 177
Greek magic and mysticism, 74, 82
Greek mythology, 8, 74, 106, 150–51, 171. *See also* gods, related to the letters.
Greek writing, 8, 14–15, 61, 77–78, 81–83, 171
Greeley, Horace, 103
Griffo, Francesco, 33
Grimm, Jacob, 55, 87
Gutenberg, Johann, 28, 31, 100–01, 183, 285
gyfu, 105
gyromancy, 138

H, the letter and its sound, 107–14
haegl, 110
Halsell, Maureen, 74, 79
handwriting, 19, 21, 30, 102–03, 246, 252
Havamal, 242
Hawthorne, Nathaniel, 54, 102–03, 109
he, 81, 108
Hebrew writing, 9, 10, 137, 160; alphabet legend, 57–58. *See also* Semitic writing.
Hegel, G.W.F., 53
Herodes Atticus, 276
Herodotus, 14
Hesiod, 259
heth. See kheth.
Hewitt, Graily, 197–98
hieroglyphic writing. *See* Egyptian writing.
Higenbottam, Frank, 280
Hölderlin, Friedrich, 96
Homer (*The Iliad*), 117
Horace, 76
hornbook, 59, 75–76, 228
hot-metal typography, 37
Howell, James, 65–66
Hugo, Victor, vi, x, 45, 84, 231, 256, 264, 271
Hugo von St. Victor, 69, 157
Humanistic writing, 29–30, 31, 155, 254

I, the letter and its sound, 115–23, 124, 125, 262
iconographic (pictographic) writing, 5–6
ideographic (hieroglyphic) writing, 6, 11, 285
idho, 122
II (double I), 120, 131
illiteracy, 2, 94–95
I-longa, 119
imp of the perverse, 185
initial letters, 121-22, 192, 193
Initial Teaching Alphabet, 290

inscriptional lettering, 18, 19, 20, 121, 200, 210
Insular writing, 23, 25, 236, 242, 287
invention of letters, 118–19
"invisible" type, 113, 234
Io, myth of, 168–70
Ionian Greek alphabet. *See* Greek alphabet.
iota, 115–16, 124, 125
Irving, John, 272, 283
is, 122
Isaiah, 95
Israelites, 215
Italian language, influence on S, 209–10
italic type, 32, 33

J, the letter and its sound, 119, 124–31, 225, 262
Jabés, Edmond, 229
Jackson, Donald, 62, 67, 197
Jacobs, Noah, 86, 289
Jakobson, Roman, 155
Jami, 85
Jarrell, Randall, 226
Jason and Golden Fleece myth, 151
Jaugeon, Jacques, 127, 145
Jennett, Séan, 37, 128, 210, 225
Jennings, Gary, 73, 213
Jensen, Hans, 66, 110
Jensen, Nicolas, 30, 32
Jerome, St., 22, 27, 58
Jesus, 131, 214–15, 217, 250
Jewish mysticism, 57, 90, 105, 110, 136–37, 292. *See also* Kabbalah.
Johnson, Dr. Samuel, 130
Johnston, Edward, 44, 113, 172
Jones, A. Lloyd, 5
Jonson, Ben, 108, 130, 141, 187, 189, 197, 208, 251
Jordan, Juno, 164, 291–92
Joyce, James, vi, 130, 135, 153, 180
Judeo–Christian tradition, writing in, 9–10
Jünger, Ernst, 55, 83, 86, 87–88, 123, 175–76, 229–30

K, the letter and its sound, 132–40
Kabbalah, 88, 131, 136–37, 156, 160–63, 292
Kafka, Franz, 135–36
kaph, 132, 139
kappa, 132
Kelmscott Press, 38
kerning, 91
kheth (*heth* or *cheth*), 81, 107, 108
King Lear (Shakespeare), 175, 269
Kinnell, Galway, 96, 199–200, 291
Kircher, Athanasius, 164
Koch, Rudolf, 115, 170, 215, 263
koph, 186
koppa, 186
Koran, 52, 187

L, the letter and its sound, 141–49
Lacedaemonian (Spartan) letter (I), 115

lagu, 148
Lamartine, Alphonse de, 135, 282
lambda, 141, 143–44
lamed, 141, 148
Landa, Diego de, 16
language, 4, 5, 10; for Greeks, 159. *See also* speech.
language sounds, correspondence with alphabet, 205, 247, 288–90. *See also* phonemes.
Latin, 263; use of Greek words, 267
Lawson, Alexander, 35–36, 39, 190, 238
left-to-right writing, 18, 200
legends relating to alphabet: Egyptian, 11–12; Greek, 1–2; Hebrew, 57–58; Irish, 8; Korean, 73; others, 8–10
legibility, 23, 27–28, 113, 145–46, 198–99, 211–12, 247, 254–55, 281
Leibniz, G.W., 71
Leiris, Michel, 139
letter correspondences, 74–75, 82, 83, 95, 116–17
lettering, 201
letters: beauty of, 104; construction of, 49–50; design of, 30–31, 32, 41, 112–13, 116–19, 127–29, 157, 172–73, 197–98, 211–12, 247; identity of, 43–44, 118–19, 235, 293; variety of, 99–100
Lévi-Strauss, Claude, 94
Lewis, John, 29
Liberal Arts, related to letters, 50, 142, 143, 154, 166, 203, 213, 250, 270
ligatures, 24, 28, 30, 33, 91, 284, 285
lipogrammatists, 85, 173, 179-80
"liquid" letters, 141, 165, 197
literacy, 28, 152–54, 188
lower-case (minuscule) letters, 20, 30, 121, 145, 146, 147, 200–01, 222, 225, 254–55, 281
Lucian, 207, 215, 220
luis, 148–49
Luther, Martin, 200–01

M, the letter and its sound, 142, 143, 150–58
Macaulay, Thomas Babington, 162
Macrobius, 117
magic, 93, 138; magic squares, 161; magic triangles, 228. *See also* mysticism.
Mainz Psalter, 121–22
majuscule letters. *See* capital letters.
Mallarmé, Stéphane, 138–39
Malory, Sir Thomas, 245
man, 156
"Man of Letters" (Tory), 50–51, *passim.*
mantras and chants, 228–29
manuscripts: ancient, 9, 10, 11, 12, 18, 20, 21, 22; medieval, 23, 24, 26–29, 120–21
Manutius, Aldus, 32, 33
Mardersteig, Giovanni, 19
Marlowe, Christopher (*Doctor Faustus*), 92–93
Marquez, Gabríel García, 283
Martius, 267
Mason, William O., 8, 284, 287, 292–93

Maximinus, 260
Mayan writing, 16
McKerrow, Ronald, 225, 232
McLean, Ruari, 183
McLuhan, Marshall, 101–02, 150–54
mem, 150, 156
Merovingian writing, 24, 192, 236
Metz, Peter, 275
Meyrink, Gustav, 90
Middle Ages (Medieval Period), writing in, 22–28,
    120–21, 191–94
Milton, John, 33, 34, 59, 62, 292; *Areopagitica*, 33, 34
minuscule letters, 23, 26, 62, 146, 190. *See also* lower-
    case letters.
Modern type style, 35
monograms, 43, 44
monumental (square) capital letters, 20, 85, 144
Moore, George, 252
Moran, Hugh, 47, 56, 98, 214
More, Sir Thomas, 226, 277
Mormons. *See* Deseret Alphabet.
Morris, William, 35, 38
Moses, 215
moveable type, 28, 100–02, 144, 153–54
Moxon, Joseph, 33, 145
mu, 150
muin, 156
Muses, related to letters, 50, 62, 68, 73, 97, 106, 116–
    17, 134, 181, 195, 216
Mycenean writing, 12, 13
mysticism and letters, 53, 58, 73–74, 90, 136–38,
    160–64, 181, 228, 255, 259, 291–92
mythology and letters, 5, 8–9, 10, 122, 150–51, 168–
    70, 242

N, the letter and its sound, 159–67
Nabokov, Vladimir, 294
names of the letters, 14, 48, 110–11, 130, 132–33, 225,
    243–44, 250, 267–68
Nerdinger, Eugen, 44–45, 98, 115, 132, 159, 170, 177,
    205, 214, 258, 264–65, 266
Nesbitt, Alexander, 30, 102
new letters, 118, 178–79, 233, 290. *See also* Utopian
    letters.
nion, 166
Norman Conquest, 99, 129–30, 243
Norse mythology, 122, 242
nu, 159, 164
"number of the beast," 162
numbers, related to letters, 159–64, 175, 195
numerology, 163–64, 291–92
nun, 159
nyd, 166

O, the letter and its sound, 168–76
Odin (Woden), 8, 166, 242
Ogham writing, 122. *See also* Beth-luis-nion.
Old Style type design, 33, 37–38

Olson, Charles, 139
omega, 131, 169, 171–72, 214, 240–41. *See also* Alpha
    and Omega.
omicron, 170–72
optical character recognition, 238–39
oracles and the alphabet, 137–38, 149
oral culture, 3, 151–52
Orcutt, William Dana, 126
orin, 175
Ormin, 99
Orphic mysteries, 171–72
orthography, 135, 136, 178–79, 219–20, 227, 245–46
Orwell, George (*Animal Farm*), 80
os, 175
ouija boards, 137
ox (bull), 47, 214
Oxford English Dictionary (*O.E.D.*), 49, 66, 82, 123,
    175, 178, 227, 262

P, the letter and its sound, 177–85, 196; words
    beginning with, 178
Pacioli, Luca, 32, 127
palimpsest, 183
palindromes, 180
pangrammatists, 180
paper, 182, 184
papyrus, 11–12, 18, 20, 182–83
parchment, 18, 20, 182–83, 184
pathboc, 184
pe, 177, 181
Pedianus, 220
Pei, Mario, 246
Pelasgian Greek alphabet. *See* Greek alphabet.
pen and ink writing, 18, 19–20, 21, 78, 102, 200, 210
Pepys, Samuel, 59, 254
permutations, 182
phi, 80, 156–57, 178
philosophical letter, 258–59
Phoenician writing, 10, 12–14. *See also* Semitic
    writing.
phonemes, 288–89
phonetic alphabets, 289–90
phonetic writing, 6
phototype, 41
pi, 177
pictographic (iconographic) writing, 5–6, 10, 11
Pindar, 180
Piontek, Heinz, 292
Placentus, Petrus, 179
Plath, Sylvia, 154
Plato: *Cratylus*, 82–83, 98, 115, 141, 164, 170–71, 197,
    206, 216, 249; *Phaedrus*, 1–2, 4, 51, 79, 164
Plautus, 143
Plutarch, 74, 82
Poe, Edgar Allen, 173, 174, 251–52, 257, 280
point (typographic measure), 211
Pope, Alexander, 59, 261
Postel, Guillaume, 95–96

power of letters and writing, 93–95, 135–36, 242
printer's devil, 185
printing: books, 28–29, 31, 33, 100–02, 153–54; letterpress, 28, 29, 32, 35, 100–01
Priscian, 107
pronunciation, 178–79, 205, 219–20, 227, 245–46, 247, 261–62, 288–89. See also orthography.
psi, 148, 178
psychic price of literacy, 151–52, 154
pugillares, 18
punch cutting, 30, 33
punctuation, 6, 22, 285–88, 291
puns, 180
Pynchon, Thomas, 78, 79, 230, 239, 264
Pythagoras, 74, 259; letter of (Y), 259, 260–61
Pythagoreanism, 74, 82, 83–84, 90, 110, 159, 160, 163

Q, the letter and its sound, 186–95; association with U, 187–88
qoph, 195. See also koph.
question mark, 285–86
quotation marks, 285, 286

R, the letter and its sound, 177, 196–204
Rabelais, François (Gargantua and Pantagruel), 75
rad, 204
religions and alphabets, 89–90, 215, 218
Renaissance designers, 32, 116, 126–28, 129. See also letters: design.
representational letters, 25, 192
resh, 196, 204
rho, 177, 196, 197
rhythm of letters, 67, 99–100, 202
right-handed people, influence of on letters, 200
Rimbaud, Arthur, 53–54, 83, 86, 123, 175, 176, 229
Rolle, Richard, 54, 84
Romance languages, 133, 207, 208, 244
Roman letters and writing, 15, 18–23, 32, 44, 77–78, 82, 104, 201, 293
roman letters and type style, 29, 30, 33
Roman numerals, 69, 79–80, 122, 148, 156–57, 160, 218, 224, 239, 255
Rousseau, Jean J., 229
rubricator, 122
Ruga, Spurius, 98
ruis, 204
runic writing, 54, 62, 92, 166, 241–43, 267
Ruskin, John, 103, 104
Rustic script, 21, 62, 78, 236

S, the letter and its sound, 205–13, 267; abbreviation for silence, 207, 213; long form, 209, 210; words beginning with, 178
Saaz, Johannes von, 162
Sacred King ritual, 215
sadhe, 205
saille, 213
samech, 205, 249

Samian letter, 259
sans serif (gothic) typefaces, 36, 39–40, 100, 210, 211, 212, 236–37
Sartre, Jean-Paul (The Repreive), 94–95
Scarfe, Laurence, 201
Schulz, Bruno, 294
scribes, 20, 21, 22, 23, 24, 28, 30, 190–91, 203
scripts, reflective of their historical period, 26, 236
Sefer Ha-Zohar (Book of Splendor), 57, 136–37
Semitic writing, 12–13, 274–75. See also Hebrew writing, and Phoenician writing.
semi-uncial (half-uncial) script, 22–23
Sephiroth, 137
serifs, 36, 118, 210–11
serpent letter, 208
Seuss, Dr., 290
Shahn, Ben, 57, 136, 201, 234
Shakespeare, William, 59, 130, 162, 175, 246, 269
shapes of letters, 118–19, 198–200
Shaw, George Bernard, 220, 246
shibboleth, 205, 261
shin, 205, 213
Sholes, Christopher, 281
shorthand writing, 253–54. See also Tironian Notes.
sigel, 213
sigma, 205, 206
signature (personal), 105, 250
signs, non-alphabetic, 288
Sinclair, Upton, 164
single-character alphabets, 147, 293
Skelton, John, 59
Smith, Percy, 104
Smollett, Tobias, 76
Socrates. See Plato.
sounds of letters, 87–88, 141, 155, 205, 228–29. See also consonants, and vowels.
Southey, Robert, 247
speech, 1, 2, 3, 4, 10, 152–53. See also oral culture.
spelling. See orthography.
Spengler, Oswald, 218
SS (double S), 210, 267, 269
stars, reading in, 95–96
Steig, William, 111
Steinberg, S.H., 32–33, 102, 157, 226
Steiner, George, 51, 105, 135–36, 137, 155
Sterne, Laurence, 162
Stevens, Wallace, 55, 70, 256–57, 272
Stevenson, Robert Louis, 106
Strauss, Victor, 212
Styron, William, 276
substitution/special requirement alphabets, 278
Sulla, 258
Sumerian writing, 10
syllabaries, 6, 12, 14, 174
syllables, 6

T, the letter and its sound, 207, 214–22
Talmud, 9, 282

tau, 214, 215, 220
Taurian Age, 47, 214
tav (*taw* or *tahv*), 214, 215, 220–21, 249
teaching the alphabet, 59, 75–76, 146–47, 276
teth, 218, 220
Tetragrammaton (Holy Name of God), 89, 131, 174, 232, 262
theta, 69, 83–84, 218, 220
thok. See eth.
Thomas, pseudo-Gospel of, 214–15
Thor, letter of, 221
thorn, 218–19, 242, 263
Thoth (Theuth), 1–2, 3, 8, 11, 12, 60
Thurber, James, 70, 173–74, 181, 182
Tinker, Miles, 281
tinne, 217
tir, 221
Tironian Notes, 253, 284
Top, Alexander, 178, 215
Tory, Geofroy, 32, 49–51, 53, 55, 62, 67, 68, 69, 72–73, 84, 97, 106, 108, 113–14, 116–18, 125–26, 133–35, 141, 142–43, 154–55, 157–58, 165, 166–67, 168–70, 172, 181, 187–88, 192, 194–95, 197, 203, 206, 213, 216, 220, 224, 243, 250–51, 259–60, 264–65, 268–70, 283, 287–88. *See also Champ Fleury.*
Tracy, Walter, 50, 86, 201
Trajan Column, x, 19
Transitional type style, 34–35
tree-alphabet. *See Beth-luis-nion.*
Trissino, Gian Giorgio, 129, 232
Trithemius, Johannes (*In Praise of Scribes*), 28–29
Tryphiodorus, 179–80
tsade, 205
Tuchman, Barbara, 94
Twain, Mark, 103
Tyndale, William, 59
type "blindness," 210
type cases, 145, 225
type families, 39–40
typewriter, 281–82, 285
typography: before nineteenth century, 30, 31, 32–34; classification, 42–43, 236; compositors, 225; design, 30, 31, 112–13, 211–12, 282; fonts, 145; founding, 34 (*see also* punch cutting); influence of, 153–54, 201–02; moveable metal, 28, 29, 100–01 (*see also* Gutenberg); nineteenth century, 35, 36–37; rhythm, 67; styles in history, 236–37; tradition, 128; twentieth century, 38–43; unobtrusiveness, 234; variety, 235–36

U, the letter and its sound, 187, 188, 223–30, 231
uath, 109
Ullman, B.L., 22, 28, 199
uncial script, 21, 22, 100, 236
universal language, quest for a, 291
Updike, D.B., 31, 37, 126, 189
upper-case letters, 145, 146, 200–01, 224–25
upsilon (*ypsilon*), 223, 231, 258, 262

ur (*ura*), 227
Utopian letters, 226–27, 277–78

V, the letter and its sound, 188, 223–25, 231–39, 240
Varro, 110–11
vau (*waw*), 89, 223, 231, 240, 248, 258
vellum, 182–83
Virgil, 20
virtues, cardinal, related to letters, 50, 84, 117, 172
Visigothic script, 24
vowels, 6, 14, 81–82, 87–88, 141, 174, 227–28, 229, 231, 232, 290

W, the letter and its sound, 240–48
Walsh, William, 103, 112, 130, 284
Warde, Beatrice, 146, 147, 202, 211, 234
waw. See vau.
wax, writing on with stylus, 18, 77
Webster, Noah, 245
wen (*wyn*), 242–43, 244
Werner, E.T.C., 9
whimsical letters, 192. *See also* fantastic alphabets.
White Goddess, 61. *See also Beth-luis-nion.*
White, T.H., 70–71, 184, 191
Wilkins, John, 291
witches, 213
Woodcock, John, 146
Woolf, Virginia, 209
Worde, Wynkyn de, 59, 245
words: shapes of and legibility, 146, 199, 281; separation of writing into, 22, 286
Wright, E.V., 85
writing: 1–5, 102, 291–92; alphabetic, 6–7; beginnings, 3, 4, 47; considered holy, 1, 8–10, 73–74; development, 5–7; power of, 16, 94–95; styles, 236; tradition, 1–2, 3, 5, 8–10
writing masters, 102, 103, 193, 194

X, the letter and its sound, 249–57
x-height, 254
x-ratings, 255
xei (*xi* or *ksi*), 249
Xenophon, 206

Y, the letter and its sound, 258–65, 267
Yciar, Juan de, 127, 129
yod, 115, 124
yogh, 99
yr, 263

Z, the letter and its sound, 98, 258, 266–73
Zapf, Hermann, 199, 236
zayin (*zain*), 266
zed, 267
zeta, 266, 267
Zolar, 58, 64, 72, 84, 108, 115, 124, 137–38, 139, 140, 148, 156, 166, 181, 195, 204, 213, 220–21, 247–48, 249, 266

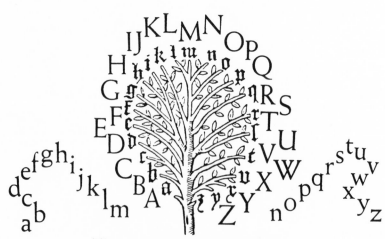

THE ALPHABET ABECEDARIUM
Book and cover design by Richard A. Firmage.
Composition and layout by the author on a personal
computer system using Aldus Pagemaker 4.01.
Text typeface is Adobe Garamond, designed by Robert
Slimbach and made available (as were also dozens of the
other typefaces shown) to the author through the kindness
of Adobe Systems Inc., which has graciously supported this
endeavor in many ways. Special thanks to Fred Brady of
Adobe for his ongoing encouragement and assistance.
The camera-ready pages were output by Fred on a
Linotronic 300 phototypesetting machine.
The book was printed and bound by
Maple-Vail Book Manufacturing
Group of Binghamton,
New York.
The text paper
is a natural, sixty-
pound, entirely acid-free sheet.